Intercultural Dialogue in Practice

MIX
Paper from
responsible sources
FSC® C018575

LANGUAGES FOR INTERCULTURAL COMMUNICATION AND EDUCATION
Series Editors: Michael Byram, *University of Durham, UK* and Alison Phipps, *University of Glasgow, UK*

The overall aim of this series is to publish books which will ultimately inform learning and teaching, but whose primary focus is on the analysis of intercultural relationships, whether in textual form or in people's experience. There will also be books which deal directly with pedagogy, with the relationships between language learning and cultural learning, between processes inside the classroom and beyond. They will all have in common a concern with the relationship between language and culture, and the development of intercultural communicative competence.

Full details of all the books in this series and of all our other publications can be found on http://www.multilingual-matters.com, or by writing to Multilingual Matters, St Nicholas House, 31–34 High Street, Bristol BS1 2AW, UK.

LANGUAGES FOR INTERCULTURAL COMMUNICATION AND EDUCATION
Series Editors: Michael Byram, *University of Durham, UK* and Alison Phipps, *University of Glasgow, UK*

Intercultural Dialogue in Practice

Managing Value Judgment through Foreign Language Education

Stephanie Ann Houghton

MULTILINGUAL MATTERS
Bristol • Buffalo • Toronto

Library of Congress Cataloging in Publication Data
Houghton, Stephanie, 1969-
Intercultural Dialogue in Practice : Managing Value Judgment through Foreign Language Education / Stephanie Ann Houghton.
Languages for Intercultural Communication and Education: 22
Includes bibliographical references and index.
1. Intercultural communication. 2. Intercultural communication--Study and teaching. 3. Language and languages--Study and teaching. I. Title.
P94.6.H68 2012
303.48'2—dc23 2012009124

British Library Cataloguing in Publication Data
A catalogue entry for this book is available from the British Library.

ISBN-13: 978-1-84769-725-7 (hbk)
ISBN-13: 978-1-84769-724-0 (pbk)

Multilingual Matters
UK: St Nicholas House, 31–34 High Street, Bristol BS1 2AW, UK.
USA: UTP, 2250 Military Road, Tonawanda, NY 14150, USA.
Canada: UTP, 5201 Dufferin Street, North York, Ontario M3H 5T8, Canada.

Typeset by Techset Composition Ltd., Salisbury, UK.
Printed and bound in Great Britain by the MPG Books Group.

Contents

     Top-Down and Bottom-Up Approaches   81
     Domains and Interfaces   85

6   Critically Analysing Self and Other   88
     Stage 1: Analytically Describing One's Own Values   88
     Stage 2: Analytically Describing the Values of Another Person   94
     Stage 3: Comparing and Contrasting Self and Other   113

7   Critically Evaluating Self and Other   116
     Stage 4: Evaluating Self and Other   116
     Stage 5: Selecting between Alternatives   132
     Savoir Se Transformer: Knowing How to Become   149
     Knowing How to Become and L2 Motivation   153

8   Shifting the Interface: From Self and Other to Self and Society   157
     Intercultural Mediation   157
     Propaganda and Persuasion   166
     Democratic Citizenship   168
     Language, Ideology and Intercultural Dialogue in Practice   176

     Conclusion   182
         Epilogue   185
     References   188
     Index   199

Figures and Tables

List of Figures

List of Tables

Series Editors' Preface

This book represents a very substantial body of empirical and reflective work, making a considered original contribution to the field of intercultural language education in the tertiary context. The focus for the complex case study model is the teaching of foreign languages in higher education in Japan, with specific attention paid to managing the evaluation of difference. The approach – a complex action research case study – is meticulously articulated and presented and is one which fits well with the developing scope of this book series. In particular, the book focuses on the role and possibility of empathy evaluation in teaching foreign language and culture, as defined and presented in Byram's model of five savoirs for intercultural communicative competence. It brings the perspectives articulated by Guilherme's development of the place of critical engagement (savoir s'engager) to bear, together with Bennett's model of cultural sensitivity and it breaks open the concept of empathy by contextualising its problematics for the individual teacher. All of this work builds on that of previous contributions to this series. The paradox, which generates the intellectual excitement in this work, grows from the encounter between empathetic, relativising judgments of cultural and linguistic difference in foreign language education, and from the place of political and ethical constructions of critical engagement. In short, the charting here of a genesis is in identity crises of multiple kinds, and its proposed solutions lie in cognitive encounters, which draw most persuasively on Piaget and Kohlberg.

In order to explore this paradox – correctly identified as a *complex* case study, the book carefully engages in painstaking qualitative data gathering, codification and analysis of substantial data. These data have not been gathered in the objective mood but rather from a clearly subjectively defined action research position as teacher–researcher. This substantive data set is of considerable value to the field, gathered in the 'researcher' mode of this hyphenated identity, as well as containing the materials, lesson plans, visual literacy resources etc developed in the 'teacher' mode. Consequently, the work gains traction over its research field in three ways: first, through objective analysis of qualitative data; second, through critical, subjective narrative reflection on the development of classroom resources focused on empathy and judgment; and third through the development of hyphenated identities for the researcher–teacher in addressing the hyphenated contexts and problems of the intercultural language field.

This is where the most original contribution to the book series and field of languages for intercultural education is to be found; it is not an easy feat and clearly offering a stimulating resource for future research in this field. This approach allows for fractal methodological possibilities that are in line with the most forward thinking action research in the social sciences to date, in particular the work of actor-network theorists.

The honesty of Houghton's narrative voice in its presentation of the difficulties of status and professionalism for a foreign national in the Japanese tertiary language education system is refreshing and of intellectual value. This is then juxtaposed with the clear and scientifically objective presentation of the data (third person narrative) relating to empathy and its analysis in terms of the problematics for intercultural language education. From this encounter of the two voices of a hyphenated identity the conclusions draw together the existing models of ethnocentrism, ethnorelativism and the psychodynamics of socialisation and difference to demonstrate the considerable difficulties of empathy in intercultural language education contexts, for teachers and learners and also for researchers. Through a development of Byram's model of intercultural communicative competence and Barnett's model of 'critical reflection' Houghton succeeds here in offering a dynamic, fractal and considered statement of both the order and the chaos, stability and flux which is present in human encounters in intercultural language education contexts.

Preface

Developed over the first decade of the 21st century, this book can be considered one of a series of three interconnected volumes that were initially sparked by the deep sense of malaise of being employed as a 'foreign' teacher at a university in Japan. Described in the introduction, the troubling employment situation in which I found myself in the year 2000 provides the social backdrop for this book, in which a case study based on action research is described that explores ways of tackling social prejudice through foreign language education. Both this study and the gradual, albeit partial, resolution of the employment problems through labour union negotiations highlighted the need to place the dynamic concept of intercultural dialogue at the centre of foreign language education, which should take as its aim the development of criticality in order to help students respond communicatively, analytically and creatively to the increasingly culturally diverse – and often problematic – world that lies outside the classroom.

For the overarching framework and steady guidance I needed to explore my ideas, I would like to extend my deepest gratitude to Emeritus Professor Michael Byram from Durham University, who supervised my studies offering many lessons for life along the way. I would like to thank my research assistant, Natsuki Sasaya, and all the students who so enthusiastically took part in the study. I would also like to extend my warmest thanks to both Damian Rivers and Etsuko Yamada for their professional companionship – to Damian for helping me explore the problematic context surrounding the employment of foreigners in Japanese universities in more depth (see Houghton & Rivers, forthcoming), and to Etsuko for helping me connect the intercultural dialogue model described in this book with other models of criticality at different levels of foreign language learning across cultural contexts, thereby extending the potential reach of my own work (see Houghton & Yamada, forthcoming).

I would like to extend my deepest gratitude to my husband, Takao Suenaga, for motivating and inspiring me to continue my life in Japan with a positive spirit. And I would also like to thank the editorial staff at Multilingual Matters for their professionalism and support.

Stephanie Houghton
November 2011

Introduction

Teachers may get their research ideas from many places. McDonough and McDonough recognise that 'unease' (McDonough & McDonough, 1997: 79) about aspects of classroom life may generate researchable issues, but this book finds its genesis in unease outside the classroom. I taught English as a foreign language in a Japanese senior high school from 1993 to 1996, where I made many close friendships and met my Japanese husband. In those early days, I found people around me to be very culturally accommodating, but I came under increasing pressure to conform to Japanese culture upon my return to Japan in 1999. In particular, the social distance between foreign teachers and other Japanese teaching staff at the university where I worked was markedly uncomfortable. As a *gaikokujin kyoushi* (外国人教師), or foreign teacher, I was prohibited from attending official meetings. Although I was eventually allowed to attend as an observer, I was prohibited from both speaking and voting. Never having been deprived of my voice before, I was unnerved. It is in this sea of tension and state of unease that my research question was born.

> Tension is defined as both an act of stretching and a state of uneasy suspense. Each definition of tension applies to teaching and research. Often, the best research questions are located in a taut spot between two points. (Hubbard & Power, 1999: 25)

Thus, negative personal experience drove me into research but the extent to which common sense forms of knowing can help us understand the world is limited, a point recognised by Cohen *et al.* (2000), who advocate the use of research to develop more systematic and reliable ways of developing an understanding of the world. Indeed, at the outset, the fact that I had no theoretical basis to understand what was happening to me left me ill equipped to deal with the problems, but I felt a sense of responsibility as a foreign language teacher to educate people to handle such intercultural problems more effectively than I could do so myself at the time, yet I did not know how.

This tension stimulated my interest in attitudes towards foreign culture and I became interested in how the issue should be handled in foreign language education. Throughout the literature analysis period (2001–2003), I was seeking strategies to cope with cultural pressure. Until that point, my strategy had been to focus on understanding Japanese culture rather than judging it, but while this approach had worked quite well in my first three years in Japan, it failed to solve culture-related problems in my life on my return to Japan as I came under increasing pressure to conform to what were, to me, unacceptable aspects of Japanese culture. Adopting more judgmental approaches with the Japanese person closest to me just seemed to ignite irresolvable arguments as we each tried to force our cultural values upon the other, and I was often surprised how the values of some Japanese people seemed to lie in diametric opposition to my own.

Further, I was often perplexed by, and objected to, apparent conceptual difference between English and Japanese speakers. Consider the following examples. Firstly, my official employment status *jokin teki na hijokin* (常勤的な非常勤) translated roughly from Japanese into English as *a part-timer who works as a full-timer*, even though it was only endowed with the legal rights of a part-timer. How could the concepts of full-timer and part-timer be conflated in such a way as to give me a similar workload to full-timers, yet deny me the same legal rights and benefits? How could this be considered fair? Secondly, Japanese nationals could be employed as *gaikokujin kyoushi* as long as they were native speakers of the language to be taught. Was it not ridiculous that native English speakers of Japanese nationality could be employed as *gaikokujin kyoushi* in Japan?

Such confusion and protest at the use of language led me to wonder about the connections between language and prejudice, and their impact on society, but my confidence in my own conceptual system and value judgments was undermined as the gap between my own perceptions and the reality around me forced me to question myself. As I grappled more generally with the question of whether or not to judge another culture and its members, I became increasingly interested in value and concept difference as reflected in language, and whether or not teachers should train students to judge cultural difference and why. I found that the conceptual link from prejudice to values can be made a few easy steps. Prejudice is a form of prejudgment (i.e. judging without first gathering information) and judging involves evaluation, which in turn involves the application of values. While this book explores the management of value judgment in foreign language education, its central concern is prejudice, which as Allport noted in 1954, can escalate in society through the five stages of anti-locution, avoidance, discrimination, physical attack and extermination. Insofar as this book takes an implicit stand against all these issues, it can be considered a contribution to peace education.

In an increasingly interconnected world, people need to learn to respond constructively to cultural difference. Since foreign language learners are regularly presented with cultural difference as a matter of course, foreign language education provides an ideal space within which to explore issues that arise. How should foreign language teachers manage the evaluation of difference in foreign language education? Hinging my early exploration of the academic literature upon judgment exposed a range of views upon its management that revealed terminological differences, which in turn reflected underlying differences in research priorities and conceptualisations of competence primarily in the European and North American contexts. Such distinctions have been explored elsewhere (Byram & Guilherme, 2010; Guo, 2010), so let me highlight some of the major differences relevant to this book.

Considerable terminological difference can be found in the definition of empathy, which along with perspective-taking and adaptability is one of three common themes that can be found 'in most Western models of intercultural competence' (Deardorff, 2009a: 265). Confusion seems rooted in the fact that empathy can be defined in communicative, cognitive and/or affective terms. Defining empathy in affective terms can lead some people to confuse empathy with sympathy, and prioritisation of the cognitive over the affective in intercultural communication can lead other people to reject empathy as a whole. Although Deardorff distinguishes empathy from perspective-taking, empathy can be defined as perspective-taking. An example is Paul and Elder's (2002) use of the term *intellectual empathy* to describe perspective-taking as a cognitive act.

This terminological confusion also seems to reflect deeper theoretical disagreement over whether or not it is cognitively possible to suspend judgment at all. The wide usage of the term *non-judgmental stance* in the North American context implies the view not only that the suspension of judgment is possible as a single cognitive act, but that it can also be a more general disposition, an implication that may be rejected outright by advocates of critical approaches to education not only on the grounds of viability but also of desirability. But this outright rejection of empathy seems to ignore the distinction between non-judgmental stance as a general disposition and the temporary suspension of evaluation for the purposes of perspective-taking.

The multi-disciplinary nature of intercultural communication naturally brings together researchers from many disciplines from cognitive and social psychology to communication studies and foreign language education, all of whom have different interests and priorities. This book makes a contribution to this multi-disciplinary discussion primarily from the standpoint of a foreign language teacher attempting to bridge the gap between theory and practice.

The question of whether or not evaluation can be suspended for the purposes of perspective-taking is easily resolved when considered from the standpoint of materials design at the task level. Yes, it can – insofar as teachers can require learners to evaluate in some tasks and suspend evaluation in others while doing other things. This is primarily a pedagogical decision, but such decisions should be theoretically sound. Providing teachers with the theoretical background they need to make such decisions in practice as they attempt to develop intercultural communicative competence in learners is an important aim of this book.

Synthesising conceptualisations of intercultural competence, Deardorff (2009a) highlights relationship development (in which empathy/perspective-taking come(s) into play), context and identity as being three over-arching themes that differing conceptualisations of intercultural competence tend to share. While the difference of opinion related to the definition of empathy presented above lies at the interface between self and other, it is primarily located in the individual. Another major difference of opinion is located at the interface between self and society, at which contextual considerations come into play. The notion of context is relevant to both teachers and learners. Regarding the former, the term context may be used in relation to research to describe the background of existing research, knowledge and understanding that informs new and ongoing research projects (Blaxter *et al.*, 2001). Consideration of context not only sheds light on the possibilities that are open to teachers and the constraints upon them, but also carries broader implications for the generalisability and validity of research, relating directly to its very paradigms. In this regard, McDonough and McDonough (1997) note that all human beings operate within a role set inhabited by others. In the case of teachers, this will comprise a network that encompasses members such as colleagues, students and administrative staff that will not only affect job specifications and teachers' perceptions of their own roles but also the ways in which they go about their working lives.

When the study described in this book was conceptualised, I had just taken up position as a *gaikokujin kyoushi* which automatically placed me outside of the institutional hierarchy. This explained why I was neither invited to nor allowed to speak or vote in any official university meetings. In practical terms, I found myself placed very much at the periphery of everyday departmental activity working unsupervised in virtual isolation on a day-to-day basis. I was left with the perplexing sense that while I was employed to teach and promote foreign language education, the university administration at the same time denied me equal employment status and full participation in the life of the university because I was foreign, which undermined my trust in my employer and many colleagues. Insofar as this negative personal experience drove me into research, the research activity that ensued was driven largely by contextual influences.

For me, research was thus a mechanism through which I attempted to constructively manage the interface between myself and the social environment, which naturally involved changing both in ways that were politically oriented to some extent. This belied my underlying view of the teacher as a *transformative intellectual* (Giroux, 2010), a term that serves to highlight the purposeful intervention of the teacher in society that can stimulate dynamic development in both.

What it means for an individual to be a member of society is explored through the concept of *citizenship* with its implicit emphasis upon social responsibility (Osler, 2000). Recognition of the increasingly international nature of societies from national to community levels has led to the classification of foreign language education as a form of citizenship education, particularly in the European context, where critical approaches to foreign language education aimed at developing critical cultural awareness are gaining ground. Notwithstanding its implicit classification of the individual as a member of society, the concept of criticality can also be viewed in purely individual terms by viewing the individual in primarily cognitive terms. But focusing upon one view to the exclusion of the other can cause confusion in the definition of criticality, which may be aggravated by lay interpretations of criticism in terms of the expression of negative evaluation only (i.e. the expression of prejudice).

While criticality is widely discussed in relation to the development of intercultural communicative competence primarily in European circles in relation to critical cultural awareness (Byram, 1997) and critical discourse analysis (Fairclough, 1995, 2010), for example, the role of criticality in intercultural communication is yet to be recognised in the North American context, where discussion seems firmly rooted in the notions of non-judgmental stance and empathy. There, the interface between self and society seems to be approached more through the conceptual lens of *context*, which is one of the overarching themes characterising conceptualisations of intercultural competence noted by Deardorff (2009a). Like citizenship, the term context is located at the interface between self and society but while the former implies social responsibility, the latter does not. The former can be considered prescriptive in orientation insofar as it invites discussion of what should be, whereas the latter merely invites description of what is, which explains why research that has been produced in the North American context may be dismissed for its lack of criticality by some European researchers.

The interface between self and society will be explored throughout this book. As selfhood is explored in relation to different cultures, important distinctions will be drawn between individuality and individualism (which is often contrasted with collectivism), and between independent and interdependent selves, all of which address the central issue of identity, which is the third main theme to emerge from Deardorff's (2009a) synthesis of conceptualisations of intercultural competence mentioned above. Consideration of selfhood will illuminate a tri-partite distinction between *being, doing* and *becoming* that contrasts the active preservation of the status quo for culture-specific purposes with the active changing of self and society. Insofar as the concept of citizenship both promotes and is premised upon the latter, it risks culture-specificity in a way that contextual description does not.

Notably, much of the research carried out in the European context is specifically designed to actively promote the development of European identity and citizenship. Citizenship in this sense is not a national but an international endeavour, which is proceeding through the formation of international agreements that allow for educational policies to be developed and implemented in the different cultural contexts that collectively constitute the European Union. But even if considerable agreement can be found in national educational policies round the world, international agreements made at the European level do not automatically apply globally. Prescriptive and/or descriptive concepts including criticality, citizenship and context need to be considered in relation to the political backdrop. An attempt will be made to explore this at a range of national, international and global levels with reference to various social and cultural contexts.

The study that will be described in this book took place in Japan. It consisted of a complex case study based on action research in which three differing approaches were taken to the management of value judgment in English language education. In one course, learners were asked to suspend evaluation to empathise with others (i.e. to take their perspectives). While learners were asked to evaluate consciously in both of the courses, learners were encouraged to evaluate freely in one, while the others were encouraged to evaluate by applying democratic values supportive of human rights. Qualitative data suggested that while empathy seemed to develop communication skills and self-awareness, it left some learners feeling insecure as they were influenced by others. But while evaluating consciously seemed to empower learners to take responsibility for their choices as they changed in response to others, others rejected the process itself in an explicitly stated bid to preserve social harmony as a cultural preference. In all cases, value and concept change seemed likely to be the likely product of encounters with cultural difference regardless of the teaching approach.

This study foregrounded, first and foremost, the dynamic nature of identity as learners developed their values and ways of thinking in response to people who differed from them in some way. Considering both theoretical and practical aspects of the findings, the intercultural dialogue model was developed to help teachers enhance the quality of self-development sparked by intercultural dialogue. The selection of the term *dialogue* is intended to draw attention to the way that people's perspectives can change dynamically in response to those of others, and perspective shift is indeed the etymological essence of dialogue as we shall see. The development and presentation of the intercultural dialogue model in this book thus represent an acceptance that identity change is an unavoidable aspect of intercultural communication, and as such, it deserves special attention in foreign language education.

Proposing a long-term policy for the promotion of intercultural dialogue within Europe and between Europe and its neighbouring regions, the White Paper on intercultural dialogue was launched in May 2008 as one of the many initiatives undertaken during the European Year of Intercultural Dialogue 2008. The term intercultural dialogue has become a buzzword at the policy level and according to Phipps (2009), there is a pressing need to synchronise the terminology of policymakers with the terminology of academics working (particularly but not exclusively) in foreign language education, who address the very same issues by using different sets of terms. Terminological gaps divide researchers in Europe and North America particularly in definitions of empathy and criticality, and fundamental disagreement over how to manage value judgment in intercultural dialogue remains; however it is phrased.

Thus, an overarching aim of this book is to explore the wide-ranging terminology relevant to intercultural dialogue, exposing areas of agreement and disagreement, not only to enhance terminological synchronisation but also to promote clearer consideration of the underlying issues. More specifically, the purpose of the book is to report the findings of a research project conducted in Japan that brought teaching practice to bear upon some of the main conflicting theoretical perspectives on how the evaluation of difference should be managed in foreign language education. At the heart of this issue lies the question of how foreign language teachers should address prejudice, which is a key dynamic in intercultural dialogue that brings many other factors into play.

Following the introduction, the book will be split into two main parts. Part 1 will explore value judgment and its psychological roots theoretically, at different levels and from different cultural standpoints. Discussion starting at the level of the individual in Chapter 1 will explore intra-individual processes such as information processing and language development, before considering social and developmental influences upon self-development in different cultures. In Chapter 2, intergroup dynamics will be considered in relation to ethnocentrism and ethnorelativism by drawing upon insights developed in the fields of social psychology and cross-cultural psychology. In Chapter 3, a range of possible learning objectives will be drawn from the discussion in the first two chapters before conflicting perspectives upon the management of value judgment are highlighted. Part 1 will conclude by focusing upon personal and social transformation.

In Part 2, a model for managing value judgment in intercultural dialogue in (foreign language) education will be presented by drawing the main conclusions of the study together into a coherent whole that pays due attention to the analysis and interpretation of research data. Having presented an overview of the model in Chapter 4, Chapters 5 and 6 will be dedicated to the presentation and illustration of issues related to the analysis and evaluation of self and other. Having considered the nature of the basic processes and their effects, Chapter 7 will then move to the meta-level at which informed decisions can be made about *how to be* and *what to do* in intercultural dialogue in the future, as part of the process of orienting self to other developing oneself in the process. Finally, Chapter 8 will show how the focus can be shifted within the model from the interface between self and other to the interface between self and society for the purposes of social analysis and transformation.

Part 1

Exploring the Roots of Value Judgment

1 Information Processing, Socialisation and the Self

The Mind as an Information Handling System

The mind can be seen as an information handling system (de Bono, 1969, 1990, 1991) whose effectiveness derives from its ability to create, store, recognise and retrieve patterns of information. The memory surface of the nerve cells of the brain provides a special, yet essentially passive, environment in which information self-organises as it impacts upon the memory surface, forming channels that guide incoming information into deepening patterns that are influenced by the sequence of arrival and the nature of the surface. Parts of the environment can be attended to selectively, but since attention span is limited, only part of the memory surface can be activated at any one time, which is affected by what is being presented to the surface at the moment and what has happened to the surface in the past.

The most easily activated areas or patterns on the memory surface are the ones that have been encountered most often because they have left the strongest trace on the memory surface, giving rise to pattern repetition or reconstruction because such patterns are recalled more readily than others. Patterns engrained in memory tend to become increasingly rigid and can be difficult to change. Since the sequence of arrival of information determines its arrangement, the information could always be arranged better. Bias is built into the mind as anything resembling a standard pattern tends to be perceived as the standard pattern as information is processed, which centres the information enabling established patterns to string together into longer sequences that may become so dominant that they start to constitute their own patterns.

As information continues to impact upon the brain, the mind builds up a stock of pre-set patterns of information held in memory that facilitate communication through which information is transmitted through codes that refer people back to these pre-set patterns. Words or partial information can be communicated to trigger the retrieval of interlinked information patterns, which means that not all the information needs to be communicated to retrieve the pattern. Word triggers facilitate the transfer of information, rendering appropriate reaction to situations possible as situations are identified from initial aspects of them. Communication through language code thus depends upon the building up of a catalogue of retrievable patterns in memory.

Words can be loaded insofar as the value of the word is not expressed through a separate adjective, but contained within the word itself, and people may use adjectives freely to pass judgment without justification. Words can trigger emotional backgrounds that are unjustified and tend to reflect crude either/or dichotomies imbued with the sense of good and bad, or right and wrong. Such dichotomies, set up through the use of the word *not*, are based upon mutually exclusive categories that can easily contradict each other facilitating the sorting of information into one category or the other, imposing a false rigidity upon perception in the process.

This description of the mind as an information handling system summarised from the work of de Bono (1969, 1990, 1991) helps us to imagine information about the world being stored in data structures that store concepts in memory in multiple locations throughout the brain in schematic networks (Rumelhart, 1980; Rumelhart & McClelland, 1986). In intercultural interaction, schemata provide a repertoire of frameworks regarding social beliefs, cultural values, expectations and assumptions that the person can use to make sense of the intercultural events and relationships (Endicott *et al.*, 2003). Culture learning itself can be conceptualised as the internalisation of information held in schemata that store concepts through which individuals classify and interpret their experience of the world, and culture learning is influenced by language since it involves concept acquisition (Byram, 1989a).

Within interlinked schematic networks of information, words cohere in layered hierarchies with other words sharing many of the same semantic features. Super-ordinate concepts, such as *living things*, may come at the top of a hierarchy above multiple layers of subordinate concepts that may each contain separate, but hierarchically linked, categories with hierarchies meshing into hetararchies, and each language–culture establishing its own hetararchy (Fantini, 1995). Much human thought involves the categorisation of new objects and events, but while categorisation processes themselves are universal, the way hierarchies and categories are set up is not. This depends upon the amount and type of information people have at their disposal and considerable variation in conceptual thought exists (Rosch, 1978).

Network and hierarchy are two of the dominant images often used to conceptualise the structures in which information is contained in the mind. While the two images are not incompatible, and are often used interchangeably, the most useful image for the purpose of this book is that of concepts being contained in hierarchies rather than networks, not only because it accords with Rokeach's description of the structure of value systems presented below, but also because the concept of hierarchy with discrete and separate elements that are evaluated and ranked relative to each other lends itself well to the structuring of teaching activities that require critical analysis and evaluation, as we shall see.

According to Rokeach (1973), values manifest themselves in everyday life as enduring beliefs that specific modes of behaviour or end-states of existence are *preferable* to others, that act as guiding *standards* for action, attitudes, ideology, self-presentation, evaluations, judgments, justifications and comparison between self and others. Highlighting the *hierarchical* structure of value systems, Rokeach notes that since any given situation will typically activate several values within that system rather than just a single one, and different subsets of the value system will be activated in different situations, a *relative* dimension comes into play when values come into competition, are prioritised and integrated into relatively stable hierarchically organised systems, wherein each value is ordered in priority or importance relative to other values.

The underlying structural similarities between the descriptions of value systems and conceptual hetararchies presented above are obvious. Further, while concept and value systems have a measure of stability, they are also dynamically under construction as new concepts and values are integrated into the existing system in order to stabilise it. What the description of the value system adds to the description of the conceptual system, then, is the *relative ranking of elements* through evaluation. Later in the book, we will see how people can actively adjust their concepts and values to those of others by applying selected evaluative standards.

This book is primarily concerned with how value judgment should be managed in foreign language education, and how language helps to shape thought insofar as it structures the way in which people view the world (Hunt & Agnoli, 1991; Lakoff & Johnson, 1980; Lantolf, 1999; Wierzbicka, 1997). Worldview is, to some extent, mediated by language and its conceptual structures and components (Fantini, 1995), and insofar as words focus attention upon particular aspects of environmental phenomena and affect their interpretation (Lantolf, 1999), they set up points during information processing at which the world is translated into the symbols and then translated back into the real world. It is at these translation points that language runs into the variability of perception and the interactive complexity of the world (de Bono, 1991).

Any links that can be found between language and thought are not, however, necessarily representative of 'incommensurate world views, or of concepts that are nameless and therefore unimaginable, or of dissecting nature along lines laid down by our native languages according to terms that are absolutely obligatory' (Pinker, 1994: 66), and the claim that language *controls* thought remains controversial (Hardin & Banaji, 1993). But the linguistically structured conceptual frameworks people use to categorise the world around them contain both *cultural* and *personal* models (Lantolf, 1999). The former are sets of conventionally constructed concepts constituting the shared cognitive resources of a community, constraining what people attend to and perceive as salient in the world. The latter are unique sets of concepts, based on life experience, that are heavily influenced by, but not totally determined by, cultural models. People generally tend to be unaware of how far their personal models are influenced by cultural models and cannot make them explicit.

Mental representations can be represented in the brain without being couched in words and reasoning, and the deduction of new pieces of knowledge from old ones takes place in sub-language systems. Representations can be considered physical objects whose parts and arrangement correspond, piece for piece, to some ideas or facts that can be symbolised consistently and processed, according to principles of logic, that can result in the alteration of the representations or the creation of new representations as pieces of the representations are copied (Pinker, 1994).

This view of mental representations as being discrete and separate elements that can be rearranged and expanded upon in the mind accords with the image presented earlier of value-laden conceptual hierarchies that are always under construction, as new concepts and values are processed and integrated into the existing system. Such basic universal cognitive processes also involve the deployment of reasoning and logic during decision-making. For example, everyone has the capability for self and other evaluation on the basis of available facts and arguments (Byram & Guilherme, 2000).

But the English language in particular does not embody the information that a processor would need to perform valid sequences of reasoning due to its ambiguity, lack of logical explicitness and synonymy, and to get languages of thought to serve reasoning properly would require them to look more like each other than their spoken counterparts. While the language of thought that best supports reasoning, or *mentalese*, is probably universal, the underlying human capacity for reasoning and logic is clouded by both language itself and communicative difficulty (Pinker, 1994).

This echoes de Bono's (1991) view that while language is a good describing system, it is not a good perceiving or thinking system because definitions depend on other definitions, frames of reference and context. Problems can arise when the words are too big and clumsy, or when we do not have words at all. And words, especially adjectives, can trigger emotional backgrounds that are unjustified when people use them freely to pass judgment without justification.

The representations underlying thought and the sentences in a language can thus work at cross-purposes, and communicative efforts may fail to transmit the vast amounts of information that lie behind utterances, which are also hampered by limited attention spans. Since selective attention is limited, details can never be focused upon in equal measure, and the selection of some points over others renders any rendition of the truth necessarily partial. When fractions of messages are communicated, listeners fill in the gaps by drawing upon prior knowledge as they attempt to grasp the meaning of utterances.

Perceptual processing, parsing and utilisation are three distinct information processing stages of language comprehension (Anderson, 1985). The first stage of perceptual processing involves the selective direction of attention onto sections of aural or written input for a few seconds, during which time preliminary analysis may convert them into meaningful representations (Call, 1985). The second stage of parsing involves the construction of further meaningful representations of input by segmenting sentences into language chunks, the size and composition of which depend on the presentation of the information and the person's general knowledge of the language (O'Malley & Chamot, 1989, 1990; Richards, 1983). The third stage of utilisation involves the decoding of chunks by matching them with meaning-based representations held in long-term memory. Meanings are then concatenated with other parsed chunks, to form a more complete understanding of the input as ideas are linked. When single concepts are evoked, connections are made with other concepts through spreading activation within conceptual frameworks.

Prior knowledge held in value-laden conceptual hierarchies assists language comprehension through top-down processing as people interpret new information in the light of old, inferring and predicting meaning when there are gaps in understanding. Alternatively, the starting point for comprehension may be the analysis of individual words to form meanings that accumulate, but lack of attention to context and first language interference make bottom-up processing inefficient (O'Malley & Chamot, 1989, 1990). Both types of processing may be misleading if prior knowledge is drawn upon inappropriately (Carrell, 1983).

Cognitive Development

In the field of developmental psychology, the development of under-standing is considered to be a social process that comprises a series of qualitatively different stages of acquisition of conceptual frameworks, 'in which more adaptive and flexible processing systems come to replace less flexible, more concrete ones' (Sercu, 2000: 64). For this reason, intercultural development is often discussed in relation to cognitive and moral development (Byram, 1989a; Doyé, 1992, 2003; Endicott et al., 2003; Sercu, 2000), in all of which a central issue is the way people respond to discrepancies between incoming information and the information already held in their mind.

Cognitive theorists propose that people are motivated to adjust their mental representations of the world to reduce cognitive discrepancies, accommodate new information and create realistic mental maps of the world. People are driven to maintain cognitive consistency because the awareness that two cognitions are dissonant (or that the attitudes are incompatible with behaviour) is so unpleasant that they attempt to reduce the discrepancy (Festinger, 1957). Festinger's concept of *cognitive dissonance* and Piaget's concept of *disequilibrium* both rest upon the view that people tend to attempt to resolve cognitive conflict when there is a discrepancy between two beliefs, two actions, or between a belief and an action (Crain, 2000).

Piaget suggested that during information processing, new information about the world can either be assimilated into existing conceptual frameworks, or the frameworks themselves may be modified to accommodate inconsistent information. The continuous processes of assimilation and accommodation can produce both adaptive change and disequilibration, both of which can trigger various readjustment mechanisms (such as selection, categorisation and combination) as individuals strive to resolve cognitive conflict. Piaget conceptualised development in terms of the assimilation of external perturbations by the internal structures of the mind, which stimulate evolution and/or innovation in the process. And contradiction works as an active force that can help consolidate and improve the system as equilibration is sought between internal conceptual frameworks and external objects, between conceptual frameworks themselves, and between individual conceptual frameworks and their larger structures (Gruber & Voneche, 1995).

Table 1.1 The general stages of development in Piaget's Cognitive-Developmental Theory

Period I	Sensori-Motor Intelligence (birth to 2 years). Babies organise their physical action schemes, such as sucking, grasping and hitting, for dealing with the immediate world
Period II	Pre-Operational thought (2–7 years old). Children learn to think – to use symbols and internal images – but their thinking is unsystematic and illogical. It is very different from that of adults.
Period III	Concrete Operations (7–11 years old). Children develop the capacity to think systematically, but only when they can refer to concrete objects and activities.
Period IV	Formal Operations (11 to adulthood). Young people develop the capacity to think systematically on a purely abstract and hypothetical plane.

Source: Adapted from Crain (2000: 113)

An overview of the general stages of development in Piaget's Cognitive-Developmental Theory is presented in Table 1.1.

Notably, when people process information about the world, they can either attempt to maintain existing impressions or to develop more accurate representations, operating either under an *impression–maintenance* or an *accuracy* mode. In the former, simplified processing strategies are adopted to maintain simple, but coherent, impressions by ignoring or distorting inconsistent information that threatens existing conceptual categories, especially when cognitive resources are scarce and/or when motivation is low. But when cognitive resources are more plentiful, motivation is higher and when people are sufficiently familiar with a target and are presented with novel and otherwise atypical information, more systematic processing strategies may be adopted that lead to the re-categorisation of information or the modification of existing conceptual frameworks. For this to occur, motivation and cognitive resources are crucial; 'people have to be willing to get involved in active information processing' (Sercu, 2000: 67).

Moral Development

From a social standpoint, the mind can be seen as a set of innate dispositions and social meanings, comprising beliefs, skills and knowledge, that are triggered and shaped by structured and interconnected webs or networks of cultural meanings, which are gradually internalised under the guidance of older people or significant others, through successive and ordered stages, or zones of proximal development, that determine the social meanings people are exposed to and influenced by from early childhood (Byram, 1989a). The processes through which people gradually become inculcated with the values and norms of society that enable them to function are a matter not only of cognitive but also moral socialisation (Doyé, 1992, 2003) and can be ideological in nature (Fairclough, 1995, 2010).

Piaget's investigation of children's social thought also included moral development and he basically found 'a series of changes that occur between the ages of 10 and 12, just when the child begins to enter the general stage of formal operations' (Crain, 2000: 149). But Kohlberg's investigation of moral development beyond that point revealed stages beyond those discovered by Piaget. An overview of the six stages, categorised into the three levels of pre-conventional, conventional and post-conventional morality, is presented in Table 1.2.

Moral development is thought to emerge from our own thinking about moral problems as information processing is stimulated by social experience, discussion and debate, all of which motivate us to develop our positions as our views are brought into question. In this process, the cognitive conflict stimulating the development of broader, more comprehensive moral viewpoints is the same kind of cognitive conflict at work in Piaget's concept of equilibration through which 'the child takes one view, becomes confused by discrepant information and then resolves the confusion by forming a more advanced and comprehensive position' (Crain, 2000: 166).

In Socratic teaching, for example, this dialectical process is actively capitalised upon by teachers who systematically probe into learner viewpoints to reveal latent inadequacies, motivating learners to formulate more comprehensive and coherent positions. Overcoming value discrepancies that emerge in this process, such as discrepancies between what people say and do in practice, can be considered a goal of intercultural education (Simon *et al.*, 1995), but the universality of dissonance-based theories has been brought into question, as we shall see.

Perspective-taking is another way in which moral development is thought to take place as other people's viewpoints are consciously taken into consideration to develop conceptions of what is fair and just. Perspective-taking, or the ability to empathise, first starts to develop as children start de-centring and learn to focus simultaneously on two dimensions of a problem. Appreciation of the different ways in which situations may be viewed by different people triggers the shift out of early egocentrism, but notable in this regard is Piaget's observation that not all adults automatically learn to engage

Table 1.2 An overview of Kohlberg's Stages of Moral Development

Level 1 Pre-conventional morality	Stage 1	Children think of what is right as what authority says is right. Doing the right thing is obeying authority and avoiding punishment.	
	Stage 2	Children are no longer impressed by a single authority; they see that there are different sides to any issue. Since everything is relative, one is free to pursue one's own interests, although it is often useful to make deals and exchange favours with others.	
Level 2 Conventional morality	Stage 3	Young people think as members of a conventional society, with its values, norms and expectations.	Young people emphasise being a good person, which means having helpful motives towards people close to one.
	Stage 4		The concern shifts towards obeying laws to maintain society as a whole.
Level 3 Post-conventional morality	Stage 5	People are less concerned with maintaining society for its own sake, and more concerned with the principles and values that make for a good society.	People emphasise basic rights and the democratic processes that gives everyone a say.
	Stage 6		People define the principles by which agreements will be most just.

Source: Adapted from Crain (2000: 155)

in the more logical, reasoned, abstract forms of thought that would enable them to consider situations from many points of view, and to focus on many different aspects of a given problem before arriving at judgments and solving problems.

Just as some people do not reach the *formal operations* stage of Piaget's theory, some people never enter the higher *post-conventional* level of Kohlberg's stages of moral development. The *higher stages* are only reached by individuals who manage to free themselves from the norms of the society into which they are born, transgressing the prescriptions of their society to follow universal rules more conducive to the development of a better society in which people coordinate their interests considering multiple perspectives, democratic processes and social justice.

While Kohlberg's post-conventional level of moral development can be seen as a desirable goal of intercultural education (Doyé, 1992, 2003), the universality of its status as a *higher* stage of moral development was brought into question on the grounds of both gender and cultural bias. Gilligan (1982) suggested that women tend to frame moral issues more in terms of care and responsibility in relationships than men who tend to frame them instead in terms of rights and rules. Within this view, the female ethic of care contrasts with the male ethic of fairness and justice. And Tronto (1987) suggested that indigenous societies may develop moral orientations more like those Gilligan articulated for women that emphasise people's *interdependence*, and the self as an extension of others, recognising the possibility that some cultures may develop more advanced moralities based on harmony and interdependence with the whole of creation.

While the emphasis of justice over the ethic of care may carry greater potential to overcome the kinds of powerful and oppressive legal systems challenged by Gandhi and Martin Luther King in the name of higher principles (Broughton, 1983), a neo-Kohlbergian approach did emerge in the 1990s in response to the criticisms of Kohlberg's original theory, as a theory of moral development was proposed that was rooted in, yet deviated from, many of Kohlberg's fundamental ideas according to Endicott *et al.* (2003). In this theory, Rest *et al.* (1999) described the development of moral reasoning in terms of the gradual replacement of more primitive forms of thinking by more complex moral schemata residing in long-term memory, which develop through the recognition of similarities and recurrences in socio-moral experience. The three moral stages characterising this approach, which forms a developmental hierarchy that parallels Kohlberg's three major levels, are listed below:

(1) The *personal interest schema* is pre-sociocentric in that it rests upon an egocentric perspective in which the concern of the individual is limited to their personal stakes in the dilemma and those of the people with whom they are closely related, and lacks any overarching, guiding concept of an organised society.

(2) The *maintaining norms schema* (usually emerging in adolescence) is characterised by a perception of a need for a society-wide system of cooperation

and the uniform application of laws and social norms, and a duty-based, authoritarian orientation.

(3) The *post-conventional schema* is the most complex of the three and is characterized by flexible thinking since multiple mental frameworks, or schemata, are drawn upon to construct a common morality based on a community's framework of shared ideals ranging from the ideals of classic Kohlbergian individual rights-based principles of justice to communitarian and other non-Kohlbergian moral principles.

Self-development

The self, emerging and establishing itself partly through cognitive and moral development over time from early childhood, can be considered an active agent, in the same way as language, that affects social behaviour by promoting differential sampling, processing and evaluation of information from the environment (Triandis, 1989).

The self-structure is an organized configuration of perceptions of the self which are admissible to awareness. It is composed of such elements as the perceptions of one's characteristics and abilities; the percepts and concepts of the self in relation to others and to the environment; the value qualities which are perceived as associated with experiences and objects; and the goals and ideals which are perceived as having positive or negative valence. It is, then, the organized picture, existing in awareness either in figure or ground, of the self and the self in relationship, together with the positive or negative values which are associated with those qualities and relationships, as they are perceived as existing in the past, present and future. (Rogers, 1951: 501)

On a cognitive level, the term *self-concept* refers to the information a person stores in conceptual frameworks in memory about their own attributes, including current and possible selves, which forms the knowledge-base for social interaction (Nishida, 1999). Over time, self-concept comes to be characterised both by autobiographical memory, which renders it somewhat personal in nature, and cultural elements that are shared with others who happen to have been socialised in similar ways. This echoes Lantolf's distinction between personal and cultural models noted earlier.

Focusing on typically shared cultural elements of self-concept between members of certain groups, Heine (2001) tracked conceptual developments in cross-cultural psychology originating in Hofstede's (1980) study of the values of IBM employees in 76 different countries, which identified *individualism/collectivism* as one major type of value difference round the world. While criticising this work for its essentialised view of culture, justifiably highlighting the dangers of stereotyping and over-generalisation, Holliday (2011) recognises that Hofstede's work 'has sustained theory-building for more than 25 years' (Holliday, 2011: 6–7). Examples of this include the work of Triandis (1989) and Markus and Kitayama (1991) who, building upon yet departing from, Hofstede's ideas went on to suggest that individualist cultures have an *independent* view of the self, whereas collectivist cultures foster an *interdependent* view of the self. Heine then distinguished these concepts even further by contrasting the following tendencies: consistency and flexibility, self-enhancing and self-critical motivation, intra-individual and extra-individual focus, malleability of self and world and relationship between self and other, each of which will be considered subsequently.

As with other value-laden conceptual frameworks, self-concept can itself be conceptualised as a hierarchy of multiple layers of subordinate concepts that may each contain separate, but hierarchically linked, categories with hierarchies meshing into hetararchies, and each self-concept establishing its own hetararchy. Much thought about the self involves the categorisation and internalisation of new objects and events, but while categorisation processes themselves are universal, the way hierarchies and categories about the self within the self are not.

One aspect of this relates to whether consistency and/or flexibility are sought. Dörnyei (2009) echoes Markus and Nurius' (1986) point that discrepancies between evaluated elements, including the ideal selves we would like to become, the selves that we could become and the selves that we are afraid of becoming, can destabilise the self, as discrepancies and contradictions cause cognitive dissonance that drives attempts to resolve ensuing cognitive conflict. People who cannot maintain a consistent self-concept and self-esteem may disown parts of themselves (Rogers, 1951, 1961, 1980). For this reason, self-actualisation through the reduction of discrepancy and the promotion of congruence between self-concepts and self-ideals are central goals of person-centred therapy. In foreign language education, the active promotion of the ideal self has been singled out by Dörnyei (2009) in relation to language learning motivation, as we shall see.

This illustrates what Heine means by the drive for *consistency*, a human tendency that is often claimed to be universal. But Heine suggests that it may be cultural insofar as Asians may behave differently, and inconsistently, across situations to meet situationally determined role requirements. This is what Heine means by the drive for *flexibility*, although this needs to be distinguished from the use of the same term to describe the cognitive act of perspective-taking to *flexibly* describe other people's points of view, and as we shall see later in the book, the drive for consistency may also be found in Asians, as ideals seemed to stimulate the self-development of the Japanese learners who took part in the study in particular ways.

As with other value-laden conceptual frameworks, the self-concept consists of hierarchies of concepts about the self that can each be evaluated separately, and the term *self-esteem* refers to a person's self-evaluations, both positive and negative. But while Heine notes that North Americans often seem to engage in *self-enhancing* strategies to protect self-esteem, East Asians show little evidence of self-enhancing biases or self-evaluation maintenance tendencies to protect self-esteem. Instead, they seem more concerned about how they are evaluated by others, or with *face*, which can be defined as the amount of public worth associated with one's social roles (Brown & Levinson, 1987; Goffman, 1959). Kanagawa *et al.* (2001) not only found that their Japanese research participants were more influenced by social situations than their North American counterparts, but also that their self-descriptions were more negative, or *self-critical*. An important point to note that is that while self-concept is made up of discrete elements that can each be evaluated separately, as illustrated in Figure 1.1, the terms self-enhancing and self-critical refer more to *evaluative tendencies*.

A third area of difference relates to the tendency to focus one's attention either on *intra-individual* or *extra-individual* information. Heine suggests that when processing information, East Asians tend to focus on information in the environment, while North Americans focus more on individual dispositions. This distinction between extra-individual and intra-individual focus echoes Hall's distinction between high and low-context culture. According to Hall, 'high-context transactions feature pre-programmed

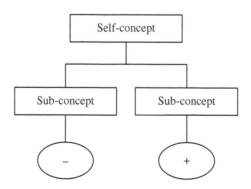

Figure 1.1 The link between self-concept and self-esteem

information that is in the receiver and the setting, with only minimal information in the transmitted message' (Hall, 1976: 101). Thus, communication can take place through the medium of silence in a high-context culture, as people rely upon shared understandings in interpretation highlighting the link between silence and contextual information and increasing the importance of both.

In contrast, in low-context culture, 'most of the information must be in the transmitted message in order to make up for what is missing in the context' (Hall, 1976: 101), and this increases the importance of explicit verbal communication. Since shared understandings are lost when one moves out of a group, the need for low-context communication increases as one moves into new contexts until shared understandings can be developed to support high-context communication. While Hall's distinction between low-context and high-context communication only reflects the degree of attention paid to context, Heine's distinction between *intra-individual* and *extra-individual* focus suggests that when people from low-context cultures are not paying such close attention to context, they may be paying more attention to the individual attributes of interactants.

Through the *associative* view of communication underpinning Hall's (1976) notion of high-context culture runs a thread that can link cultures in the Arab world, within which communicators tend to seek meaning more from the context than from the code or message as in low-context culture (Zaharna, 2009). One aspect of this, non-verbal communication, is highlighted in Nwosu's (2009) portrayal of African culture:

> In this context, the burden of communication is on the listener to decipher what the speaker is saying. Because messages tend to be covert and implicit, there is a greater reliance on non-verbal symbols. Reactions to certain messages are reserved as a way to save face and minimise conflicts. In a speaker-responsible culture, the burden of meaning in communication contexts is for the speaker to be clear and precise. (Nwosu, 209: 174–175)

A further area of difference relates to a set of perceptions related to the *malleability* of self and the world, which in turn underpin cultural orientations to change. In essence, Heine suggests that Westerners who tend to view the world as being malleable may be more inclined to try to change it because it can be brought into line with the self. In contrast, East Asians who tend to see the world as being rather fixed may be more inclined to bring themselves into line with the world instead. The concept of the malleability of the self also finds expression in Manian and Naidu (2009) portrayal of Indian culture in relation to reincarnation and karma, and in Nwosu's (2009) portrayal of

African culture, within which human events are seen as being determined by fate as part of a general orientation to *being*.

> African's conception of activity is also one that values a 'being' orientation, as opposed to a 'doing' or a 'becoming' orientation. In this regard, there is a belief that all human events are determined by fate and are therefore inevitable. A 'becoming' orientation sees individuals as evolving and capable of changing, whereas a 'doing' orientation places significance of change and control. (Nwosu, 2009: 173)

The final area of difference highlighted by Heine relates to the relationship between self and other. Those who see themselves as being *interdependent* tend to value group recognition and the maintenance of harmonious intergroup relationships, a view that depends upon the clear delineation of boundaries between in-group and out-group members. This is less important to those who see themselves as being *independent* from others, since such boundaries play a lesser role in identity construction. The concept of the interdependent self also finds expression in Nwosu's (2009) portrayal of African culture where an emphasis is placed upon community rather than the individual. Within this worldview, the subordination of the self, deference to the group, reverence for age and status and the valuing of interdependence are some of the features that define the African self-orientation to others:

> Communalism, as a way of life, has been elevated to the status of a communal religion in most of traditional Africa (Taylor & Nwosu, 2001), in the same manner that individualism, as a concept, has been elevated to status of a national religion in the West. (Nwosu, 2009: 176) (Figure 1.2)

While the distinctions between the independent and the interdependent self are notable as a set of concepts that are rooted in, yet departed from, the earlier concepts of individualism and collectivism, the latter two terms may still be used to describe cultural traits even today (Hofstede, 2009), although *individualism* defined in terms of the tendency to be independent from a group should be distinguished from *individuality*, which 'refers to the person's freedom to act differently within the limits set by the social structure' (Condon & Yousef, 1975: 65). This point is noted by Zaharna (2009) who suggests that while cultures in the Arab world are often described as being collectivist, individuality (as opposed to individualism) may still be prevalent.

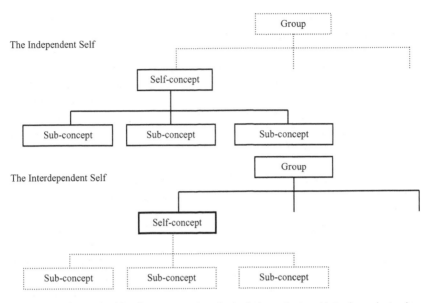

Figure 1.2 Alternative identity constructions in the independent and interdependent selves

Examples of culturally shared elements of self-concept between members of certain groups have been highlighted in this section across some of the key dimensions used in the analysis of intercultural communication to give a taste of the ways in which self-concept can differ *culturally*, although the brief overview presented above can by no means be considered exhaustive. It should also be borne in mind later in the book that the kinds of culturally shared elements of self-concept presented above influence not only intercultural communication but also researcher conceptualisations of intercultural competence in different parts of the world (Deardorff, 2009a).

2 Ethnocentrism and Ethnorelativism

It was noted in Chapter 1 that in the field of developmental psychology, the development of understanding is considered to be a social process that comprises a series of qualitatively different stages of acquisition of conceptual frameworks in which more adaptive and flexible processing systems come to replace less flexible, more concrete ones. For this reason, intercultural development is often discussed in relation to cognitive and moral development.

Insofar as multicultural experiences are related to both moral and intercultural development in terms of increasing socio-cognitive flexibility, Kohlberg's Stages of Moral Development can be connected to Bennett's (1993) Developmental Model of Intercultural Sensitivity (Endicott *et al.*, 2003). In the latter, it is assumed that the differentiation and attachment of meaning to social phenomena varies depending on the individual and the culture, and worldview is defined in cognitive terms as a particular configuration of cultural categories held in the mind about reality, or patterns of differentiation of phenomena, that are culturally determined and shared. Such patterns were explored in brief above in relation to self-development in terms of culturally shared elements of self-concept.

Bennett's model is framed in terms of category development rather than schemata, though the two approaches are not inconsistent as noted earlier. Further, it highlights the particular role of in-group–out-group dynamics and exposes a wide range of possible responses to difference in worldview ranging from ethnocentrism to ethnorelativism, both of which add new perspectives to the knowledge framework that has been constructed so far. Ethnocentrism and ethnorelativism will be considered separately and related to other theories and models below.

Ethnocentrism

The term ethnocentrism, first coined by Sumner (1906), refers to 'the tendency to identify with our group (e.g. ethnic or racial group, culture) and to evaluate out-groups and their members according to those standards' (Gudykunst & Kim, 2003: 137). Ethnocentrism has two key facets (Gudykunst, 1998).

The first facet of ethnocentrism relates to the inability to conceive of perceptions of reality other than our own, or the 'assumption of similarities' (Barna, 1998: 173). It applies when our lack of knowledge about other groups leaves us with no option other than to draw upon the information already stored in our minds to interpret what is happening, which can lead us to interpret strangers' behaviour from own cultural frame of reference, perhaps causing misunderstandings in the process. In short, the highly ethnocentric individual 'suffers from a form of cultural myopia' (Wiseman *et al.*, 1989: 364).

The second facet of ethnocentrism relates to evaluation from our own cultural standpoint, which can lead us to reject out-groups seeing them as inferior (Gudykunst, 1998), a tendency that may be universal (Brewer & Campbell, 1976). The evaluative facet of ethnocentrism is said to affect memory, insofar as we tend to remember more favourable information about in-group members, and less favourable information about out-group members (Hewstone & Giles, 1986).

The central problem, however, is a way of thinking that is firmly centred in the self. Just as egocentric people assume their existence is central to the reality perceived by everyone else, ethnocentric people assume that their own worldviews are central, and sociocentric people assume that the ways of their own society are central to all reality. Ethnocentrism, then, involves presumptions of both similarity and superiority, but development through and out of ethnocentrism into ethnorelativism may occur in ways that resemble cognitive and moral development through ongoing exposure to people from other cultures. But when an individual lacking such exposure has no, or very poorly defined, cognitive categories to describe cultural difference, the evaluation of cultural difference can be impossible in the very early stages of ethnocentrism (Bennett, 1993).

Along with increased exposure to cultural difference, cognitive categories developing in the mind to account for and explain the cultural difference become increasingly defined and more evaluative in nature. Denigration may set in if cultural difference is perceived as threatening and evaluated negatively as a form of defence. This may give way to feelings of superiority if positive evaluations of one's own culture are made to boost self-esteem and subjugate the cultural difference. Furthermore, individuals may start to evaluate the other culture more positively than their own by recognising its superiority, although this is ethnocentric insofar as the only real change is the shift of the centre from one culture to another (Bennett, 1993).

With ongoing cognitive development in response to cultural difference, similarities are noticed and super-ordinate conceptual constructs are created that incorporate previously irreconcilable elements into more complex cognitive structures. The recognition of sameness, or the identification of similarities, characterises the appeal to universal or transcultural values often found in national educational policies and curriculum documents (Parmenter, 2010).

While this may be accompanied by a decrease in evaluative tendency as cultural universals are recognised, cultural difference may be minimised as similarities are made the object of attention. Insofar as the increase in cognitive complexity minimises the difference by swallowing it up into a new and larger whole, giving the impression that differences do not really exist and we are all the same underneath, cultural difference is denied. For this reason, universalism can be categorised as a form of ethnocentrism (Bennett, 1993) (Figure 2.1).

As noted above, the evaluation of cultural difference can be impossible in the early stages of ethnocentrism due to a lack of cognitive categories to describe cultural difference, but poorly defined cognitive categories can be termed as *benign stereotypes* (Bennett, 1993) because they are non-evaluative, although stereotypes can become evaluative in the later stages of ethnocentrism.

The term *stereotype* was first coined by Lippmann (1922) to describe the way we conceptually categorise ourselves and other people into groups just as we categorise information about the world. But, while earlier definitions of them tended to focus on their flawed nature, more recent definitions have tended to recognise their status as necessary cognitive processes (Dovidio *et al.*, 1996). From this standpoint, stereotypes can be considered basic to human thought insofar as they help us to make sense of the complex world around us, and they can sometimes provide useful sources of reasonably accurate information to make inferences when there is a lack of information to draw on(Hamilton & Neville Uhles, 2000).

However, stereotypes form as we categorise people based on visually obvious attributes, such as race or gender. Once a conceptual category has been set up in the mind, knowledge, beliefs and expectancies are added, and individuals within the category are thereafter imbued with the characteristics attached to the category. Such categorisation processes form and

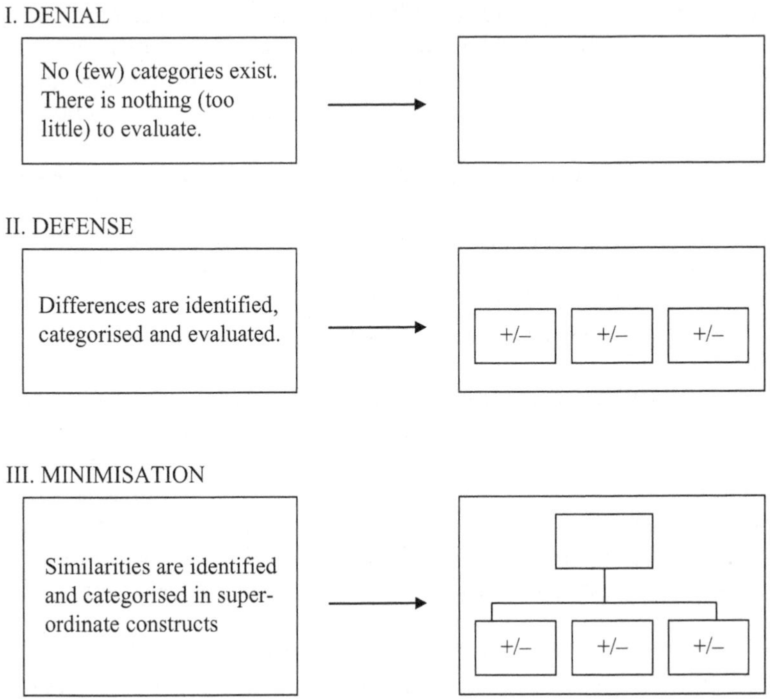

I. DENIAL

> No (few) categories exist.
> There is nothing (too
> little) to evaluate.

II. DEFENSE

> Differences are identified,
> categorised and evaluated.

+/−   +/−   +/−

III. MINIMISATION

> Similarities are identified
> and categorised in super-
> ordinate constructs

+/−   +/−   +/−

Figure 2.1 The ethnocentric stages of Bennett's (1993) Developmental Model of Intercultural Sensitivity

maintain the group boundaries that underpin ethnocentrism and prejudice (Brislin, 1986; Levine & Campbell, 1972; Rubovitz & Maehr, 1973). Stereotypes are transmitted through language and can perpetuate prejudice if language is commonly used to describe members of stereotyped groups in a biased way (Allport, 1954; Maas & Arcuri, 1996).

Notwithstanding their status as necessary cognitive processes, stereotypes can have a negative impact on perception, communication and behaviour by distorting perception (Barna, 1998), leading people to remember more favourable information about in-group members and less favourable information about out-group members (Hewstone & Giles, 1986), and causing inaccurate predictions about behaviour (Gudykunst & Hammer, 1988; Kim & Gudykunst, 1988). Stereotypes can also constrain behaviour as people seek confirmation of them during interaction, sometimes triggering a self-fulfilling prophesy in the process (Hewstone & Giles, 1986).

But as with other information contained in value-laden conceptual frameworks in the mind, stereotypes can change. Through interaction with people who do not fit into the broader category, category sub-types may be set up to account for the differences, which contain more detail than the main category. Alternatively, atypical members may be conceptually isolated from the main category preserving the existing stereotype in the process, so stereotype categorisation may or may not break down in response to new information (Hamilton & Neville Uhles, 2000). This echoes the point made by Sercu (2000) above in relation to cognitive development. As people process information about the world, they can either attempt to maintain existing impressions or develop more accurate representations, either operating under an *impression–maintenance* or an *accuracy* mode. For the latter to occur, motivation and cognitive resources are crucial; people have to be willing to actively process and restructure information.

Stereotypical categorisations of self and other help define group boundaries and lie at the heart of inter-group attitudes. The identity of any given individual consists of both personal and social identity accordingly. The term *personal identity* refers to conceptual categories about the self that define the perceiver as a *unique individual* in contrast to other individuals. While the term *social identity* refers to conceptual categorisations of the self, it can also refer instead to self-categories that define the individual in terms of *shared similarities* with members of certain social categories, in contrast to other social categories (Hamilton & Neville Uhles, 2000). Personal and social identity, as two interconnected dimensions of self-concept, are the foundational concepts of Social Identity Theory, which suggests that the social categorisation of people into distinct groups causes discrimination as the in-group is favoured over the out-group, the drive for which is psychologically rooted in a basic human need for self-esteem (Tajfel, 1982; Tajfel *et al.*, 1971; Turner, 1987), although the cultural universality of this phenomenon was brought into question by Wetherell (1982). The process is described using the term Othering by Holliday (2011):

> The process of Othering is complex and in many ways basic in the formation and maintenance of group behaviour. It can be defined as constructing, or imagining, a demonized image of 'them', or the Other, which supports an idealized image of 'us', or the Self. Othering is also essentialist in that the demonized image is applied to all members of the group or society which is being Othered. Othering operates at all levels of society, as a basic means whereby social groups sustain a positive sense of identity .... (Holliday, 2011: 69–70)

Individuals identify with a group such that positive self-identity is main-
tained and that this motivation is enacted in such interrelated forms as
in-group bias, in-group commitment, in-group loyalty, and out-group
discrimination. (Kim, 2009: 55)

Unfair negative attitude toward out-group members, or prejudice, also
underpins group identification and social categorisation processes (Dovidio
et al., 1996). Essentially, prejudice involves pre-judgment based upon labels
that are applied to people originating in sometimes superficial factors used
to differentiate people (such as race, sex, skin colour, occupation, religion or
political affiliation). Judgments, or evaluations, can be prejudicial insofar as
people are judged based on their perceived membership of the labelled category, rather than upon their individual characteristics. In addition to making
judgments about facts, individuals also make judgments about the goodness,
worth or desirability of other people based on the labels applied. These are
sometimes so strongly held that they are impervious to the introduction of
new facts which, from a rational point of view, should affect attitudes
towards others (Brislin, 1986).

This observation echoes Sercu's point that when people process information about the world, they can either attempt to maintain existing impressions or to develop more accurate representations. People are not always
willing to actively process and restructure new information with an *open
mind*, perhaps because prejudice can sometimes help people avoid punish-
ment, gain reward, protect self-esteem, express values or it can help them
develop the knowledge they need to function effectively in society (Brislin,
1986; Katz, 1960).

Ethnorelativism

When people process information about the world, including about other
people, they can attempt to develop more accurate representations about
them as noted above, which can bring identity into play. Kim (2009) identifies a range of concepts used by researchers to refer to an *inclusive identity
orientation*, including cognitive differentiation, multiple categorisation, decat-
egorisation, recategorisation and wide categorisation.

These concepts generally refer to a degree of cognitive refinement that
allows for a less stereotypical and more personalised way with which
to perceive and orient oneself to culturally dissimilar others. (Kim,
2009: 56)

As we have seen, intercultural development is integrally related to both cognitive and moral development, and a central issue is the way in which people respond to discrepancies between incoming information and prior knowledge. As with cognitive and moral development, intercultural development can be considered as a social process that comprises a series of qualitatively different stages of acquisition of conceptual heterarchies, in which more adaptive and flexible processing systems come to replace less flexible, more concrete ones. When people process information about the world, they can gradually develop more accurate representations if they are willing to actively process and restructure information.

With ongoing exposure to cultural difference, cognitive development takes place as similarities are noticed and super-ordinate conceptual constructs are created that incorporate previously irreconcilable elements into more complex cognitive structures. While this may be accompanied by a decrease in evaluative tendency as cultural universals are recognised, cultural difference may be *minimised* as similarities are focused upon. Then, if people no longer feel threatened by difference, they may actively attempt to elaborate new conceptual categories to accommodate difference, rather than simply preserving existing ones; this may be accompanied by non-evaluative acceptance of behavioural and value difference (including language) as the belief that there are no absolute standards of rightness or goodness becomes more difficult to justify (Bennett, 1993).

Just as empathy plays an important role in cognitive and moral development as egocentric people learn to take the perspectives of other people, it also plays an important role in intercultural development as ethnocentrism gives way to ethnorelativism. This can be characterised by a paralysis of judgment as the belief that there are no absolute standards of rightness or goodness is challenged. Empathy, or perspective-taking, requires at least a temporary suspension of one's own value-laden conceptual frameworks if another person's perspective is to be explored with minimal distortion from one's own.

The ability to empathise also characterises Rogers' (1980) description of the person-centred therapist who listens closely and attempts to view the world through the clients' frame of reference by suspending analysis and evaluation from within their own frame of reference, and setting aside their own values through non-judgmental stance and perspective-taking to nurture in their client a congruent self. This approach has also been applied to nurture the development of teachers who can temporarily suspend critical, evaluative thought to confirm understanding (Edge, 1992).

Communicatively, empathy can involve the overt signalling of understanding and concern through verbal and non-verbal cues (Gudykunst, 1998).

But communicative behaviour and skill may differ significantly depending upon the foreign language ability of the person (Nishida, 1985) and/or the culture concerned (Abe & Wiseman, 1983), although empathy, respect and non-judgmental stance may still be universal even if they are variously expressed in different cultures (Olebe & Koester, 1989).

In Japanese communicative behaviour, for example, it has been suggested the prioritisation of relationship maintenance leads to forms of communication that are more reserved and more attentive to social norms than in the United States. Communicative patterns that involve self-disclosure or the verbalisation of evaluations of other people may also differ (Olebe & Koester, 1989). For this reason, it is important to remember that private, unverbalised evaluations of self and other may exert an influence upon surface level communication when considering research that has been conducted into *non-evaluative empathy* as a form of communicative behaviour (Koester & Olebe, 1988).

At a deeper level, however, empathy has both cognitive and affective components. Affectively, it involves vicariously experiencing the emotions of another, which causes some people to confuse sympathy with empathy. But cognitively, empathy involves perspective-taking, and being able to take the perspective of another person to see the world from their point of view seems to play an important role in cross-cultural adaptation. Research suggests that those who are most non-judgmental in terms of interaction posture, and most relativistic in their orientation towards knowledge, may experience greater culture shock than those who are not, which implies that the greater the awareness of the limitations of one's truths, the greater the likelihood is that one will be influenced by people who have different worldviews to one's own. Such receptivity towards other life orientations may thus generate intra-personal turmoil and confusion as attempts are made to resolve value contradictions and discrepancies (Ruben & Kealey, 1979).

For this reason, empathy is considered to involve adaptation as extensive exposure to different worldviews leads to the development of a more pluralistic orientation towards cultural difference, resulting from the internalisation of two or more cultural frames of reference and commitment to their co-existence within the self. This means that as cultural difference is internalised as part of the self, what used to be respect for cultural difference can gradually turn into self-respect (Bennett, 1993) (Figure 2.2). Kim coined the term intercultural identity to refer to an achieved self–other orientation developed by an individual with an *inclusive indentity orientation* over time:

> Intercultural identity is thus conceived as a continuum of adapative changes over time from a mono-cultural to an increasingly complex and inclusive character. (Kim, 2009: 56)

IV. ACCEPTANCE

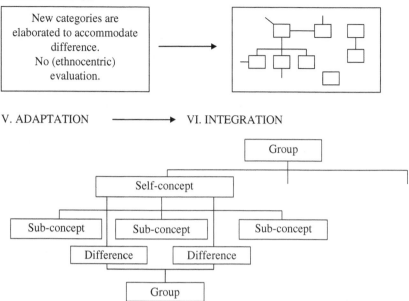

V. ADAPTATION ⟶ VI. INTEGRATION

Figure 2.2 The ethnorelative stages of Bennett's (1993) Developmental Model of Intercultural Sensitivity

> The brain is an open system (you can learn), you have choices (you can communicate one way or another) and your actions produce a response. (you do something to other people) (Samovar & Porter, 2004: 283)

As we have seen, non-judgmental stance and the development of adaptive skills play an important role in the development of intercultural sensitivity, but the development is neither linear nor guaranteed as the paralysis of judgment in the face of alternative perspectives may cause some people to retreat to the surer ground of ethnocentrism. But others may develop the ability to consciously analyse and evaluate situations from various cultural perspectives before proceeding to make their own evaluations as they make decisions and choices. The former type of evaluation can be considered contextual and the latter can be considered critical, both of which are qualitatively different from ethnocentric evaluations that are bound by the value system formed during socialisation:

> Should you marry him? the question comes in English.
> Yes.

Should you marry him? the question echoes in Polish.
No. (Hoffman, 1989: 199)

In contextual evaluation, possible evaluations from standpoints other than one's own are identified. In critical evaluation, one's own evaluations are arrived at through the careful consideration of possible evaluations from standpoints other than one's own, regardless of whether they are ultimately selected or rejected as decisions are made. In critical evaluation, a number of cultural frames of reference may be applied as a range of possible evaluative standards are identified and applied by choice. Insofar as this carries implications for self-development, both contextual evaluation and critical evaluation play a role in identity-development. As Bennett (1993) notes, integrated people who consciously select cultural options by taking different cultural frames of reference into consideration are thus choosers of alternatives, although the concept of critical evaluation is not explicitly recognised or incorporated into his model.

Coming to grips with a multiplicity of realities on a cognitive level can involve the conscious restructuring of identity to incorporate other worldviews as disparate new elements are actively integrated into a new whole. The conceptual frames of reference of individuals with an *inclusive identity orientation* described by Kim (2009) above may experience culture shock that can lead to the loss or rejection of primary cultural affiliation according to Bennett (1993), echoing Rogers' (1951, 1961, 1980) concern that people who cannot maintain a consistent self-concept and self-esteem may disown parts of themselves.

Another important identity factor at play in intercultural communication in this regard is *identity security* (Kim, 2009) that is used to describe the degree to which people feel secure in their own changing identity which serves to integrate other related terms such as risk taking, self-confidence, self-esteem and hardiness, which tends to manifest itself in 'generally positive attitudes toward and evaluation of oneself and others' and as a kind of 'self-trust that allows individuals not to cripple themselves with irrational feelings of inferiority or defensiveness and instead to seek more practical and adaptive alternatives when interacting interculturally' (Kim, 2009: 57–58).

Thus, as Bennett (1993) notes, any subsequent disintegration of identity that leaves an individual in marginal existence on the periphery of two or more cultures may be coupled with the understanding that identity emerges from the act of defining identity itself. By suggesting that such people are best placed to mediate cross-culturally, since they are not enmeshed in any reference group and are able to construct each appropriate worldview as needed, Bennett introduces the notion of citizenship, a theme that will be revisited later in the book.

3 Theoretical and Political Perspectives upon Value Judgment

Theoretically Driven Learning Objectives

In this chapter, we will consider some of the learning objectives implied by the previous two chapters related to the management of value judgment, highlighting areas of theoretical disagreement towards the end. The mind was presented as an information-handling system that gradually accumulates retrievable patterns of information that are stored in memory in value-laden conceptual hierarchies serving as sources of prior knowledge that help us interpret the world around us. Furthermore, identity can be considered in cognitive terms with self-concept consisting of value-laden conceptual hierarchies that contain information about one's own attributes developed partly through personal experience and partly through social influence largely occurring unconsciously.

Declarative knowledge warrants special attention in two regards. First, reflection upon the content of the conceptual categories to which learners refer when describing themselves and the world around them is needed and second, the relationships between conceptual categories and their relative rankings need to be considered when reflecting upon values. In this process, attempts can be made to identify and recognise the possible influences of the linguistic and cultural environment upon the development of concepts and values. Theoretical knowledge of the social processes that tend to shape knowledge and personal development in identifiable ways also warrants special attention.

> Knowledge has two major components: knowledge of social processes, and knowledge of illustrations of those processes and products; the latter includes knowledge about how other people see oneself as well as knowledge about other people. (Byram *et al.*, 2009: 25)

But an attitudinal dimension comes into play that constitutes an *orientation* to knowledge. It involves the recognition of the boundaries and limitations necessarily placed upon one's own knowledge and identity by one's lack of experience and limited social exposure, coupled with a recognition that the knowledge bases of others will naturally differ from one's own in significant ways that can undermine communicative processes. Intercultural misunderstanding can be rooted in the ethnocentric projection of one worldview onto another as the perception of other perspectives gets distorted. Recognition of this point and the willingness to actively overcome it out of respect for others, to enhance communication with them, depends upon the existence of attitudes that are characterised by curiosity, openness and the readiness to suspend disbelief about other cultures and belief about one's own (Byram, 1997).

> Respect for otherness is manifested in curiosity and openness, readiness to suspend belief about (the 'naturalness' of) one's own culture and to believe in (the 'naturalness' of) other cultures. (Byram *et al.*, 2009: 23)

Naturally, foreign language learners may lack awareness of the extent to which their knowledge frameworks are personal or cultural in nature. Also, the lack of conceptual categories about particular kinds of cultural difference resulting from a lack of prior exposure to it can render evaluation impossible if there is too little information to evaluate. But experiencing another culture can illuminate one's own as the complex unconscious presuppositions of worldview are made more conscious, and encounters with cultural difference can naturally highlight the particularity of one's own worldview, stimulating self-reflection in the process (Bennett, 1993; Hall, 1990). Cultural awareness and consciousness-raising activities can be developed to this end.

Cultural knowledge has been identified as an important dimension of intercultural communicative competence (Byram, 1997). As it develops, it can provide a source of information that can be used to interpret and predict the behaviour of people from other cultures (Fiedler *et al.*, 1971), minimising misunderstanding in the process (Gudykunst & Kim, 2003; Miller & Steinberg, 1975; Wiseman *et al.*, 1989). This can include developing an awareness of the existence of, and potential impact upon communication of, different linguistic, verbal and non-verbal conventions.

Communicative awareness: an ability to recognize different linguistic conventions, different verbal and non-verbal communication conventions – especially in a foreign language – and their effects on discourse processes, and to negotiate rules appropriate for intercultural communication. (Byram *et al.*, 2009: 24)

The knowledge frameworks of others can be systematically explored and described by learners if they are taught how to develop and deploy the skills of discovery and interaction, paying attention to linguistic and cultural influences in the process. Actively seeking out other interpretations of familiar and unfamiliar phenomena both in one's own and in other cultures, questioning one's own culture (Byram, 1997) and tolerating ambiguity are all part of this process as one gathers the information on offer while also actively looking for 'the hidden and the unexpressed' (Holliday, 2011: 27) and 'the "unsaid" (implicit propositions)' (Fairclough, 2010: 27) in which ideology tends to lie.

Skills of discovery and interaction are the ability to acquire new knowledge of a culture and cultural practices and the ability to operate knowledge, attitudes and skills under the constraints of real-time communication and interaction. (Byram *et al.*, 2009: 25)

Tolerance for ambiguity is the ability to accept ambiguity and lack of clarity and to be able to deal with this constructively. (Byram *et al.*, 2009: 24)

When learning to explore and describe the perspectives of others, learners can focus their attention upon the affective and behavioural dimensions of the process, but cognitively speaking, empathy involves the temporary suspension of one's own value-laden concepts and evaluative processes, as attention is selectively directed instead onto another person's perspective with the specific goal in mind of exploring and describing it as accurately as possible.

Empathy is the ability to project oneself into another person's perspective and their opinions, motives, ways of thinking and feelings. (Byram *et al.*, 2009: 24)

As new conceptual categories are generated in response to ongoing exposure to cultural difference, similarities and differences can then be identified, categorised and evaluated, although the identification of similarities is the main cognitive process through which concepts are linked together into conceptual frameworks in super-ordinate constructs. But the declarative knowledge stored in conceptual categories about people can give rise to the development of stereotypes, which are a particular type of cognitive category that forms as information about a group of people is linked into a conceptual framework contained within a rather fixed boundary, and distinctions drawn between groups of people naturally result from the identification of differences between them. The identification of differences underpinning such processes also has an evaluative dimension as people tend to remember more favourable information about in-group members and less favourable information about out-group members, perhaps to boost their own self-esteem as we have seen.

Grouping and boundary-setting processes can both be considered cognitive processes operating within the mind of any given individual. Rigid in-group and out-group social boundaries are supported by stereotyping tendencies to some extent, as people tend to perceive more similarities between out-group members than between in-group members in biased ways. Engaging in this prejudiced form of evaluation, or displaying an unfair negative attitude towards out-group members may result in the affectively driven cognitive blocking of the introduction of new information into existing value-laden conceptual categories that *should* affect the evaluation from a rational point of view.

The ability to compare and contrast by identifying similarities and differences thus presents itself an important *analytical* learning objective in which careful and conscious attention is paid to grouping and boundary-setting patterns and tendencies, along with their underlying affective influences, during information processing. Recalling that people *can* ignore stereotypes and form more individualised impressions of others when they not only have information but also the ability and motivation to actively process it with an open mind, learner attention can be systematically directed onto both similarities and differences through carefully designed tasks to develop their ability to reflect upon and take greater conscious control over their grouping and boundary-setting tendencies, and underlying affective motivations. In this way, learners can develop more individualised impressions of others using information that is as accurate as possible, rather than relying on pre-existing stereotypes. The teacher has an important role to play not only in motivating learners but also in building their cognitive resources to increase their willingness to make the shift from operating in an *impression-maintenance* mode to an *accuracy* mode by actively processing and restructuring information (Sercu, 2000).

Individuation involves a clear self-definition and definition of the other as a singular individual rather than as a member of a conventional social category. Within this capacity, one is better able to transcend conventional in-group out-group boundaries and to see oneself and others on the basis of unique individual qualities. (Kim, 2009: 56)

Reflective self-observation is thought to generally facilitate foreign language learning by helping learners to take strategic control of their own thought processes, and exposure to cultural difference can bring the largely unconscious complex of one's own worldview to the fore. Self-reflective observation opens up the possibility of control over one's cognitive and affective responses to cultural difference as they happen, which can limit their potentially negative impact upon intercultural communication. This can in turn encourage the development of meta-cognitive and meta-affective awareness.

Reflective self-awareness underpins emotional intelligence as ongoing attention is paid to one's own internal states during which the mind observes itself. This critical awareness of one's own thoughts and emotions, otherwise known as meta-cognition and meta-mood, was described by Freud as an 'evenly hovering attention' (Goleman, 2004: 46) that takes in whatever passes through awareness with impartiality, as an interested yet unreactive witness, although it may also be judgmental in nature. Such reflective self-awareness is the basic building block of competence upon which self-control can be built, and the development of *mindfulness* in communication is considered to play an important role in communication with strangers partly by encouraging awareness of other perspectives and openness to information. Importantly, mindfulness, or reflective self-monitoring, can facilitate reflection upon the way people are categorised which creates the opportunity to reconsider and revise cognitions accordingly (Gudykunst, 1998).

Indeed, people with lower prejudice levels seem to consciously attempt to prevent negative stereotypes from influencing their behaviour because they are more likely to have personal standards prescribing that they behave in non-prejudiced way towards another person. They experience more compunction and guilt when they deviate from these standards, which in turn motivates efforts to behave in a less biased way in the future. The application of personal standards when monitoring and controlling one's own thought processes involves both meta-cognitive and meta-affective awareness and control, and attempts to combat racism and discrimination have thus involved making people aware of the dangers of using facile stereotypes in decision-making processes in the hope that they will choose not to let stereotypes influence their behaviour (Devine & Monteith, 1993; Hamilton & Neville Uhles, 2000).

The development of meta-cognitive and meta-affective awareness and control are considered important learning objectives not only in education generally (Anderson & Krathwohl, 2001; Bloom *et al.*, 1956), but also in foreign language learning more specifically (O'Malley & Chamot, 1989, 1990). When intercultural elements are introduced into foreign language education, self-reflection and consciousness-raising can help circumvent the problem of foreign language learners merely encoding their own culture-specific meanings in the foreign language, which involves both reflective and comparative processes that lead to the development of cultural awareness (Byram, 1989a).

In addition to analytical tasks aimed at engaging learners in the identification of similarities and differences, *evaluation* also presents itself as a learning objective. When Sumner first coined the term ethnocentrism in 1906, he also recommended the sharpening of the *critical* faculty as the only antidote to ethnocentrism, defining *criticism* as the examination and test of propositions of any kind that are offered for acceptance to establish the extent to which they correspond to reality. The historical roots of critical thinking can be traced back to the ancient Greeks:

> The word 'critical' derives etymologically from two Greek roots: 'kriticos' (meaning discerning judgment) and 'kriterion' (meaning standards). Etymologically, then, the word implies the development of 'discerning judgment based on standards'. In *Webster's New World Dictionary*, the relevant entry reads 'characterized by careful analysis and judgment' and is followed by the gloss, 'critical – in its strictest sense – implies an attempt at objective judgment so as to determine both merits and faults'. Applied to thinking, then, we might provisionally define critical thinking as thinking that explicitly aims at well-founded judgment and hence utilizes appropriate evaluative standards in the attempt to determine the true worth, merit, or value of something. The tradition of research into critical thinking reflects the common perception that human thinking left to itself often gravitates toward prejudice, over-generalization, common fallacies, self-deception, rigidity, and narrowness. (Foundation for Critical Thinking, undated)

Critical thinking essentially involves the development of discerning judgment based on standards, but the critical thinking movement seeks to enable people to govern their thoughts more generally in recognition of the fact that much human thought, left to itself, is biased, distorted, partial, uninformed or down-right prejudiced (Paul & Elder, 2002). This spontaneous and non-reflective thinking, otherwise known as *first-order thinking*, may contain insight, prejudice, truth and error, indiscriminately combined. Indeed, the academic literature is replete with wide-ranging examples of cognitive distortions, many of which have affective underpinnings and behavioural consequences, such as focusing on information that confirms judgments to the exclusion of that which does not, the use of various mental shortcuts in reasoning that lead to inaccurate conclusions and the hasty formation of premature impressions and snap judgments in social perception.

Since we cannot attain reliable self-knowledge through our senses because the senses do not exactly mirror reality, Socrates suggested that we should study ourselves through rational thought and introspection, and Socrates' injunction *Know Thyself* remains a motto of psychological thought even today (Rathus, 1985). Such *second-order thinking* can be considered first-order thinking raised to the level of conscious realisation before it is analysed, assessed and carefully and consciously reconstructed. Learning how to govern our thoughts as critical thinkers involves analysing, exposing and scrutinising the egocentric roots of our way of thinking to identify and replace inappropriate evaluative standards with sound ones through conscious choice. In this way, we can free ourselves from many of the traps of undisciplined and instinctive thought, taking command over our self-development and the directions in which our lives are heading (Paul & Elder, 2002).

It was noted earlier that in Socratic teaching, learner viewpoints are systematically probed to reveal their inadequacies and motivate learners to formulate better positions. In this way, Socratic questioning can be used to promote second-order thinking in ways that include questioning ends and objectives, the status and wording of questions, the sources of information and fact, the method and quality of information collection, the mode of judgment and reasoning used, the concepts that make reasoning possible, the assumptions that underpin concepts in use, the implications that follow from their use and the points of view that frame reasoning (Crain, 2000).

However, it was also noted above that Kohlberg's Stages of Moral Development were criticised for both gender and cultural bias by suggesting that the ethic of care is located at a lower stage of the developmental hierarchy than rationality. The critical thinking tradition has also been criticised by de Bono (1990) who argues that critical thinking alone cannot construct anything new from its parts because of its emphasis upon analysis of closed conceptual systems. This is because a line must be drawn during the process of analysis to enclose what is relevant, meaning that a decision needs to be taken as to what to include or exclude from the system before the factors and the inter-relationships are then analysed.

Arguing that this is both preceded and affected by perceptual limitation, de Bono (1990) recommends the development of lateral thinking instead, which involves making side-ways leaps between conceptual patterns, and looking between and around conceptual boundaries, to discover new ways of perceiving the world beyond that which we can already imagine in order to restructure our own patterns through conscious choice. But as we have seen, perspective-taking also involves making side-ways leaps between conceptual patterns, and looking between and around conceptual boundaries, to discover the different ways in which the perspectives of others differ from our own. This suggests that we can restructure our own conceptual patterns through conscious choice to some extent in response to cultural difference.

As noted earlier, Socratic questioning is only one of the ways in which moral development can occur, and perspective-taking also finds its place in contemporary critical thinking as one of six intellectual traits that support the development of fair-mindedness. Fair-minded judgment requires a good-faith effort to acquire accurate knowledge about another person's point of view through perspective taking, or *intellectual empathy* (Paul & Elder, 2002).

The critical thinking movement thus calls for the development of intellectual traits that require the application of intellectual standards to thought itself and more specifically, to reasoning processes or the transformation of information to reach conclusions (Paul & Elder, 2002). This is a call for increased meta-cognitive awareness and control, but since the mind is a pattern-making and pattern-recognition system, and can always be better organised since its arrangement depends partly upon the order in which information is received, it needs to restructure itself constantly.

Thus, attempts should be made to reorganise information gathered during perspective-taking into new conceptual patterns by consciously engaging in the processes of analysis and evaluation. Although the word *critical* etymologically refers to evaluative processes, and still does in contemporary thought, evaluation can be suspended temporarily *as part of the critical process* to allow ideas to survive longer in the mind to breed further ideas, to allow other people to offer ideas that might otherwise have been rejected, to accept ideas and allow them to stimulate existing patterns, or to allow ideas previously considered evaluated to survive long enough to highlight ways in which the current frame of reference might be altered and improved upon. Ultimately, through intercultural communication, individuals should be 'able to expand their repertoire of cultural engagement and carry practices from one society to another, to share underlying universal cultural processes with people from other societies, and to dialogue with the environment provided by national social structures' (Holliday, 2011: 36).

Evaluative processes cannot be switched off completely but evaluation can be suspended to make way for other forms of explorative thought by *postponing* evaluation until later (de Bono, 1990). Acting interculturally requires a willingness to suspend one's values, 'at least temporarily, in order to be able to understand and empathise with the values of others that are incompatible with one's own' (Byram, 2008: 69). On this, Holliday (2011) highlights the importance of being able to adopt a non-judgmental stance temporarily to interrogate ideology through intercultural communication by bracketing:

> Putting aside established descriptions relates to the discipline of bracketing. Often associated with phenomenology, this can be described as locating prejudices which will colour the viewpoint of the researcher and consciously putting them aside, to 'temporarily suspend all common-sense assumptions' in order to set aside judgements about the expected 'nature', 'essence' and 'reality' of things (Schutz, 1970: 316), and to make visible the practices through which taken-for-granted realities are accomplished. (Gubrium & Holstein, 1997: 40) (Holliday, 2011: 31)

Dewey (1997) highlights the role of suspended judgment in problem-solving through critical thinking:

> The essence of critical thinking is suspended judgment; and the essence of this suspense is inquiry to determine the nature of the problem before proceeding to attempts at its solution. (Dewey, 1997: 74, cited in Houghton & Yamada, forthcoming)

While teachers can help learners to explore and identify the different ways in which situations may be evaluated from various personal and cultural standpoints through carefully designed tasks, they can also help learners to consciously and reflectively scrutinise their own evaluative processes, along with their underlying affective motivations. Learners can thus hold themselves up to conscious analysis *by themselves*, suspending evaluation until the initial analysis is complete. Genuinely taking the perspectives of others into consideration while critically reflecting upon themselves can enhance the quality of learners' evaluations of self and other insofar as the standards of the base culture are not automatically and ethnocentrically applied without critical self-reflection coupled with the careful consideration of alternative viewpoints.

As we have seen, personal development can be seen in terms of existing worldview giving way to the internalisation of other cultural frames of reference through empathy, which can transform identity and equip people to mediate between cultures. By encouraging learners to evaluate with conscious reference to their own value-laden conceptual frameworks, and to justify their evaluations with reasons, critical cultural awareness (Byram, 1997) may develop if attention is paid to the various ways in which incoming information is analysed, evaluated and integrated into existing knowledge frameworks, identifying discrepancies and making appropriate adjustments to one's way of thinking in the process to develop more logically consistent, reasoned forms of thought:

> Critical cultural awareness: an ability to evaluate, critically and on the basis of explicit criteria, perspectives, practices and products in one's own and other cultures and countries. (Byram *et al.*, 2009: 25)

Similarities and differences not only between cultures but also between self and other can be systematically sought, identified, analysed and evaluated with conscious reference to one's own value-laden conceptual frameworks with a view to *mediating* between conflicting interpretations of phenomena, resolving cultural and linguistic mismatches and identifying irresolvable differences, all of which rests upon the ability to interpret and relate alternative systems (Byram, 1997).

> Skills of interpreting and relating: the ability to interpret a document or event from another culture, to explain it and relate it to documents from one's own. (Byram *et al.*, 2009: 25)

Mediation in this sense involves mediating between oneself and others by 'taking an "external" perspective on oneself as one interacts with others and to analyse, and where desirable, adapt one's behaviour and underlying values and beliefs' (Byram, 2008: 68). Intercultural mediation is both cognitive and moral in nature, but the discussion on cognitive and moral development earlier in this book suggests that those who reach the highest stages of each should be able to engage in higher forms of thought by focusing on many different aspects of a given problem before arriving at judgments. However, not all adults reach these higher stages of cognitive and moral development, and there is good reason to encourage both cognitive and moral development, both of which underpin intercultural development, through education.

Conflicting Perspectives upon the Management of Value Judgment

In the previous section, an attempt was made to construct bridges between intercultural communication theories and the practice of foreign language education by presenting a range of learning objectives related to value judgment, rooted most deeply in cognitive and moral development, implied by the theoretical background presented earlier in this book. While it is assumed throughout this book that regardless of local cultural context, learning objectives will generally be set for learners who will mostly be assessed as *individuals* in class, it is also recognised that the determination of learning objectives within a lesson plan, syllabus or broader curriculum can also have a *social* dimension insofar as their formulation may be influenced in a top-down manner by national education policy or curriculum documents.

Recognition of the co-existence and interconnectedness of these individual and social dimensions allowed for theoretically driven learning objectives to be considered in direct relation to the political and cultural context of the Council of Europe through Byram's (1997) Model of Intercultural Communicative Competence, an earlier version of which was incorporated into the Common European Framework of Reference for Foreign Languages, and the Autobiography of Intercultural Encounters (Byram *et al.*, 2009), an educational instrument that was designed to support the implementation of the White Paper on Intercultural Dialogue (2008) mentioned in the introduction to this book.

The previous section as a whole points to a theoretically driven vision of intercultural communicative competence that has both individual and social dimensions, but as noted earlier, researcher conceptualisations of intercultural competence in different parts of the world can be culturally influenced just as intercultural communication can be influenced by culturally shared elements of self-concept (Deardorff, 2009a). In this section, an attempt will be made to highlight some of the differing views on the ways in which value judgment should be handled in intercultural communication bringing some of the main areas of underlying disagreement into sharper focus.

The word evaluation has been used in different ways in relation to value judgment so far. Before proceeding, let us review some of the key uses of the term before taking a historical look at the different ways in which they have been viewed by some of the authors cited. The following distinctions made in passing so far are notable at this point:

- Evaluation involves the application of values to arrive at positive or negative judgments about an object's worth.
- Evaluation can be suspended at least temporarily to (re)consider information.
- Prejudiced evaluation involves hasty evaluation that is biased.
- Ethnocentric evaluation involves the unreflective application of the values of one's own culture without considering alternatives.

- Contextual evaluation involves identifying the different ways in which an object can be evaluated from different standpoints.
- Critical evaluation involves evaluation with conscious reference to one's own values.

It was noted above that Bennett (1993) introduced the question of citizenship into his account of the development of intercultural sensitivity by suggesting that people in marginal existence on the periphery of two or more cultures may be best placed to mediate cross-culturally, since they are not enmeshed in any reference group, and are able to construct appropriate worldviews as needed through contextual evaluation. The interconnectedness of global citizens is noted by Ashwill and Du'o'ng (2009), yet the political, social and historical contexts within which intercultural interaction occurs has largely been neglected in *Western* models of intercultural competence according to Deardorff (2009a), although her recent synthesis of conceptualisations of intercultural competence was admittedly written 'from a U.S. perspective' (Deardorff, 2009a: 264). In foreign language education, within the European context at least, the political, social and historical contexts have been taken into greater account within the concept of intercultural citizenship as an element of intercultural communicative competence related to *critical cultural awareness*, or the ability to 'evaluate critically and on the basis of explicit criteria perspectives, practices and products in one's own and other cultures and countries' (Byram, 1997: 63), which is a matter of *political* education.

Byram's definition of critical cultural awareness presented above drew upon views developed within the German context (also see Moosmüller & Schönhuth, 2009) focusing particularly upon Doyé's application of Gagel's distinction between the cognitive, evaluative and action orientations to foreign language education. More specifically, Gagel's evaluative orientation referred to the ability to explain, mediate and use values to make political judgments. Both Doyé and Byram agreed that when making judgments, foreign language learners should respect the norms of other societies and evaluate them in an unprejudiced way, echoing Bennett's (1993) distinction between ethnocentric and contextual evaluation.

But Byram's position on the issue of evaluation changed significantly between 1994 and 2002. While initially recognising that the 'neutral empathetic construction of cultural norms is necessary to appreciate the relevant cultural construct' (Byram *et al.*, 1994: 29), he also noted an uneasy uncertainty in the literature as to the nature of the cognitive dimension of empathy, and a general tendency for it to be explained in terms of feelings and sympathy, a point recognised by Gudykunst (1998) who also distinguished its cognitive and affective dimensions as we have seen. Claiming that the desire to simplify and stereotype may frustrate the development of empathetic understanding even if critical thinking training is used to enhance empathetic skills (Byram *et al.*, 1994: 30–31), Byram (1997) rejected the viability of empathy as a learning objective for foreign language learners for being uncritical and normative, while recognising the potentially negative impact of ethnocentric evaluation upon intercultural interaction.

Rejecting Damen (1987) and Robinson's (1988) work for their lack of criticality, Guilherme (2002) supported Byram's rejection of empathy on the grounds that learners are simply expected to accept and understand the other viewpoint rather than taking a critical, analytical stance because value-free interpretation is unlikely to happen, endorsing his recommendation that an evaluative approach should be taken towards other cultures to allow the conscious control of biased interpretation. Noting disagreement between foreign language teachers over whether or not the mere act of cultural comparison necessarily involves value-judgment, or whether it can remain a neutral recognition of similarities and differences, Guilherme took the view that since comparisons rooted in the perspective of the onlooker *necessarily* involve judgment, a non-judgmental stance should succeed and not precede the deployment of critical awareness (which involves judgment, or evaluation), if it is to be attempted at all.

The ongoing underlying disagreement over the relative value of non-judgmental stance versus judgmental stance seems to have obscured interpretations of academic contributions in the field to some extent. While endorsing Foucault's description of power relations as enabling and generative of cultural production, Guilherme (2002) failed to recognise Damen's (1987) synthetic, dynamic level as providing the potential for critical cultural transformation, while simultaneously recognising the generative aspect of cultural production in Kramsch's (1993) model, which emphasised the importance of self-understanding, making oneself understood and understanding others. Placing the focus upon dialogue and the production of meaning across cultures that can constitute a third perspective where culture is dialogically created through discourse, Kramsch recognised the importance of the sociocultural context of the learner, of the school and the classroom cultures, and the role of language in changing people's perceptions and visions, although discussion lacked explicit social and political commitment according to Guilherme (2002).

But as noted earlier, lower-prejudiced people may have personal standards that allow them to control prejudicial thought as it arises, which implies the cognitive viability of controlling evaluative processes to some extent. Even so, Byram *et al.* (2002: 36) *absolutely* rejected the notion of non-judgmental stance, recommending teachers to reflect instead upon how the ways in which their own stereotypes and prejudice affect teaching and learning, which was essentially a call for increased meta-cognitive awareness but *not* for meta-cognitive control. In contrast, de Bono (1990) argued that the suspension of judgment is the *essential* mechanism through which other frames of references can be fully appreciated through lateral thinking, which is hindered by the closed-minded analysis and evaluation of closed conceptual systems as alternative avenues of thought are hastily closed down. Further, de Bono argued not only that lateral thinking could support the development of democratic society, but also that non-judgmental stance is the primary cognitive mechanism through which self-transformation occurs. From this standpoint, self and society can be developed consciously through the temporary suspension of judgment because this cognitive act clears the way for the active generation of new options through the unblinkered consideration of social phenomena in new ways that are relatively unconstrained by the limitations of existing conceptual frameworks. This view is supported by Holliday (2011) in relation to bracketing and the opening up of cultural possibilities as noted earlier.

While Byram drew upon Doyé for support of judgmental stance (Byram, 1997; Byram & Guilherme, 2000), Doyé (1992, 2003) recognised the educational viability and desirability of both evaluative and non-evaluative approaches to intercultural education, drawing partly upon Piaget and Kohlberg's models of cognitive and moral development. While Doyé highlighted the role of perspective-taking in equilibration, and multi-perspective educational approaches that nurture the ability to work with multiple-mental models as a matter of cognitive socialisation (also see Rest *et al.*, 1999), he also highlighted the role of evaluation in Kohlberg's post-conventional stage of moral development at which judgment is made with reference to universal principles rather than to one's own social norms. Insofar as this involves the unbiased registering of the representations of others, rather than disqualifying them as being strange or either inferior or superior to one's own, Doyé highlighted the importance of non-judgmental stance, which involves the suspension of evaluation.

It seems from the discussion above that writing from within the European context, Byram and Guilherme were taking a dichotomous view within which non-judgmental stance and empathy were being rejected in favour of critical evaluation, partly because it was less normative and thus carried greater potential for political and social transformation. Yet Doyé, who was also writing from within the European context, did not see critical and evaluation and empathy as being mutually exclusive. Not only were they seen as co-existing, they each had a distinct and important role to play in intercultural development.

As we have seen, the cognitive, affective and communicative components of empathy have caused definitional confusion in the academic literature that can still be found today. But when defined in *cognitive* terms, as perspective-taking, empathy can be considered a political act that supports both justice and democracy within Kohlberg's post-conventional stage of moral development because it involves considering social situations from different viewpoints. This kind of contextual evaluation (Bennett, 1993) can be distinguished from critical evaluation (Byram, 1997) insofar as it involves taking other perspectives into consideration prior to passing one's own judgment, both of which carry the potential to be relatively unprejudiced forms of evaluation. In this sense, empathy as perspective-taking underpins an *action orientation* to intercultural communication that is socially oriented insofar as it grasps and takes seriously the opinions and arguments of others, according personal recognition to people of other opinions and putting oneself into the situation of others (Byram *et al.*, 2009), which are some of the communicative activities and skills needed by democratic citizens:

> Action orientation is the willingness to undertake some activity alone or with others as a consequence of reflection with the aim of making a contribution to the common good. (Byram *et al.*, 2009: 25)

Insofar as this emphasis of the action orientation encourages people to change the world that is seen as being inherently malleable, rather than bringing their malleable selves into line with it, this emphasis exemplifies the kind of cultural expression often found in the West that was highlighted by Heine (2001) in his distinctions between the independent and interdependent selves, the latter of which can be exemplified by countries in East Asia. As noted earlier, the concept of the malleability of the self also finds expression in Manian and Naidu (2009) portrayal of Indian culture in relation to reincarnation and karma, and in Nwosu's (2009) portrayal of African culture, within which human events are seen as being determined by fate as part of a general orientation to *being*.

Personal and Social Transformation

The distinction between the individual and the social has been a recurrent theme in this book. The setting of learning objectives aimed at promoting the development of individual learners in particular directions is paralleled in national education policy and curriculum documents that implicitly or explicitly set learning objectives, contained within overarching educational goals aimed at stimulating the development of large groups of learners in society, in particular directions. The implication of this is that social development in particular directions can be stimulated by guiding learner development in particular directions in the first instance, which means that any consideration of learning objectives needs to take into consideration not only their individual and social dimensions, but also the relationship between, and relative prioritisation of, the two.

What it means for an individual to be a member of society is addressed through the concept of *citizenship* and this too can have personal and social dimensions, either of which may be favoured over the other. Guilherme (2002), for example, endorsed Soysal's (1998) post-modern description of citizenship based on *personhood* rather than on *nationhood*, favouring the view of individuals and societies as culturally complex and essentially fragmented entities with permeable boundaries. Noting Mouffe's (1992a, 1992b) position that identities must be constantly deconstructed and reconstructed giving rise to citizenship as a form of constructed identification, Guilherme (2002) supported Pennycook's (1994) call for the integration of critical pedagogy into English language education to address identity problems rooted in post-colonial power relations to stimulate the development of a decentred and redefined post-colonising self, empowering it in the process, a view supported by Canagarajah (1999) and Holliday (2011).

While this focus upon the political, historical and social contexts of intercultural competence tends to be viewed through the conceptual lenses provided by the *criticality* movement within the European context in relation to critical pedagogy and critical thinking for example, they tend to be viewed, instead, in terms of *context* from 'the U.S. context' (Deardorff, 2009a: 264) in relation to 'the role of equality and power in intercultural competence, as well as the impact of such historical contexts as colonialism and its subsequent effects upon indigenous culture' (Deardorff, 2009a: 267). Notably, the index of the *SAGE Handbook of Intercultural Competence* (Deardorff, 2009c) only has one reference each to the concepts of critical cultural awareness and citizenship education in Byram's Model of Intercultural Communicative Competence (2009), and one reference to critical thinking in Deardorff's (2009b) discussion on intercultural competence assessment, in contrast to the many references made to context.

Parmenter's (2010) comparative analysis of national educational policies in 65 different countries suggests that while personal and social transformation are both key aspects of interculturality (see Table 3.1), justifications for the inclusion of interculturality as a policy or curriculum goal tend to be framed in terms of social ideals, political ideals, individual identity development and national interests, with the former two being cited far more frequently than

Table 3.1 Conceptualising interculturality in national education policies: An overview of key concepts

(1)	Recognition of sameness	• Awareness of the commonality of being human • Recognition of human dignity • Recognition of human rights and equality • Solidarity, connectedness, fellow feeling, commonality of cultures • Appeal to universal or transcultural values

(2)	Tolerance/Respect for otherness	• A range of desired attitudes towards otherness
		  ○ Openness (neutral)
		  ○ Tolerance (acceptance)
		  ○ Respect (positive evaluation)
		  ○ Appreciation (positive evaluation)

(3)	Engaging with otherness	• Knowledge • Interpersonal and communication skills (in general or in a particular language) • Affective involvement (including empathy) • Action
(4)	Learning to live together	• Co-existence • Cooperation • Harmony at interpersonal, intercultural and international levels

(5)	Transformation and action	• Self-transformation
		  ○ Internalisation/use of attitudes/values developed through intercultural learning
		  ○ Lifelong learning
		• Social transformation
		  ○ Social responsibility
		  ○ Social justice
		  ○ Social agency/making a difference

Source: Adapted from Parmenter (2010)

the latter two. This implies that the social dimension of intercultural education tends to be prioritised over the individual dimension among many national policy-makers, although the importance of the 'skills, knowledge, values and attitudes key to the development of an intercultural person' (Parmenter, 2010: 76) is well recognised.

Table 3.1 shows that the recognition of sameness forms part of the conceptualisation of interculturality, and this involves the cognitive identification of similarities, which is another recurrent theme in this book. This recognition of sameness involves a basic awareness of the commonality of being human and recognition of human dignity that leads to the recognition of human rights and equality, which often includes appeal to *universal* or *transcultural values* (Parmenter, 2010). But as we have seen, universalism rooted in the identification of similarities can be categorised as a form of ethnocentrism when considered in cognitive terms.

According to Bennett's (1993) description of the development of intercultural sensitivity, focusing upon similarities between cultures and constructing super-ordinate conceptual constructs to incorporate previously irreconcilable elements into more complex cognitive structures may be accompanied by a decrease in evaluative tendency, coupled with the minimisation of cultural difference, including areas of value difference that are neither universal nor transcultural, as similarities are selectively focused upon. Notwithstanding the fact that the list of categories presented in Table 3.1 do not constitute a developmental model, it can be seen that a range of desired attitudes towards otherness – or cultural *difference* – are prioritised by policymakers that seem to range from neutral to positive, excluding the negative, although Parmenter (2010) highlights the increasingly common linkage between intercultural learning and critical awareness when intercultural teaching approaches are considered:

> The second category covers a range of desired attitudes to otherness from openness, through tolerance, to respect and appreciation. These attitudes form a continuum of neutral to positive attitudes to otherness. The negative end of the continuum is obviously not useful for intercultural engagement, and is not explicitly promoted in national education policies anywhere. (Parmenter, 2010: 78)

Seen in terms of its personal and social dimensions, regardless of where the emphasis is placed, the reach of the concept of *citizenship* extends beyond consideration of what it means for an individual to be a member of society. It extends into the ways in which individuals and societies can develop together through targeted education, from the macro-level in the form of educational policy down to the micro-level in the form of particular individual learning objectives that are part of a lesson plan.

An important new theme emerging in relation to evaluation, then, is the deliberate transformation of self and society, and the question arising is what role teachers should play in this with regard to the management of value difference. Guilherme (2002) endorsed Osler and Starkey's (1996) position that teachers should deliberately attempt to bring learner values into line with universal values based on democracy and human rights, although universal values referred to in national policy and curriculum documents are rarely defined (Parmenter, 2010).

Byram (1997) took the view that instead of trying to change learner values, teachers should encourage learners to adopt a judgmental stance by making the basis of their evaluations explicit in general support of freedom of choice as foundation of democratic society, and claimed that learner choice of other evaluations of phenomena in their own society could count as evidence of intercultural communicative competence in assessment. However, despite Byram's (1997) claim that teachers should not deliberately try to change learner values, he went on to recognise and possibly endorse the positions of Guilherme, Osler and Starkey outlined above by claiming that 'human rights may provide foreign-language and culture education with culture-universals, basic principles, and values that traverse cultures' (Byram & Guilherme, 2000: 70), also suggesting that teachers might refer to documents produced by international organisations as sources of universal values, following Osler and Starkey (1996).

This lay in stark contrast to Byram's earlier position, when he claimed that 'taking international standards of human rights as a base-line for evaluation is not of course a ready-made answer to the question of what standard should, or could be recommended, since interpretations of human rights differ' (Byram, 1997: 44). More recently, however, his view that respect for human dignity and equality of human rights should be the democratic basis for social interaction seems to have established itself more firmly:

> It is important to make one's values explicit and conscious in any evaluative response to others. There is nonetheless a fundamental values position which has to be accepted, a position which acknowledges respect for human dignity and equality of human rights as the democratic basis for social interaction. (Byram *et al.*, 2009: 25)

This position appears to have considerable political support by many national governments (Parmenter, 2010).

> (I)ntercultural learning is a real concern of many education policy-makers around the world, and that it is seen as a positive trend by the majority. It also shows that the big ideals – peace, social justice, democracy and sustainability – remain the dominant rationale for intercultural learning in schools, at least at policy and curriculum level. (Parmenter, 2010: 84–85)

While some national governments prefer to assign responsibility for intercultural education to the subjects of social studies and foreign languages, others tend to take a more cross-curricular approach (Parmenter, 2010). This opens the way for the kinds of multi-disciplinary educational approaches advocated by Guilherme (2002) that combine foreign language education, human rights education and education for democratic citizenship, which has been explicitly linked to Byram's concept of critical cultural awareness as a form of political education, as noted earlier (Byram, 1997).

There seems to be considerable international agreement that ideals related to peace, social justice, democracy and sustainability should form the dominant rationale for intercultural learning in schools. This agreement has naturally given rise to internationally agreed laws and educational policy documents to which foreign language teachers are sometimes recommended to refer as sources of universal values that can guide intercultural education. Regardless of the extent to which international agreements may be (dis)approved of by particular (groups of) individuals or national governments that did not agree to them in whole or in part, they may be still seen as giving teachers greater license to guide learner values in certain directions than the kinds of national educational policy and curriculum documents analysed by Parmenter (2010).

Examples of human rights treaties agreed to at the inter-governmental level that might be used as points of reference in education include the International Convention for the Elimination of All Forms of Racial Discrimination (ICERD) and the Convention for the Elimination of All Forms of Discrimination against Women (CEDAW). Although the formation of such international agreements may give the general impression that the values expressed within them are fully accepted and agreed upon by the national governments concerned, along with the groups of people they represent, national governments can make explicit reservations limiting the obligations placed upon them after the agreement has been put into effect.

Constructed international agreements can be considered super-ordinate conceptual constructs that come into being as common ground is found between the governments concerned and they are rooted in the identification of similarities. As we have seen, focusing selectively upon similarities may minimise differences in the process (Bennett, 1993), so it is important to recognise differences between the positions of national governments as international agreements are considered in terms of the universal and trans-cultural values they may express. For example, formal reservations to CEDAW made by the Kingdom of Saudi Arabia (United Nations, undated) were stated as follows:

Saudi Arabia
Reservations:

1. In case of contradiction between any term of the Convention and the norms of Islamic law, the Kingdom is not under obligation to observe the contradictory terms of the Convention.
2. The Kingdom does not consider itself bound by paragraph 2 of article 9 of the Convention and paragraph 1 of article 29 of the Convention.

This example illustrates the way in which a set of universal ethical precepts formally fixed through inter-governmental collaboration can be modified in ways acceptable to the international community to suit the requirements of a particular government as it asserts its own culture in the face of newly emerging international standards. Attending to the way each particular culture views the world on the one hand while seeking fixed and universal ethical precepts that apply to all cultures, requires a balance to be struck between the culturally relativist and universalist points of view that seem to shape the dynamic interplay between global and local forces sketched out above, in which international agreements are formed while allowing for disagreement.

Samovar and Porter (2004) attempt to strike such a balance by proposing a set of guidelines for *an intercultural ethic* that include being mindful that communication produces a response, seeking commonalities among people and cultures, recognising the validity of differences, taking individual responsibility for one's actions and respecting the worth of an individual. Regarding the latter, the relevance of articles 1, 18 and 19 of the Universal Declaration of Human Rights are singled out for special consideration in intercultural communication.

Article 1

All human beings are born free and equal in dignity and rights. They are endowed with reason and conscience and should act towards one another in a spirit of brotherhood.

Article 18

Everyone has the right to freedom of thought, conscience and religion; this right includes freedom to change his religion or belief, and freedom, either alone or in community with others and in public or private, to manifest his religion or belief in teaching, practice, worship and observance.

Article 19

Everyone has the right to freedom of opinion and expression; this right includes freedom to hold opinions without interference and to seek, receive and impart information and ideas through any media and regardless of frontiers.

A prominent group of Saudi women who exercise their rights to freedom of thought, opinion and expression by exercising their social agency as intellectuals either as writers, university professors and in one instance, as head of a department attached to the Islamic World League, collectively discourage women from participating in the public sphere and criticise masculine and patriarchal *Western* society for imposing upon women the burden of political responsibility, although they themselves hold positions of social responsibility (Tsujigami, 2009, 2011). Since they oppose CEDAW and speak disparagingly of women who support gender equality, they were labelled the *anti-Cedawīyāt*, a term used by one of Tsujigami's interviewees.

By exploring and giving voice to their positions, Tsujigami recognises the validity of their difference of opinion as recommended by Samovar and Porter (2004), yet consideration of the opinions themselves reveals how the values contained in a human rights treaty such as CEDAW can be rejected by some of the very people they were designed to protect:

By directly criticizing 'the West' as masculine and patriarchal, they are indirectly critiquing the 'masculine' perspectives and means of the United Nations' world-wide campaign to co-opt 'the Other' into its hegemony. They are resisting to the hegemonic campaigns such as CEDAW and the 'Women and Millenium Goals' which often lack consideration for culture and religious differences. (Tsujigami, 2009: 27)

In the light of the above, what role should teachers play in this area with regard to the management of value difference? Two options identified so far involve teachers actively raising learner awareness of their own values or purposefully attempting to bring learner values into line with universal values based on democracy and human rights, but the more basic connection between language, conceptualisation and identification deserves special consideration at this point. It was noted earlier in this book that words can be loaded insofar as the value of the word is not expressed through a separate adjective but contained within the word itself (de Bono, 1991), and the use of the term *the West* in the extract above provides a good example. Tsujigami (2009) notes that despite demonstrating hostility toward *the West*, the concept forms an integral and necessary part of the identity construction of members of the *anti-Cedawīyāt*, who refer to the theories of *Westerners* and utilise *Western* discourses to support their arguments:

> For the 'anti-*Cedawīyāt*', 'Westerners' are often hostile but simultaneously a necessary 'Other' for the formation of Saudi Women's identity. This infers that the 'anti-*Cedawīyāt*' are not isolated from the globalization, but they are an integral part of it: they self-imagine via imagining 'the Other' the 'Westerners'. This self-imagining essentially means that they are forging identity via 'counter-othering'. In other words, they are speaking for themselves instead of being spoken for, and grounding their agency in their own religio-cultural foundations. Their discourses are the counter-arguments to the tacit imperialist strategy to co-opt and uniform 'the Other'. It is also an implicit appeal by the 'anti-*Cedawīyāt*' on who has the authority to decide what is just and what is not. (Tsujigami, 2009: 27)

The negative evaluation attached to *the West* in the extract above seems to illustrate how a word can trigger an emotional response, reflecting a crude either/or dichotomy (e.g. *either* Saudis *or* Westerners) imbued with the sense of good and bad, and right and wrong that is set up through the use of the word *not* (e.g. Saudi women are *not* Westerners), that some may consider an unjustified and stereotyped over-generalisation. Recalling de Bono's (1991) point that this use of mutually exclusive and contradictory conceptual categories to readily sort information into one category or the other imposes a false rigidity upon perception, the need to consider basic categorisation and labelling processes, in relation to evaluation, presents itself as a consideration in foreign language education.

As noted earlier in this book, the concept of citizenship embraces notions of what it means for an individual to be a member of society, but clearly, visions of this can vary widely both personally and culturally. For this reason, Guilherme (2002) recommended that teachers pay attention to culturally variable notions of citizenship by referring to contradictory world-views and dichotomous concepts such as the defence of the national perspective, multi-cultural perspectives and individual and communitarian points of view, which may differ both in the relative prioritisation of individual or collective interests, and in the vertical or horizontal arrangement of relationships.

Both positive and negative visions of the future may shape evaluative preferences at the social level as well as at the personal level. Bennett's (1993) point that the identification of similarities may result in the minimisation of differences has been noted before partly in relation to Parmenter's (2010) point that the recognition of sameness is one factor that gives rise to the recognition of human rights and universal values. While generally supporting that, Guilherme (2002) rejected the view of foreign language education as subjective involvement with another culture that leads to a synthesis of both cultures where 'differences between people will be decreased' (Robinson, 1988: 101, cited in Guilherme, 2002: 139) for its underlying harmonious and consensus-driven idea of intercultural relations and lack of criticality.

However, as we have seen, some cultures may prioritise social harmony over social justice, and Kohlberg's suggestion that harmony-oriented social systems are at a lower stage of moral development than justice-oriented ones was criticised on the basis of cultural and gender bias. While Eastern and Western values are often seen as being mutually exclusive and diametrically opposed (Matsuda *et al.*, 2001), Lee (2001) rejects such dichotomous categorisations by encouraging the development of finer conceptual distinctions to overcome rigid conceptual categories, the importance of which has been highlighted before.

Returning to the discussion of Saudi Arabia, recognition that the *anti-Cedawīyāt* discourse involves some women 'speaking out for themselves and creating their own narratives to construct their own gendered power relations based upon their own interpretations of Islam' (Tsujigami, 2009: 17) raises the further question of whether teachers should seek to play a guiding role in the identity-construction of learners. Notwithstanding the express reservations of the Kingdom of Saudi Arabia noted above, CEDAW is an internationally-agreed human rights treaty designed to protect the rights of women. And many national policy and curriculum documents go 'beyond mere recognition of human rights and equality to require commitment' (Parmenter, 2010: 76). However, while Parmenter's comparative analysis of national education policies suggested that although the concept of becoming intercultural seems to be generally embraced positively, the issue of how to maintain the balance between the influence of other cultures and traditional cultural values and practices also appears occasionally, with reservations sometimes being explicitly stated. The clearest case was from Saudi Arabia, where the 2004–2014 Ten Year Plan identified one of the challenges facing education as 'the cultural invasion and its results', emphasising the need to adopt:

a balanced approach that will allow learners to enjoy the benefits of technology (which, in turn, will benefit the community) while maintaining the Kingdom's values and faith, and that is able to protect them from the risks that might harm them as individuals and groups and that might negatively affect Muslim society. (Kingdom of Saudi Arabia Ministry of Education, 2005) (Parmenter, 2010: 70)

The complex range of issues outlined above, including the link between evaluative processes and personal identity development, may be explicitly recognised and addressed in international agreements and their supporting documentation. The UNESCO Declaration and Integrated Framework of Action on Education for Peace, Human Rights and Democracy (UNESCO, 1995) is a good example. It recognised the importance of nurturing personal identities oriented towards mutual understanding, respect and equality in the face of difference. More specifically, it recommended that education must cultivate in citizens the ability to make informed choices, basing their judgments and actions not only on the analysis of present situations but also on the vision of a preferred future.

The distinction between evaluations based upon the analysis of present situations from those based upon visions of a preferred future is notable. As we have seen, discrepancies between (1) 'the ideal selves we would very much like to become'; (2) 'selves that we could become'; and (3) 'selves we are afraid of becoming' (Markus & Nurius, 1986: 954, cited in Dörnyei, 2009: 12) can destabilise the self as the discrepancies cause cognitive dissonance that drives attempts to resolve ensuing cognitive conflict (Nishida, 1999; Triandis, 1989), especially if *consistency* is sought (Heine, 2001). This point will be returned to later in this book.

The United Nations Educational, Scientific and Cultural Organization (UNESCO), a specialised agency of the United Nations, is one of two institutions that will be considered below that develop international agreements related to education, the other being the Council of Europe. Both were founded in the 1940s just after the Second World War to promote democracy and human rights. UNESCO aims to promote peace through dialogue in the fields of education, science, culture and communication, while the Council of Europe aims to promote unity between parliamentary democracies and seeks to harmonise the policies of its member states in fields such as education, culture, social welfare, health, the environment, local government and justice. The similarities between their overarching aims are obvious, but the main purpose of the Council of Europe is to develop education to meet the needs of modern European society and to foster the emergence of European identity.

Two comparable documents produced by these institutions include the UNESCO Delors Report (Delors, 1996), which presents a set of general educational guidelines that continue to influence national educational policies and curriculum documents (Parmenter, 2010), and the Common European Framework of Reference for Foreign Languages (CEFR) (Council of Europe, 2001), which presents a set of guidelines specifically for foreign language education. While the documents were developed and released around the same time, the similarities between them are entirely coincidental and deserve special attention.

It can be seen in Table 3.2 that the UNESCO Delors Report (1996) recommends that people should learn through education how to know, do, live together and be. While the first two categories seem cognitive and skills-oriented, the concept of learning to live together arose out of the recognition of the important role played by education in guarding against the conflicts and violence that have scarred human history. The value of *non-judgmental*

Table 3.2 An overview of the general educational guidelines provided by the UNESCO Delors Report (1996)

(1)	Learning to know	• Learning how to learn ○ Concentration, memory skills and ability to think ○ Practical problem-solving and abstract thought ○ Deductive and inductive reasoning to pursue a logical train of thought
(2)	Learning to do	• Skills training linked to personal competence ○ Interpersonal skills/communication ○ Team/problem-solving skills ○ Learning to act appropriately in unfamiliar situations ○ Shaping the future through social innovation
(3)	Learning to live together	• Peace-oriented education ○ Stand against prejudice, in-group bias, racism and violence ○ Emphasise the discovery of other people/involvement in common projects with common goals ○ Learn about human diversity ○ Notice the similarities and interdependence of all people ○ Develop a spirit of empathy to enhance understanding of other people's reactions by actively looking at things from their point of view
(4)	Learning to be	• Fulfillment of each and every human being in all their capacities

stance is hinted at in the recognition given to the important role played by empathy when trying to understand the viewpoints of others.

Through the concept of *learning to be*, it is suggested that the aim of education should be the complete fulfillment of each and every human being in all their capacities. As catalyst to the human being, seen both as an *individual* rich in potential and an interactive *social* being, education can be considered a form of personality training. The active promotion of freedom of thought, judgment, feeling and imagination throughout the Delors Report (1996) was claimed to be more than a mere cry for individualism as personality differences, independence, personal initiative and even the ability for upsetting the established order, were identified and singled out as being guarantors of creativity and innovation. This point needs to be considered in relation to distinctions made earlier in this book between interdependent and independent selves made by Heine (2001) in relation to malleability of the self versus malleability of the world. In particular, it echoes Condon and Yousef's (1975) distinction between individualism and individuality noted by Zaharna (2009) in relation to self-development earlier in this book.

As noted above, the CEFR contains a set of guidelines that apply specifically to the teaching of foreign languages. In the early 1990s, Michael Byram and Geneviève Zarate were commissioned by the Council of Europe to provide input to the CEFR, which would allow the assessment of *sociocultural competence*. Together they developed a model that conceptualised *intercultural competence* – changing the term used to be more precise in meaning – in terms of having the declarative knowledge of a culture, the ability to learn cultures, the ability to apply intercultural skills and a general disposition of respect and tolerance toward cultural difference. Their model was first presented in a Council of Europe publication (Byram & Zarate, 1997) whose influence upon the CEFR is somewhat apparent in the sections listed below (Council of Europe, 2001: 101–106). These four general competences were supplemented in the CEFR (2001) by communicative language competences that included linguistic, sociolinguistic and pragmatic competences.

- Section 5.1.1: Declarative knowledge: *Savoir*
- Section 5.1.2: Skills and know-how: *Savoir-faire*
- Section 5.1.3: Existential competence: *Savoir être*
- Section 5.1.4: Ability to learn: *Savoir apprendre*

Declarative knowledge was divided into intercultural awareness and sociocultural knowledge, including knowledge about everyday living, living conditions, interpersonal relations, values, beliefs and attitudes, body language, social conventions and ritual behaviour. Knowledge of the world, embracing factual knowledge, knowledge about classes of entities and their properties and relations, was considered to derive from experience, education or information sources. This component impressed upon teachers the need to consider the kinds of knowledge foreign language learners would need to communicate effectively, particularly in the societies where the target language is spoken. Declarative knowledge needs to be considered in conjunction with the other knowledge-related component, the ability to learn, which involves gathering knowledge in new situations before integrating it effectively with existing knowledge.

Skills and know-how were considered to include social skills, living skills, vocational and professional skills in addition to leisure skills, all of which were thought to require foreign language learners to bring the culture of origin and the foreign culture into relation with each other with cultural sensitivity, using strategies, mediating between cultures and overcoming stereotyped relationships in the process. The development of an intercultural personality was considered an educational goal in its own right, insofar as the role played by the self in intercultural encounters was highlighted. Wide-ranging factors such as attitudes, motivations, values, beliefs, cognitive styles and personality factors were brought into close relation in the concept of existential competence, in which it was recognised that such factors affect not only the communication process but also foreign language learning itself.

When the Council of Europe incorporated the model into the CEFR, Byram and Zarate signed away their rights to the model by contract. Once this separation had taken place, Byram (1997) went on to develop the model independently of Zarate in part by adding critical cultural awareness/political education, or *savoir s'engager*, as a fifth component. An outline of the resulting model (Byram, 1997: 34) is presented below, where it can be seen that only the first three components had found some expression in the CEFR (Council of Europe, 2001):

- *Savoir être*: Attitudes
  - Curiosity and openness, readiness to suspend disbelief about other cultures and belief about one's own.
- *Savoir*: Knowledge
  - Of social groups and their products and practices in one's own and in one's interlocutor's country, and of the general processes of societal and individual interaction.
- *Savoir apprendre/faire*: Skills of discovery and interaction
  - Ability to acquire new knowledge of a culture and cultural practices and the ability to operate knowledge, attitudes and skills under the constraints of real-time communication and interaction.

- *Savoir comprendre*: Skills of interpreting and relating
  - Ability to interpret a document or event from another culture, to explain it and relate it to documents from one's own.
- *Savoir s'engager*: Critical cultural awareness/political education
  - Ability to evaluate critically and on the basis of explicit criteria perspectives, practices and products in one's own and other cultures and countries.

Byram's 'list model' suggests a range of teaching objectives that can be used by foreign language teachers when planning teaching and assessment without specifying 'links of dependency or interdependency among the competences' (Byram, 2009: 325). The aim of the model, then, is to 'help foreign language teachers to plan more deliberately than they often do, to include intercultural competence in their pedagogical aims' (Byram, 2009: 324). In Byram's view, critical cultural awareness/political education is the most educationally significant of the savoirs (Byram, 2008: 236) because it fundamentally re-characterises language teaching and learning as education for citizenship and democracy, which brings into question the relationship between teacher and learner values as we have already seen.

Although Byram went on to claim that there is a fundamental values position that has to be accepted in foreign language education, which 'acknowledges respect for human dignity and equality of human rights as the democratic basis for social interaction' (Byram *et al.*, 2009: 25), he did suggest that teachers who do not wish to interfere in the views of their learners for ethical reasons 'can encourage them to make the basis of their judgments explicit and expect them to be *consistent* in their judgments of their own society as well as others' (Byram, 2008: 233, emphasis mine). In 1997, Byram had recommended the following learning objectives to teachers to develop critical cultural awareness in learners:

- Identify and interpret explicit or implicit *values* in documents and events in one's own and other cultures.
- Make an *evaluative* analysis of the documents and events, which refer to an explicit perspective and *criteria*.
- Interact and mediate in intercultural exchanges in accordance with explicit *criteria*, negotiating where necessary a degree of acceptance of them by drawing upon one's knowledge, skills and attitudes. (Byram, 1997: 53, emphasis mine)

At the heart of each of these learning objectives, and indeed at the heart of critical cultural awareness itself, lies the issue of judgment which involves applying values as specific standards or criteria for evaluation. Sensitivity to values can help us to identify and interpret values in documents or events. Once we have analysed them, we can make judgments by applying our values as standards or criteria during evaluation. Having critical cultural awareness is essentially about knowing how to bring to different kinds of cultural experience 'a rational and explicit standpoint from which to evaluate' (Byram, 2008: 233).

But the concept of critical cultural awareness did not feature in the original version of Byram and Zarate's (1997) model or in the CEFR (Council of Europe, 2001). Added later by Byram (1997), it is taking time to establish itself as a concept in the political arena. It can, however, be seen impacting upon recent European policy contained in the Council of Europe's White Paper on Intercultural Dialogue (Council of Europe, 2008) through the vehicle of the *Autobiography of Intercultural Encounters* (Byram et al., 2009: 25), which is a set of theoretically driven self-assessment materials developed to support the implementation of the White Paper through language education. It can be seen in the extract below that critical cultural awareness is starting to gain some political recognition as a concept:

- The *Autobiography of Intercultural Encounters* has been developed as a follow up to the Council of Europe's White Paper on Intercultural Dialogue 'Living together as equals in dignity' (www.coe.int/dialogue), and in particular in application of Section 5.3 Learning and teaching intercultural competences (page 25, paragraph 152):
  - Complementary tools should be developed to encourage learners to exercise independent critical faculties (emphasis mine) including to reflect critically (emphasis mine) on their own responses and attitudes to experiences of other cultures. (Byram et al., 2009: 25)

It was noted above that critical cultural awareness is essentially about knowing how to bring to different kinds of cultural experience 'a rational and explicit standpoint from which to evaluate' (Byram, 2008: 233). However, reflecting upon the concept in the light of Wringe's (2007) views on moral education, Byram has suggested recently that his past emphasis upon the development of an explicit rational standpoint may have been too narrow, in recognition of the fact that making critical evaluations may lead to evaluations being made that are 'not according to criteria of rationality but of "maximising happiness", "communitarianism" or "caring"' (Byram, 2009: 324). This can be considered the expression of a values position that acknowledges difference.

Increasing recognition of the *relational* aspects of intercultural competence, in which the relationships between the interactants are brought into sharper focus, is prompting reconsideration of existing definitions of intercultural competence that have focus mainly upon the individual to date (Deardorff, 2009a). The notion of the relational serves as a useful conceptual bridge between the Arab world (Zaharna, 2009), Africa (Nwosu, 2009), Latin America (Medina-López-Portillo & Sinnigen, 2009), China (Chen & An, 2009) and Vietnam (Ashwill & Du'o'ng, 2009), along with the many other countries and cultures that have been described as collectivist to varying degrees (Ting-Toomey, 2009):

(R)egarding the pivotal role of identity in intercultural competence, it seems that transcending boundaries in regard to one's identity in crucial in developing intercultural competence. In this age of globalization that often leads to politicized cultural identities, the transcendence of one's identity seeks to defy simplistic categorisations of cultural groups, addresses the adaptive and fluid nature of multicultural identities, and strives to understand the fullness of who one is, moving beyond the traditional dichotomous ingroup/outgroup mentality to one that embraces and respects' others' differences as well as commonalities and, in so doing, keeps the focus on the relational goals of engagement. (Deardorff, 2009a: 267)

Part 2

Managing Value Judgment in Foreign Language Education

4 Overview of the Study

Introduction

In Part 1 of this book, we explored what it means to be intercultural through discussion on information processing, socialisation and the development of the self before the concepts of ethnocentrism and ethnorelativism were compared, contrasted and brought into relation. Special focus was placed upon the role of value judgment, and as potential learning objectives were drawn from the literature analysis, particularly for use in foreign language education, conflicting perspectives upon the management of value judgment emerged that pointed the way to the overarching themes of personal and social transformation.

In this process, many similarities between national educational policies and curricula were identified but 'there seems to be little coherence in many countries when it comes to the concrete policies of how to achieve the goal of becoming and being intercultural' according to Parmenter (2010: 82–83), who echoes UNESCO's (2009) view that there needs to be much greater comparative in-depth study of a whole range of countries and contexts, at the macro-level of general policy statements to curricula down to the micro-level of syllabuses, materials, classroom practice and teacher and learner identities.

The contribution made in Part 2 of this book comes from the micro-level, although guidelines from the macro-level were considered in its development. A bottom-up approach will be taken within which suggestions are made from a particular local context as to how the gap between theories on intercultural competence and teaching practice can be bridged, in foreign language education in particular, notwithstanding the wider connections that can ultimately be made to the field of intercultural communication as a whole. A teaching model, labelled the Intercultural Dialogue (ID) Model for reasons that will be explained later, will be presented to help foreign language teachers attempting 'to include intercultural competence in their pedagogical aims' (Byram, 2009: 324) to better organise their teaching activities, considering syllabus and materials development, classroom practice and teacher and learner identities.

Many models considered in Part 1 of this book differ in terms of their conceptual underpinnings and goals. Spitzberg and Changnon (2009) categorise models of intercultural competence into five main types, an overview of which is presented in Table 4.1, although the categories may overlap, and the same model may be categorised in different ways. For example, while Byram's (2009) Model of Intercultural Communicative Competence was categorised as a co-orientational model in Spitzberg and Changnon's (2009) analysis, it may also be categorised as a compositional model, insofar as the lists of teaching objectives do not suggest 'links of dependency or interdependency among the competences' (Byram, 2009: 325), perhaps because the model was theoretically generated in the first instance. Since the model does not suggest 'a didactic ordering of which aspects of which competences should be taught prior to others' (Byram, 2009: 325) and 'because the model is a schematization and does not specify in every detail an intercultural speaker, the prescription of how learners should develop is limited' (Byram, 2009: 325).

In contrast to Byram's model, the ID Model to be presented in Part 2 *does* suggest a didactic ordering of which aspects of which competences should be taught prior to others, and in this sense it rests upon an underlying view of

Table 4.1 An overview of the main types of intercultural competence models

Model type	Main features
(1) Compositional	A list of components of intercultural competence without a specification of the relations between them
(2) Co-orientational	A conceptualisation of the interactional achievement of intercultural understanding
(3) Developmental	A specification of stages of progression or maturity through which competence is thought to evolve
(4) Adaptational	A model of the processes of mutual adjustment between multiple interdependent interactants
(5) Causal	A specification of the relations between components of intercultural competence typically in a path model with an identifiable set of distal-to-proximal concepts leading to a downstream of outcomes that mark or provide a criterion of competence

Source: Adapted from Spitzberg and Changnon (2009)

the ways in which learners can and should develop that took shape in the course of the study to be described. The model was designed primarily to help teachers organise their teaching activities but despite its highly practical orientation, it remains informed by the wide-ranging theories considered in Part 1 of this book. While the model is causal insofar as it specifies the relations between components of intercultural competence in a path model that suggests the sequencing of specific tasks and outcomes as indicators of competence, the main priority of the model is *not* to describe the ways in which competence tends to develop within the individual, as in developmental models.

The priority is placed instead upon making a concrete set of suggestions to teachers as to how they can organise their teaching activities better when they attempt to include intercultural competence in their pedagogical aims, considering syllabus and materials development, classroom practice and teacher and learner identities. For this reason, practical considerations affecting teaching and learning activities within and surrounding the classroom *context* played important guiding roles in its development.

In Part 1, a special focus was placed upon the role of value judgment in intercultural communication, and conflicting perspectives upon the management of value judgment emerged through detailed analysis of the relevant academic literature as noted above. Value judgment serves as the linchpin of the ID Model, insofar as it provided the central research focus of the study that led to its development. Focusing on value judgment shed light upon the relations between other components of intercultural competence when viewed from a *pedagogical* standpoint.

In the academic year 2003–2004, an empirical study based on action research was conducted (Houghton, 2007, 2009a, 2010) to explore and reflect upon the kinds of learning objectives that can and should be set when foreign language teachers attempt to manage the issue of evaluation of difference in foreign language education, in general recognition of the complex relationship between values, prejudice (pre-judgment) and evaluative processes. While the development of critical cultural awareness (Byram, 1997) was recognised as one possible approach, it was not accepted at face-value because alternative and conflicting approaches were identified in the academic literature.

At the time the study was conceptualised, Byram was taking the position that teachers should train learners to adopt a judgmental stance focusing their attention squarely back on themselves to develop critical awareness of their own evaluative processes to control them, recommending that teachers should not try to change learner values. This approach, however, seemed too weak for Guilherme, who suggested that teachers should also aim to bring learner values into line with universal values supportive of democracy and human rights to promote social justice, recommending that teachers should try to change learner values if necessary. This view gradually came to be supported by Byram as research into intercultural competence started to fuse with that being done on citizenship education in the European context.

Despite subtle differences between the positions of these European researchers at different times, what they all shared was a rejection of non-judgmental stance in intercultural communication, which was precisely what was being advocated by many researchers of intercultural communication in North America, by de Bono and indeed by Byram and Zarate in their early work. Bennett, Gudykunst Paul and Elder, among others, all seemed to agree upon the importance of learning to adopt a non-judgmental stance when communicating with others different from ourselves, to engage in intellectual empathy and appreciate different perspectives upon social phenomena. Notably, in the European context, Doyé recognised the importance of both.

From a theoretical standpoint alone, it was impossible to reconcile the differing approaches to evaluation outlined above and action research was brought to bear upon them with a view to illuminating gaps, weaknesses or inconsistencies within the theoretical standpoints from practical points of view. From the outset, then, the study described in this chapter was never solely aimed at transforming the state of the researcher's own knowledge and improving her own and other teachers' practice, although it attempts to do both. It was to ultimately refer theory-driven practice back to the theory itself to provide concrete examples from practice that may either validate or invalidate various conflicting claims identified in the literature analysis. This research priority corresponds closely to Hopkins' view of action research presented below:

> Action research might be defined as 'the study of a social situation with a view to improving the quality of action within it'. It aims to feed practical judgment in concrete situations, and the validity of the 'theories' or hypotheses it generates depends not so much on 'scientific' tests of truth, as on their usefulness in helping people to act more intelligently and skilfully. In action research, 'theories' are not validated independently and then applied to practice. They are validated through practice. (Hopkins, 2002: 43)

Thus, the detailed presentation of the ID Model in this book, which was developed in a particular local context, throws a loop from theoretically driven practice back to the theory itself with a view to illuminating both in new ways that may prove useful to theorists and practitioners alike.

Overview of the Study

Three distinct approaches towards the management of value difference in foreign language education were identified in the academic literature.

(1) Teachers should train learners to suspend evaluation and intellectually empathise with others instead.

(2) Teachers should train learners to make conscious evaluations and focus their attention squarely back on themselves to develop critical awareness of their own biases to control them, but teachers should not try to change learner values.

(3) Teachers should basically follow the second approach just noted, but should also aim to bring learner values into line with democratic principles and human rights promoting social justice, changing learner values if necessary.

To explore these three teaching approaches, three separate courses of study were designed, without reference to existing textbooks, by taking a bottom-up approach through which specific learning activities, contained within teaching materials in individual lesson plans, were built upon foundational sets of learning objectives broadly related to evaluation into three overarching syllabuses. They were implemented over one academic year over a nine-month period (October 2003–January 2004) in three different upper-intermediate English language classes at a university in southern Japan, where the author of this book was teaching English as a foreign language. The 36 learners who took part in the study were split randomly into three groups, each of which consisted of 12 female Japanese learners in their second year of study in the Faculty of Humanities, and the author as teacher-researcher.

Qualitative data were gathered mainly in English. Data collection techniques included the audio recording of lessons, the gathering of learner classwork and homework as forms of documentary data and post-class learner and teacher diaries. The different perspectives of research participants were taken as separate data sources, and triangulation was taken to mean the gathering of valid data from these different sources. In terms of the people involved, the main data sources were the learners and the teacher-researcher. There was no separate observer in lessons but the audio-recordings allowed the teacher-researcher to listen to the lessons during the data analysis period, from the standpoint of a researcher, to provide a third perspective on the phenomena under investigation. This overcame the limitation imposed upon this kind of research by the fact that the teacher and researcher were one and the same person. Ethical issues related to anonymity, for example, were duly considered following guidelines laid out by McDonough and McDonough (1997), Cohen *et al.* (2000) and Creswell (2003).

Despite the differences between them, the three syllabuses mentioned above shared a core course that was based upon theoretical areas of the academic literature that did not seem to be in dispute. In general, it was designed to systematically raise selected parts of the largely unconscious bodies of learner values and perspectives, let us call them presuppositions, to the surface to expose differences between learners in what seemed to be a monolingual, mono-cultural group. The three courses, which were spread over two terms of study and contained a total of 27 lessons each, all ran through five interlocking stages containing core course and course-specific components related to value judgment that sometimes overlapped.

In stage 1 (weeks 1–8), a conceptual framework was provided within which learner presuppositions were raised to the surface in working configurations to reveal differences between them that could be utilised later in experiential learning activities. Themes selected reflected teacher perceptions of underlying teacher and learner cultural and conceptual differences between the Japanese and English languages based on personal experience. Having distinguished values from beliefs and norms in week 1 using Lustig and Koester's (1999) definition of culture, the concept of values was broken down into more detail in weeks 2–5 to set up enough conceptual categories to reveal value difference between learners using a set of values that seem to be universal (Schwartz & Sagiv, 1995; Schwartz *et al.*, 1997):

Week 2: Power and Achievement
Week 3: Benevolence and Universalism
Week 4: Tradition, Security and Conformity
Week 5: Hedonism, Stimulation and Self-Direction

The list of values presented above was used as an overarching conceptual framework within which to structure learner reflection in the core course through targeted learning activities. First, the values were illustrated in short dialogues and having identified *possible* values being expressed (there were no right or wrong answers), with reference to definitions of the values, learners were then asked to reflect on and discuss their own values with other learners by considering the definitions in relation to new topics that expanded upon the existing conceptual framework. This was followed up with homework activities in which learners had to write a series of four paragraphs reflectively describing their values, with a view to making presentations about them to other learners in speeches in weeks 6–8. In addition, learners were asked to make a value chart in which they had to rank their relative prioritisation of the values on a scale from –5 to +5.

Course-specific components differed in three important ways. One group of learners was asked to suspend evaluation to intellectually empathise with other learners by deploying specific communication skills, while members of the other two groups were asked to evaluate consciously. In these two courses, the concept of critical evaluation was defined for learners in terms of comparing, contrasting, judging (evaluating) and justifying judgments (evaluations) with reasons; but while learners were left to evaluate freely in one course, a conscious attempt was made to change learner values in specific ways in the other. Particular values from the taxonomy that seemed more desirable than others in intercultural communication were selected and presented to learners in the form of a list, and their agreement was sought.

For example, since intercultural communication often involves getting to know new people and places, novelty and new challenge were prioritised as target values, as were the promotion of equality and the welfare of all people, since such concepts seem supportive of human rights. However, neither tradition nor conformity was set as a target value, since they both involve commitment to one's own culture and following social norms. None of the values were explicitly discouraged, however, and the choice of target values was subjective on the part of the teacher.

In stage 2 (weeks 8–12), attempts were made to expose all learners to value difference before asking them to respond in course-specific ways. This was achieved by asking learners to rank each of the 10 values numerically from –5 to +5 in a value chart. See the task described below for further detail, in which an illustrative example is provided of a learner's value chart.

Task

Reflect on which of the 10 values are the most and least important to you. Shade in the Value Chart below. Do not show other students.

KEY	
B: Benevolence	U: Universalism
P: Power	A: Achievement
C: Conformity	T: Tradition
Sec: Security	H: Hedonism
St: Stimulation	SD: Self-direction

YOUR VALUE CHART										
+5						✕	✕			
+4	✕							✕		
+3		✕								
+2				✕						
+1										
0	B	U	P	A	C	T	Sec	H	St	SD
–1			✕						✕	
–2										✕
–3				✕						
–4										
–5										

Having identified areas of value difference between learners by juxtaposing their value charts, they were then paired up and asked to discuss the value difference before imagining a potential problem that might be caused by it and writing a short dialogue to illustrate it. When learners presented their conflict dialogues to the class, other learners were asked to respond in course-specific ways. A third learner was then placed into some pairs to mediate conflict in course-specific ways. Learners were given a chance to reflect upon the activities in follow-up homework essays.

Stage 4 (weeks 2–25) was divided into three sub-stages. In sub-stage 1 (weeks 2–14), learners had to write three questions for each of the 10 values outlined in weeks 2–5, to develop a questionnaire with which to interview a foreigner about their values in the summer assignment, before responding in course-specific ways. This central task was enveloped by sub-stage 2 (week 14, summer assignment and week 15) when the stage 3 discussion of *concept*, which took place chronologically after stage 2, was extended to include stereotypes as a particular kind of concept used to categorise people. While week 14 activities focused on defining and examining the nature of stereotypes, week 15 focused on whether or not learner stereotypes had been broken by their foreign interviewees. Learners were asked to write reflective essays on group interviews held at the end of the first term.

In sub-stage 3 of stage 4 (weeks 23–25), learners had to present their course-specific summer assignments in speeches to other learners, who were asked to respond in course-specific ways. They were also set a number of other tasks during this stage within which previous work was recycled back into the course to promote further reflection and discussion of learner-generated themes. In some cases, learners' views expressed in their home-work or diaries were presented to other learners for consideration. An end-of-course assignment was also set towards the end of stage 4 in which they were asked to transcribe recordings of their pre-course interviews, before writing a reflective essay on how their ideas had developed during the course. They were also asked to submit discussion points for the end-of-course group interviews.

Stage 5 (weeks 16–27) was structured around the concepts of power distance, individualism/collectivism, masculinity/femininity and uncertainty avoidance, which were presented as four major areas of value difference round the world (Hofstede, 1980). Having tried to identify these values in dialogues and video clips, learners were asked to respond to them in course-specific ways, before mediating conflict dialogues written by the teacher that illustrated differences in value and concepts between Japanese and English. In week 18, learners following the third teaching approach described above branched off further to focus on democracy as a political system by comparing and contrasting their definition of democracy with other learners and considering the political nature of Japanese society. They were asked to evaluate, not with reference to their own values, but with reference to universal values contained in international human rights treaties, prior to conducting a democratic citizenship project following the example set by the teacher as a role-model.

Data were analysed after the courses had finished and once decisions had been made as to the extent the various learning objectives had been met, and judgments had been made about their viability and desirability, the bodies of data generated by the three courses were examined and brought into relation as they were treated as a single complex case study. As a result of data analysis, the ID Model was developed to help structure and sequence the management of value judgment in the foreign language classroom with a view to supporting intercultural dialogue in the real world outside the classroom by equipping learners with the requisite skills inside the classroom. ID can be considered both an acronym for intercultural dialogue and an abbreviation of identity, and through recognition of these points, the ID Model emphasises the importance of identity management in intercultural dialogue.

It is envisaged that having interacted with and gathered detailed information about others, suspending evaluation in the process, learners then go on to evaluate both self and other with reference to clear and conscious standards. Having considered a range of new potential options generated by interaction with others and the discovery of difference, the subsequent selection between alternatives that have been generated carries profound implications for self-development as learners embark upon decision-making processes that helped determine the kinds of people they wanted to become in the future. This sometimes involved them in making conscious attempts to bring order to internal chaos.

To some extent, casting foreign language learners as citizens who have potentially important roles to play in society can downplay the development of personal identity in policy documents that tend to focus upon social development. This concern is echoed in Kim's (2009) discussion of the identity factor in intercultural competence, but intercultural communication is characterised in the first instance as being intensely personal in nature in the ID Model. Its elaboration can be considered a call for more explicit attention to be focused upon the ways in which structured self-reflection can cause learners to start reconsidering and redefining themselves as they attempt to explore, interpret and evaluate themselves, others and the world around them.

5 The Intercultural Dialogue Model

Top-Down and Bottom-Up Approaches

The course of learning envisaged in the ID Model can be broken down into the five stages listed in Table 5.1, all of which involve learner attention to task, learner change and learner development of awareness at meta-levels, the last of which comprises self-awareness, meta-cognitive awareness and meta-affective awareness. The course of learning is conceptualised as revolving primarily around the analysis of value systems (VS) but can be extended from higher levels to incorporate the analysis of social systems, as we shall see.

As can be seen in Table 5.1, the ID Model starts in stage 1 with learners' analysis of their own value systems (VS1). Learner self-reflection and self-analysis were systematically scaffolded using value taxonomies as overarching conceptual frameworks for self-reference as noted in the previous chapter. While the value taxonomies used in the study suggested by Schwartz and Sagiv (1995) and Schwartz *et al.* (1997) will be the main points of reference in this book, Hofstede (1980), Forgas and Bond (1985), Kluckhohn and Strodtbeck (1960), Heine (2001) and Markus and Kitayama (1991) all offer alternative conceptual frameworks that could be used.

The use of ready-made value taxonomies or self-awareness inventories to scaffold self-reflection (Fowler & Mumford, 1999) can facilitate course planning by providing clear sets of conceptual categories that can serve as common points of reference in syllabus and materials design, functioning as ready-made receptacles for content, allowing inter-learner comparisons to be made and giving teachers some control over classroom processes. However, they are necessarily over-simplistic in comparison with the complexity and dynamism of the value systems themselves. The internal structuring of value taxonomies and self-awareness inventories are unlikely to ever sufficiently

Table 5.1 The Intercultural Dialogue (ID) Model: Stages in the course of learning and meta-levels

Stages in the course of learning	Meta-levels
(1) Learner descriptive analysis of own value system (VS1)	Development of awareness
(2) Learner descriptive analysis of the value system of another person (VS2) having gathered information through empathy-oriented communication	• Self-awareness • Meta-cognitive awareness • Meta-affective awareness
(3) Juxtaposition, comparison and contrast of the two value systems (VS1 and VS2) to identify similarities and differences	
(4) Learner evaluation of the value systems of self and other (VS1 and VS2) with reference to a standard	
(5) Learner orientation of self to others by selecting standards and evaluative tendencies	

parallel the internal structuring of actual value systems to allow for adequate expression of them, so teachers need to keep this in mind.

In recognition of this problem, Kelley and Meyers (cited in Fowler & Mumford, 1999) note that learners may answer self-awareness inventories based on their ideals rather than their actual selves, and recommend teachers to advise learners to answer on the basis of how they perceive themselves in the present. But considering that learner values may conflict with each other at any one time, and that reflection over time is an important aspect of consciousness-raising, even the approach recommended by Kelley and Meyers above may distort learner values through over-simplification and the neglect of self-discrepancy.

An even more basic question arises as to the relative merits and demerits of selecting abstract, overarching conceptual frameworks within which to structure the consciousness-raising process. But grappling with, and bringing abstract conceptual frameworks into relation, may be considered a legitimate goal of higher education that aims to promote critical forms of mental life (Barnett, 1997), echoing the need for learners to develop the ability to work with multiple-mental models (Doyé, 1992, 2003; Rest et al., 1999). Barnett (1997) posits a framework of rules, values or theories as a condition for developing critical mentality in tertiary education, suggesting they be used as mounts for critical commentary that themselves can be criticised in relation to competing frameworks not favoured or selected by teachers. Barnett relates this to the development of understanding, autonomy and contemplation, claiming that working with multiple intellectual frames develops understanding of any one frame, increasing the possibility for autonomous thought as critical space opens up between learner and the world. In this way, intellectual frames can be considered resources to be deployed imaginatively to illuminate the world.

However, a potential problem with top-down approaches is that teachers select the overarching conceptual framework that learners are expected to refer themselves. Insofar as the introduction of the overarching conceptual system itself may trigger learner change in ways that are influenced by the structure itself, the very selection of a particular value system to scaffold self-analysis may be considered the kind of imposition or recommendation of a particular set of values upon learners rejected by authors such as Freire (1990). As Holliday (2011) warns in relation to Hofstede's taxonomy of values, for example, 'the temptation to be essentialist is quite deeply rooted to a desire to "fix" the nature of culture and cultural difference' (Holliday, 2011: 6). In relation to self-awareness inventories, Brown and Knight (cited in Fowler & Mumford, 1999: 24) emphasise the need for learners to interpret the results of self-awareness inventories for themselves rather than being given teacher interpretations to offset this problem, but learner change may be generated all the same.

Alternatively, Freire suggests a bottom-up approach that takes as its point of departure the fact that language cannot exist without thought, and neither language nor thought can exist without a structure to which they refer, implying there is no need to provide a conceptual structure for self-reference, since the structure already exists and simply needs unveiling. From this standpoint, teachers should strive to understand the structural conditions to which learner thought and language refer, or, in other words, they should attempt to explore the generative themes held in the thought-language of learners' thematic universes. Freire recommends teachers to help learners to deconstruct swathes of their own reality by analysing and decoding situations in their lives, splitting wholes into parts during description to discover interactions between the parts that shed new light on the whole, and encouraging learners to perceive and behave differently towards the original situations, armed with new understanding.

Despite the difference of opinion over the legitimacy of introducing external conceptual frameworks, both Freire (1990) and Barnett (1997) share the aim of developing critical forms of thought; but, regardless of whether a top-down or bottom-up approach is used, failure to bring learners into a state of difference with each other in the beginning would place both approaches outside the boundaries of the ID Model, for the exploration of value difference is its central theme. However, it will become clear that although a top-down approach is taken in stage 1 of the model, and a bottom-up approach is subsequently taken in stage 2 as learners are asked to gather information about the value system of another person (VS2) using the cognitive skill of intellectual empathy, which itself necessitates the use of bottom-up information processing skills. Having gathered information about VS2, learners then go on to analyse that information in the latter part of stage 2.

Indeed, the importance of analysis recognised in the ID Model, by breaking wholes into parts and considering relations between them, was also recognised by Freire (1990). However, whereas value taxonomies are used in the model to illuminate areas of value difference between learners in the classroom, Freire advocates the ethnographic study of people in everyday life, functioning naturally across situations, and the gathering of information on talk, lifestyle and behaviour to gain insight into thought construction. While this may be difficult, if not impossible in many cases, for learners to carry out in the foreign language classroom, the point remains that thought construction can potentially be accessed through those channels, and analysis remains the aim in both cases.

In stage 3 of the ID model, learners are expected to juxtapose, compare and contrast VS1 and VS2 to systematically identify similarities and differences between them. Similarly, Freire recommends the juxtaposition of learner essays on how they perceive certain situations to (a) present them with a range of alternative interpretations on the same events; and (b) encourage them to consider the viewpoints of others, reconsidering their own in the process. In this way, Freire claims that differing views can feed dialogically back into discussion evoking new analysis and generating new understandings in spiral fashion. This is also recommended in the ID Model, but in more systematic ways.

Perhaps the most striking similarity between Freire's approach and mine lies in our recognition of the importance of contradiction that arises naturally from analytical processes. Freire highlighted the emergence through dialogue of nuclei of contradictions that can facilitate the meaningful structuring of content, since they represent situations that have trapped learners. The traps inherent in contradiction open up new possible courses of action in the future, promising liberation from the traps as selections are made and learners move out of, and push people out of, contradictory states by choice. This resembles the dynamic emergence of new ways of thinking that arose in the empirical study described in this book, whereby change was often seen to accompany the resolution of contradiction and discrepancy.

Freire's view of personal history developing through the dialectical interaction of ideas, concepts, hopes, doubts and values accords with the picture of value built up in the study upon which this book is based in which internal components were often seen to come into conflict within the same individual, generating change in that individual, as previously unnoticed discrepancies and contradictions were consciously attended to. So, the ID Model aims to focus learner attention upon such dynamics with a view to taking increased conscious control to enhance self and social development. In stage 4, this involves the careful evaluation of VS1 and VS2 with reference to a clear standard before going on to make more careful selections of evaluative standards and tendencies as meta-cognitive and meta-affective awareness and control increase over time.

However, Freire does *not* prioritise the self as the primary object of analysis in the first place. While recognising that learners should develop self-awareness of their own aspirations, motives and objectives, he suggests that the primary focus of attention should be on the analytical penetration of problems faced by people in situations, connected to the social fabric as a whole. Thus, the primary interface for Freire (1990) is between person and situation in society. But in the ID Model, the primary interface is between self and other, with the interface between self and society being approached at higher levels as learners develop the ability to work at increasing levels of abstraction in the foreign language. Self and other are the primary objects of analysis in the ID Model, at least in the beginning. However, if we think in terms of different domains of operation and the interfaces between them, activity can clearly be located in many different places.

Domains and Interfaces

Let us focus on the structural issues of domain and interface. Barnett (1997) suggests that domains lie in knowledge, self and the world, and that three separate objects of critical thinking can be focused on in the same purposeful act, although their individual purposes may differ:

(1) *Knowledge* in the forms of propositions, ideas and theories (including value taxonomies, for example) can be taken as objects of analysis and opened up to criticism.

(2) *The self* can be taken as object for analysis and opened up to criticism through what Barnett calls, 'critical self-reflection', which is prioritised throughout the ID Model. On this, Barnett (1997) recognises that higher states of mind in academic life reside as much in intra-learner dialogue as they do in consenting inter-learner dialogue.

(3) *The external world* can be taken as object for analysis and opened up to criticism, which Freire prioritises in the first place and which is approached from higher levels of the ID Model.

Further, Barnett (1997) splits each of these three domains into the six clearly defined levels listed in Table 5.2. As discussion of the ID Model proceeds, Barnett's levels will be considered where relevant, but they are only outlined here. Barnett's levels and the ID Model can be distinguished in terms of domain. Whereas the former places the three domains of knowledge,

Table 5.2 Domains and levels of critical thought

	Domains		
Levels	Knowledge	Self	World
(1) Critical thinking skills			
(2) Meta-critical capacities			
(3) Critical thinking			
(4) Critical thought			
(5) Philosophical meta-critique			
(6) Sociological meta-critique			

Source: Barnett (1997)

self and the world at equal standing, the latter prioritises the internal domain of self over the two external domains of knowledge and the world.

Although analysis of the other can spark self-reflection and analysis naturally (Yamada, 2010), analysis of the self *precedes* analysis of the other in the ID Model, which can be implemented with any group of learners, even mono-lingual, mono-cultural groups. Production of the written documents containing the separate analyses of self and other can be considered the production of new forms of knowledge in two concrete documents, which can then be compared, contrasted and analysed prior to evaluation of self and other, ultimately leading to personal reorientation to others and the world more generally.

The prioritisation of experiential learning explains why the production of knowledge generated by the exploration of self and other through interaction with real people is also considered important. This is how the knowledge domain sits most comfortably within the model, but experiencing one complete cycle of the model would position learners to apply the same principles and procedures to activities situated in different domains lying at different interfaces. Thus, knowledge-laden documents authored by people learners have never met could potentially be juxtaposed and subjected to the same analytical procedures with learners reflecting back on their own reactions in order to work at the interface between the self and knowledge domains. This type of approach, which characterises the *savoir* component in Byram's (1997) Model of Intercultural Communicative Competence, which was also incorporated into Section 5.1.1 of CEFR to some extent, provides an alternative starting point for learners, just as the interface between self and world domains can provide an alternative starting point, as suggested by Freire. This interface is also addressed in Holliday's critical interpretivism (Holliday, 2011) and critical discourse analysis (Fairclough, 1995, 2010).

On a final note, let me highlight one point that will be revisited later regarding the reconstruction of self and society. The later stages of Freire's (1990) approach involve teachers challenging learners to problematise and externalise views on the contradictions in the world before preparing further teaching material to recycle ideas back into dialogue, which treats people as transforming rather than adaptive beings. Freire's characterisation of humans as historical and uncompleted beings with a sense of the past, present and future accords with the emphasis placed in the ID Model upon the time factor, as learners reflect upon their past, present and future selves during self-analysis, perhaps reorienting themselves towards the future.

For this reason, learners may return to previous steps for reconsideration as they proceed through the stages of the ID Model, and the course, which prioritises real-time communication between real people over other forms, can be summed up as an orientation to otherness within which the conscious and considered selection of values and evaluative tendency are encouraged. This developmental and future-oriented view echoes Barnett's (1997) point that autonomy can increase through critical forms of education as learners learn to build their own cognitive universes. Through the processes of self-interrogation and the gradual recognition of the validity of other viewpoints possibly over one's own, Barnett suggests that new thinking and new acts may emerge as learners widen over time. Through the processes of self-interrogation and the gradual recognition of the validity of other viewpoints, possibly over one's own, Barnett suggests that new thinking and new acts may emerge as learners widen over time, a view echoed and elaborated upon by the Colombian Ministry of Education:

A constant task of schooling at all levels should be the development of autonomy in learners. Educating people to think for themselves, to act from personal conviction and to have a critical sense of taking responsibility requires recognizing their capacities to assume values, attitudes and norms transmitted through different areas of socialization, while also recognizing their ability to actively appropriate these cultural aspects, recreate them and construct new values. This means encouraging the development of an autonomous moral conscience, which emphasizes the deep-set roots and dependence of human beings on the cultural context in which they are formed, while simultaneously recognizing their capacity for reason and abstraction, which allows them to distance themselves from the taken-for-granted, judging it critically from the perspective of values and principles reflecting universalizable content, an example of such content being human rights. (Colombian Ministry of Education, cited in Parmenter, 2010: 83–84)

6 Critically Analysing Self and Other

Stage 1: Analytically Describing One's Own Values

Barnett (1997) conceptualises disciplinary reflection in terms of learners reflecting on their own disciplinary competence as conversation within the academic discipline becomes inner dialogue and so learners interrogate their own understandings. Focusing on self-referencing, Barnett's use of the term *inner dialogue* suggests not only that ideas interplay within a single individual but that the individual comes to be reshaped by this dialogue 'forming a disciplinary person who comes to see the world through a particular set of cognitive spectacles' (Barnett, 1997: 95–96). In stage 1 of the ID Model, learners are expected to grapple with, and refer themselves to, abstract value taxonomies generated in the field of intercultural communication brought into relation to foreign language learning.

Inner dialogue capable of transforming the self can be generated as learners refer themselves, or relate their ideas to, disciplinary dialogue. But addressing self-concept is what initially leads learners to perceive themselves in new ways, which characterises Barnett's third level of critical reflection, and links levels 1 and 3 of Barnett's critical reflection directly. Also, since learner accounts of their own values generated at this early stage constitute the generation of new knowledge about the self with reference to the abstract conceptual framework provided, stage 1 of the ID Model can be linked not only with Barnett's domain of knowledge but also with Byram's two dimensions of *savoir* and *savoir être*. The conceptual links between stage 1 of the ID Model, Byram's Model of Intercultural Communicative Competence (ICC) and Barnett's levels of critical reflection are presented in Table 6.1.

As noted in the previous chapter, values can be distinguished from other components of culture such as beliefs and norms when defining values for learners in the early stages of a course. And the concept of values itself can

Table 6.1 Conceptual links between stage 1 of Houghton's (2007, 2009a, 2010) Intercultural Dialogue Model, Byram's (1997) Model of Intercultural Communicative Competence and Barnett's (1997) levels of critical reflection

Houghton: ID Model: Stage 1	Byram: Model of ICC	Barnett: Levels of critical reflection
1 Analysis of self Self-reflection Self-analysis	*Savoir* Generation of new knowledge about the self	Disciplinary Conversation within the academic discipline becomes inner dialogue within learners as they interrogate their own understanding
	Savoir être Partial description of own values with reference to overarching conceptual disciplinary frameworks	Critical New way of perceiving oneself by addressing self-concept, divesting old conceptions of the self, of the world and of the self in relation to the world
Contradiction within the self can be expected to emerge		Societal The world presents situation-specific problems, which are susceptible to purposive intervention through skill-deployment

be broken down into enough detail to set up conceptual categories to structure learner self-reflection and analysis. This can ultimately reveal specific areas of value difference between learners using a taxonomy of values, for example, that can provide a clearly defined set of concepts that can be used to guide syllabus and materials design to help learners see how the same kinds of values manifest themselves in different people and cultures.

It was also noted in the previous chapter that since people tend to be unaware of how the extent to which their personal conceptual frameworks are influenced by culturally shared conceptual frameworks, the provision of an overarching conceptual framework in teaching materials to which learners can refer during self-reflection can help raise their unconscious presuppositions to more conscious levels in working configurations, ultimately to reveal specific areas of learner difference. This is possible even in a mono-lingual, mono-cultural group of learners.

Examples are provided below that illustrate how a taxonomy of values can serve as a conceptual framework for the construction of dialogues that express hidden values that have been stacked and layered for learners to discover through reading comprehension activities. Having read and answered questions about the dialogue presented in Task 4.1, learners can then re-read the dialogue in the light of the value definitions presented in Task 4.2 to identify the hidden values expressed in them, before going on to complete sentences about their own values and discussing their answers with other learners. Such an approach to the definition of values can not only give learners a chance to reflect on, identify and describe their values to others, but can also introduce new topics to the discussion to expand the existing conceptual framework.

Learner reflexivity can be enhanced by asking them to write a paragraph about their values after each class for homework, with some critical distance from the lesson. Over a number of weeks, learners can then reflectively develop their paragraphs into an essay as a piece of process writing that they can later present to the class in the form of a speech. They can also make a value chart ranking the relative strength of each of their 10 values numerically to help them reflect upon their relative prioritisation of the values and to facilitate superficial comparison with other learners early in the course.

Task 4.1
(Sample conversation)

Alison: Hi, Stephen. How are things? Do you have any plans for the summer?

Stephen: No, not really. I think I'll just relax and take it easy. Jane and I really should start saving up to get married. We'll probably just go down to the pub as usual and spend time with friends. We see the same people there every week, which is nice. And we'll probably have a few day trips in the countryside ... visit a few country pubs!

Alison: Well, we'll probably go to Scotland to see some friends. We want to go to the Edinburgh festival in August and see some traditional Scottish dancing. I love all those kinds of traditions. I really want to see the Military Tattoo.

Stephen: Sounds like fun.

Task 4.2: Who values tradition, conformity and security?

Read the paragraph about tradition, conformity and security and then read the two conversations again. What do you think each person values, and why?

Reading: Tradition, Conformity and Security

People who value tradition accept, respect and are committed to their culture, its religion, customs and ideas. They accept their role in life and are humble. People who value conformity care about respecting social expectations and norms. They do not wish to upset or harm others and value restraint. They are obedient, value self-discipline, politeness and honour their parents and elders. People who value security care about safety, harmony and the stability of society, relationships and the self. They value family security, national security and social order. They believe that if someone does you a favour, you should do them a favour back. They also tend to value cleanliness. (Adapted from Schwartz & Sagiv, 1995; Schwartz *et al.*, 1997)

Let us consider the kind of work that may be produced by learners if teachers follow the teaching approach recommended above. In the three extracts presented below, it can be seen that learners C12, C7 and C5 claimed that they valued tradition at +4, +3 and 0, respectively, on a scale that ranged from −5 to +5. The data extracts presented below illustrate the kinds of examples they chose to provide when describing their tradition-related values following a period of reflection upon the class.

Learner C12: Week 4 Homework Paragraph

Tradition (+4)

About tradition in my life, I feel the traditional event on anniversary should keep be following. Actually, my family always follow these customs, for example, the winter solstice, the Star Festival, and the Doll's festival. These customs are the characteristic as Japanese. So I think we have to protect these customs.

Learner C7: Week 4 Homework Paragraph

Tradition (+3)

I value tradition, especially its culture. I respect Japanese picture or object of Buddha. Also, I think it is connect with recent Japanese culture so deeply in heart. I like folding paper, and toss beanbags, this is good example Japanese culture.

Learner C5: Week 4 Homework Paragraph

Tradition (0)

In the near future, I'll work at office after graduation if I'm employed. My parents wish that, too. Then there is conformity (I conform to the company), security (I can get salary) and tradition (the company has history). However I must restrain my idea, be obedient sometimes.

By reflectively analysing their values with reference to an overarching conceptual system in this way, learners can gradually come to see themselves in terms of discrete, valenced categories they can use to interpret their present, reinterpret their past and orient themselves to the future. Going through the process of reflective self-analysis, with clear and conscious reference to an overarching conceptual system engages learners in the analytical process of breaking wholes into parts, using concepts held in language. Gradually, learners may come to see themselves in terms of discrete elements or categories, identifying positive and negative points in themselves as they respond to others, and perhaps using the given conceptual systems to reinterpret their past or reorient themselves to the future. In addition, learners may also identify inconsistencies in themselves or contradictions in their own positions.

The identification of self-discrepancy may occur as learners identify discrepancies between what they claim to value, what they do in practice and their ideals and hopes for the future; and becoming aware of these discrepancies may disconcert or upset learners. Learners may also find any given concept or value can be broken down into sub-components, each of which can be evaluated either positively or negatively, putting learners in a position to select between their own conflicting values and concepts. Through consciousness-raising activities, learners may notice new parts of themselves, or they may identify discrepancies within their analytical self-accounts between various combinations of their stated values, values evident in their behaviour, real, ideal or target values. Such self-discrepancy is evident in the data extracts presented below.

Learner A7: Learner Diary: Week 2

I think I want to be the power type, because that personality is strong and has power to everything. I don't have such a strong nature and such a responsibility, so maybe I am the achievement type. I have one question for you. What do you think about your ambition type? I think your job, to teach people, is some kind of work that needs power. I want to be a teacher in the future, so do I need to be power type??

Learner A7: Speech on Values: Week 6

I don't value power well. I like to lead people, though I don't have such a confidence. Certain leader needs as such confidence, so I cannot be a leader. I just do my best for myself.

This suggests that while teachers cannot work with the entire value system at once, they too need to work at three main levels: (1) with a selected part of the whole; (2) its individual parts; and (3) between its parts by taking a step-by-step approach. We can envisage learners who have familiarised themselves with a range of different values, reflecting upon the definitions provided and relating them to their own personal experience in the process. This naturally entails breaking a value and concept system down into component parts through self-analysis with reference to the overarching conceptual framework in order to describe one's values with reference to it.

While learner values are likely to differ, they can be conceptualised as complex, hierarchically organised and possibly internally inconsistent and rather unstable systems. They are partly held unconsciously and contain various interconnected parts that may underpin, yet also contradict, behaviour. Each valenced part may itself comprise further parts which may each be valenced either positively or negatively, bringing parts into potential conflict with each other as discrepancies are noticed. Values can thus be conceptualised either as discrete parts of a system or the system that itself comprises the parts.

Further, since all the various components and sub-components of the system as a whole may conflict when considered together, and can be evaluated separately and differently, learners may notice discrepancies and internal inconsistencies within their own systems that can generate change as learners select, reject or reprioritise values, concepts and their sub-components. While some learners may accept discrepancy, others may feel disturbed by the gap, resolving to improve, expressing the inclination to change now or perhaps later. In any case, analytical consciousness-raising can empower learners to consciously reprioritise or select between their own conflicting values. Change may start to occur within learners even at this early stage as they notice new parts of themselves, as their attention is drawn to misapprehensions about themselves and as they select between their own discrepant conflicting values. Analytical self-analysis may thus generate change.

A comparison of the series of data extracts generated by learner A7 presented above and below show that while she claimed that she did not value power but wanted to in weeks 2 and 6, she shifted position over time as she considered whether or not her hopes reflected her values. By week 24, she had clarified her ideas by comparing and contrasting herself with learner A9 and concluded that while she *did* value power, she distinguished leadership (which she wanted) from wealth and social status (which she did not). This point will be considered later in relation to motivation, language identity and the L2 self (Dörnyei, 2009).

Learner A7: Learner Diary: Week 10

I ask you again that I am confusing whether I should include my HOPE in the values or not.

Learner A7: Speech on Summer Assignment: Week 24

Considering power, we have different idea about it. Learner A9 doesn't value so much though I do. The one of our differences between us is that I think it is important to have a leadership. The common point is that we both think it is not necessary to seek for wealth or high position in social status.

This process may be impacted upon by others through interaction at different stages either consciously or unconsciously. Time is another important dimension insofar as learners may be considering past, present or future selves during self-analysis, perhaps reorienting themselves to the future in the process. Further, teachers who want to guide learner values can draw their attention to their internal discrepancies but regardless of teacher position, learner change seems to be a likely product of analytical consciousness-raising.

Stage 2: Analytically Describing the Values of Another Person

Having engaged in reflective self-analysis, learners are then expected to analyse the values of another learner in stage 2 of the ID Model. Barnett identifies as key features of the second level of critical reflection the development of self-control, breadth, tolerance of perspectives and mutual understanding, and the appreciation of the limitations of own perspective. This involves moving beyond current understandings, stepping outside one's own perspective to appreciate those of others, and prioritising truth and precision in communication and analysis as matters of disposition and stance. This implies that as they progress through stage 2 of the ID Model, learners need to function within the domains of both self and other with a view to consciously selecting their dispositions in later stages (Table 6.2).

In stage 2, however, the emphasis is first placed upon learners exploring each other's perspectives in practice, deploying empathy-oriented communicative

Table 6.2 Conceptual links between stage 2 of Houghton's (2007, 2009a, 2010) Intercultural Dialogue Model, Byram's (1997) Model of Intercultural Communicative Competence and Barnett's (1997) levels of critical reflection

Houghton: ID Model: Stage 2	Byram: Model of ICC	Barnett: Levels of critical reflection
2 Analysis of other	*Savoir apprendre/faire*	Educational
This relies upon the successful deployment of empathy-oriented communication skills	Eliciting information about interlocutor perspective real-time clarifying points and developing detail.	(1) Determination to search deeper and seek breadth not resting on current understandings (2) Willingness to step outside own perspective to appreciate others (3) Concern for truth and precision in communication and analysis
	Savoir Generation of new knowledge about the other	
Contradiction within the self can be expected to emerge		Social formation Reflection anchors in dialogue as learners go openly into the language and perspectives of others and springs out of the inner disturbance caused by unfamiliar social interaction
		Societal The world presents situation-specific problems, which are susceptible to purposive intervention through skill-deployment

skills that facilitate the production of accurate accounts of the perspectives of their interlocutor. This process, which involves the generation of new knowledge, carries the potential to impact upon the world by injecting new meanings into it, so we can link this stage with Byram's dimensions of *savoir* and *savoir apprendre/faire*. In the latter, learners are required to elicit information from their interlocutor by deploying empathy-oriented communication skills, clarifying information and developing detail. This can be linked with the fourth level of Barnett's critical reflection at which learners are expected to read situations selectively and deploy specific competences. But it also relates to level 8 of Barnett's concept of self-reflection, within which the world presents situation-specific problems susceptible to purposive intervention through skill-deployment.

The emergence, through analysis, of contradiction is a point that deserves special attention. This could constitute internal contradiction within one's own value and conceptual systems or between self and situations in the world, as noted by Freire (1990). The seventh level of Barnett's concept of critical reflection, within which reflection anchors in dialogue as learners engage openly with the language and perspectives of others, also comes into play. As contradiction springs from the inner disturbance caused by unfamiliar social interaction, social development is stimulated. This is consistent with the view taken in stage 2 of the ID Model that interaction between self and other generates inner disturbance that can then be explored systematically as learners gradually learn to draw on others for self-realisation.

Intellectual empathy

Intellectual empathy and information processing

Intellectually empathising with another person involves processing information provided by that person about their own perspective or viewpoint, which is expressed through sets of interconnected, value-laden concepts. As they pay attention, learners selectively focus upon sections of the input for a few seconds to convert information into meaningful representations through preliminary analysis, before segmenting sentences into language chunks to construct further meaningful representations. Finally, learners decode chunks by matching them with meaning-based representations held in their long-term memory to form a more complete understanding of the input by linking ideas.

As conceptual connections are evoked through spreading activation within their own sets of interconnected, value-laden concepts, learners may engage in top-down processing by using prior knowledge to assist comprehension, interpreting new information in the light of old, inferring and predicting meaning when there are gaps in understanding. Alternatively, they may take the analysis of individual words as their starting point allowing meaning to accumulate, although lack of attention to context and first language interference may render this bottom-up processing inefficient. Both top-down and bottom-up processing may misguide learners through misinterpretations resulting from the inappropriate use of conceptual frameworks. Conceptual differences arising not only between individuals but also between languages can be focused on at this stage following Byram (1989a), for example, who suggests that self-reflection and consciousness-raising can help circumvent the problem of foreign language learners merely encoding their own culture-specific meanings in the foreign language.

From the standpoint of information processing, intellectual empathy is clearly a bottom-up process that requires learners to develop their understandings of their interlocutor, based on information provided by the interlocutor. This process contrasts with top-down processing, through which learners make use of their own prior knowledge to develop their understandings. The use of top-down processing may lead some learners to inject their own ideas into written accounts of interlocutor values or confuse their own ideas with those of their interlocutor. This may explain why some learners claim to find it easier to empathise with similar or familiar others, with television characters having seen the whole programme rather than just a clip, or with unfamiliar fictional characters who display familiar cultural traits. It may also explain why some learners claim to find it more difficult to empathise with different or unfamiliar others, since they have less prior knowledge upon which to draw. This would, in turn, necessitate the use of bottom-up processing to build up new knowledge from scratch. Thus, learners who claim they find it easy to empathise with others may be more skilful bottom-up processors than those who claim to find it difficult.

The practice of intellectual empathy, through which learners can start to decentre as they start considering different viewpoints, seems to help reduce their resistance to the ideas of others. But if so, this would suggest that something more than just bottom-up information processing is at work. Specifically, it suggests that such learners must be relating information contained in incoming viewpoints to their own, triggering other cognitive processes such as those described by Rumelhart (1980) and Piaget (Crain, 2000), through which learners integrate incoming information, and modify their existing information networks, possibly creating new information structures in an attempt to resolve discrepancy in the process. Since meta-cognitive awareness also seems to develop in learners as a result of this process, their attention could be drawn to these processes systematically, which is recommended since a negative effect of empathy may be the feeling of sinking under the influence of others, as we shall see.

This points us towards Byram's notion of *savoir apprendre/faire* within which learners are recommended to develop the ability to discover and build knowledge about different ways in which phenomena are culturally perceived by interacting directly with culturally different others real-time. Since this involves the deployment of the skills of discovery and interaction in the absence of knowledge, *savoir apprendre* is in keeping with the empathy stage of the ID Model. But this dimension was split into two separate dimensions in Sections 5.1.2 and 5.1.4 of the CEFR. In the CEFR version, *savoir faire* focuses on the deployment of various kinds of sociocultural knowledge *in situ*, whereas *savoir apprendre* highlights the need for information processing skills that support the integration of new knowledge into old, modifying the latter if necessary. While Byram's version of *savoir-apprendre/faire* also highlights knowledge acquisition, the need to elicit information from the interlocutor in the first place is also recognised. Likewise, the CEFR version of *savoir apprendre* specifically includes a range of cognitive, heuristic skills such as analysing, inferencing and memorising.

To this discussion of top-down versus bottom-up processing, we can add that if incoming information about the interlocutor conflicts with prior knowledge, held in the form of stereotypes, for example, empathy is likely to be further complicated as attention is drawn away from bottom-up processing towards the discrepancy, perhaps through surprise. As with the teaching of receptive language skills, teachers of intellectual empathy should consider the roles of both top-down and bottom-up information processing in language comprehension, and the possibility of interference from existing conceptual frameworks. Just as listening and reading strategies can be taught that seek to maximise learner command over each of these areas, intellectual empathy strategies can be taught that help learners build cognitive maps of the perspectives of others that are as free as possible from personal cognitive and affective interference.

The position taken in this book is that empathy should be treated as a cognitive skill that involves bottom-up processing, in which the learning objective is to explore and map out the interlocutor's perspective as accurately as possible, suspending evaluation to a later stage. This position accords with de Bono's (1990) suggestion that evaluation can be suspended to make way for other forms of explorative thought, with Paul and Elder (2002) who recognise that intellectual empathy is a cognitive move exercisable at will, and with Doyé (2003) who recognises the role of empathy, or perspective-taking, as one aspect of cognitive socialisation, echoing the discussion of the need to learn to work with multiple mental models. This theme was also highlighted in Piaget (Crain, 2000) and Kohlberg's (Crain, 2000) stages of cognitive and moral development, respectively. However, it is also recognised that learners can be influenced through empathy as they make conscious or unconscious evaluations and selections, as they try unsuccessfully to suspend their own values and concepts. So, this issue will be revisited later in relation to evaluation of self and other and the selection from alternatives.

Intellectual empathy in practice

In practice, intellectual empathy can be conceptualised in basic three stages, framed in terms of specific communication skills that can help learners construct accurate mental maps of perspectives endorsable by the interlocutor (Edge, 1992):

(1) *Reflect*: Mirror a point back to the speaker using the same or similar words to give the speaker a chance to correct any misunderstandings.
(2) *Focus*: Focus on a point made by the speaker to develop speaker ideas and detail.
(3) *Disclose*: Offer ideas to the speaker to prompt new information.

Although learners may already be using such communication strategies in everyday life, at least unconsciously, they may have difficulty using them consciously if they lack meta-cognitive awareness and control, have trouble expressing themselves in English or are unsure of their own ideas. But even if they find the communication strategies hard to use to begin with, they may get to them over time and come to recognise their importance as their skills develop.

However, to empathise successfully with an interlocutor learners must temporarily suspend evaluation to a later stage. Learners may fail to empathise effectively with their interlocutor by injecting their own point of view, perhaps accidentally, into written accounts of interlocutor values, comparing and contrasting interlocutor values and ideas with their own, sometimes judging. To help them decentre, teachers can point out when learners are allowing their own ideas to intrude into their description of their interlocutor's position, or if they are failing to suspend evaluation. Since learners have their own pre-existing value systems, it is difficult and perhaps impossible for them to imagine other perspectives without having similar thoughts in their minds.

Learner B7: Week 15 Homework

In the class, we learned about some communication skills, and must not rely on our values. But in the communication, we tend to use our values and we resist or judge or empathise. So if other person has quite different values, it is hard to understand. Because it is difficult to imagine other person's perspective without having similar thought in our mind.

A wide range of factors can facilitate or complicate the process of intellectual empathy. Whether or not learners find it easy to empathise with their interlocutor seems to depend partly on the degree of similarity and difference between self and other. Learners who find it easy to empathise with similar others because it is easy to imagine what they are thinking may be relying upon their own values and concepts rather than the decentring, and learners may be mistaking the opinions of similar others for their own.

Learner B9: Week 15 Homework

Many learners said it is hard to empathize if someone else has very different values. And it is easy to empathize with people who have similar ideas to ourselves but harder when the person has very different ideas. Of course, I agree with these suggestions.

While teachers should be aware that familiarity with their interlocutor can complicate intellectual empathy, it should also be noted that learner recognition of the influence of their own perspectives upon their perceptions of their interlocutor indicates not only that decentring is taking place but that meta-cognitive awareness is also developing, both of which are considered to be desirable forms of intercultural development in the ID Model. Empathising with different others may seem more difficult but at least similarity is not presumed. Greater suspension of the self may be required to develop a detailed description of another person's values. Also, prior knowledge seems to facilitate intellectual empathy, although this probably indicates utilisation rather than suspension of one's own conceptual system. This is evident in the data extract below when learner B10 made use of background knowledge about her foreign interviewee to analyse his values.

Learner B10: Summer Assignment

(Stimulation)

I think he values stimulation the most. He mentioned many times that having a good time or enjoying himself is important during the interview. Moreover, he loves slightly dangerous sports, for example skiing fast, and walking in nature. *Although he did not state this in the interview, I know that he also likes backpacking and traveling* (emphasis mine).

However, some prior knowledge probably contains stereotyped information about the perceived interlocutor group that may not apply to the interlocutor, surprising learners if they notice the discrepancy, which can in turn impact upon and complicate empathy-oriented communication. Intellectual empathy may also be complicated by cultural tendencies. For example, Japanese learners who claim to value silence, self-restraint and sensitivity over interlocutor status may feel inclined to hide their personality, but they get used to talking about themselves over time, coming to value communication itself more.

Learner B9: Week 15 Homework

Many learners thought it is hard to tell people about themselves because of Japanese education system. Actually I have not practice presentation in the presence of other people or tell about my own thought. And learner B7 thought it is hard to tell people about herself because Japanese people value silence. And learner B3 suggested it is hard for Japanese people to talk about themselves because they value self-restraint, hide their personality, tend not to judge and regard conflict as negative. I think that their opinions may have relevance to Japanese education system.

More generally, foreign language learners may find intellectual empathy particularly difficult if they are communicating in the target language, are in the mental habit of argument (if they are members of a debating club, for example), if they are uncertain of their own ideas or if their interlocutor is not empathising in return. Such considerations all relate to the characteristics of speaker and interlocutor and the relationship between them. The wide-ranging factors that seemed to make empathy easier or more difficult are presented in Table 6.3.

Despite the various limitations of intellectual empathy, there are many compelling reasons to teach such skills in the foreign language classroom. An important positive effect of having learners attempt empathy-oriented communication is the development of meta-cognitive awareness and decentring as learners identify and describe their own tendencies and reactions while they monitor their implementation of communication strategies, and the ways in which their own values and concepts affect their perception of others, despite attempting to suspend both.

As learners start monitoring their own and the speech of others, and deploying meta-cognitive awareness more consciously, they may start commenting on communicative tendencies, such as going off the point during a speech or selecting some aspects of the values to focus on whilst ignoring others, despite having been explicitly asked to focus on all of the values that had been covered in class. In the data extract below, learner B5 is starting to

Table 6.3 Factors complicating or facilitating empathy

Factors complicating empathy	Factors facilitating empathy
Fictional characters	
When fictional characters are non-Japanese	When fictional characters are Japanese or aspects of them approximate Japanese culture because one can draw on prior knowledge in interpretation
If you have not seen the whole film from which clips were taken and lack information to draw on	If you have already seen the whole film from which clips were taken because one has extra information to draw on
Real people	
Debating habits: Raising objections	Debating habits: Restraining opinion to argue against someone you agree with
When using the target language	Learning by watching others
Feelings intrude	Learning through practice
Uncertainty about own ideas	Having a clear opinion of one's own
When communicating with different others because one has to suspend aspects of oneself to understand them	Knowing the interlocutor well because one can draw on prior knowledge
When communicating with similar others because it is easy to mistake their opinion for one's own	When communicating with similar others because it is easy to imagine what they are thinking
When guessing the values of others	When information-gathering
As one judges others by own values/ stereotypes	
Empathising with a non-empathising interlocutor such as respected or idolised authoritative figures	
Perceived Japanese Tendencies	
Japanese people find it hard to express themselves to others because they value silence or because of the Japanese educational system	
Japanese people find it hard to talk about themselves because they value self-restraint, hide their personality, tend not to judge and regard conflict as negative	

(continued)

Table 6.3 Continued

Japanese culture prioritises the group over the individual so people are not used to talking about themselves
Japanese people may be influenced by others as they tend not to express their opinions just agreeing with others out of respect
Senior status of interlocutor

recognise that rather than using the communication strategies independently of the teacher as instructed, they tended to simply request from the speaker the repetition of certain parts of the speeches. Examples that illustrate the development of meta-cognitive awareness more generally are presented in Table 6.4.

Learner B5: Week 8 Learner Diary

I noticed we tend to ask the explanation about their value again, it means we tend to just confirm the point. I think to check the point clear is important, but in QA period, we should ask speaker by using Reflecting, focusing and disclosing before the teacher say 'Focus' or such things. Because in QA period speaker tend to just repeat [read] their speech what they said before.

Table 6.4 Examples of meta-cognitive awareness

I'm not using the communication strategies
I should use communication strategies independently of the teacher rather than requesting repetition of speech parts
I went off the point during the speech
I focus on some aspects of certain values whilst ignoring others
My own values influenced the way I identified those of others especially when I couldn't understand accurately. I need more information
It is easier to suspend my own ideas or values if I have enough information about my interlocutor to identify their values
I noticed my stereotypes
I tend to be influenced by other people's opinions, but is this partly culturally-determined?

In addition to promoting the development of meta-cognitive awareness, intellectual empathy can support relationship development to some extent by enhancing communication, understanding, conflict-management and cultural bridging. Further, it seems to be able to help learners understand different others and open their minds, reducing resistance to the ideas of others, sometimes overcoming conflict, and possibly developing consideration in the process.

Learner B5: Week 15 Homework

As I said before, I think empathy can help prevent conflict. Without it, we can never understand others. Because when we face to some problems with someone, we tend to think only ourselves, and we cannot open our eyes widely. But thanks to 'empathy', we can reconsider the problem in a wide view like 'If I were the person, I would think ....' So, when we face to some problems, we need to stop thinking, and change the position in our mind to understand others as much as possible.

Intellectual empathy also seems to support the communication process by generally helping people get to know each other better. Not only can it enhance information-gathering, interlocutor self-expression, idea clarification and confirmation, it can also encourage the development of detail and information-accuracy using bottom-up information processing, which is important because it supports the gathering of detailed and accurate information that can be critically evaluated later.

The link between information-gathering and its evaluation, which takes place in stage 4 of the ID Model, deserves special consideration at this point. When learners start to critically evaluate each other's value descriptions, information-gathering seems necessarily *partial*, insofar as the identification of key points through information-gathering involves the selection of some points for consideration and the rejection of others as learners decide how to make notes on their interlocutor's values. Whether or not learners manage to critically evaluate the interlocutor's values having made notes depends largely upon the amount of information they managed to gather in the early stages of the critical evaluation task series.

Learner A8 Week 15 Homework

When I missed to hear and note other's presentation, to recall them was so difficult and more, it was serious, because I had to compare and judge them later. I thought I could not say anything when I don't grasp it, because my statement may make someone uncomfortable and give mis-understandings, especially in this case, about values.

Intellectual empathy and influence

Having attempted to empathise with an interlocutor, even learners who produce satisfactory written descriptions endorsed by both interlocutor and teacher are likely to react to their experience later, perhaps changing in response. The issue of influence in empathy thus needs to be accounted for, but there seem to be competing schools of thought. On the one hand, some learners may recognise the possibility of being positively influenced by others by broadening their point of view as they integrate new concepts into their own. But they may wish to avoid being negatively influenced by placing the emphasis on knowing their own minds and valuing their own attributes before empathising with, considering and deciding whether or not to accept other viewpoints. They may confuse their own ideas with those of others or be shocked by the ideas of others, perhaps changing their own minds in response, especially if they lack confidence in their own opinions.

On the other hand, however, their peers may claim that such learners are being influenced because they have failed to empathise effectively, also claiming that effective empathy is precisely what holds their own ideas in tact as they are held in suspension during communication. Such learners may claim that they are not influenced during empathy because their attention is devoted instead to the implementation of communication skills and active perspective-mapping during that stage. They may also claim that empathy is a separate mental process from evaluation, that evaluation follows empathy and that influence takes place during the evaluation phase but not the empathy phase. Even learners who counter-claim they can be influenced at any stage may recognise the separation of empathy and evaluation as an ideal way of thinking, since it flexibly allows evaluations to change in response to new information gathered through empathy, noting the need to evaluate based on detailed information rather than on stereotypes.

Indeed, information-gathering and evaluation are integrally linked. Gathering information about the perspectives of others seems to be necessarily partial insofar as the identification of key points involves the selection of some points and rejection of others. Initial failure to gather enough information may render later critical evaluation difficult, if not impossible, if learners cannot remember all the content.

The basic complexity of value systems and their underlying alternative classifications of elements renders evaluation necessarily complex, so detailed information-gathering in the early stages and appropriate worksheet design are vital. If information-gathering takes place during empathy and is also a pre-requisite for evaluation, then empathy-oriented information-gathering tasks should precede those involving evaluation. But, concern about the unconscious influence of empathy is a strong argument in favour of *not* stopping the process there, but continuing on to *conscious* evaluation to help learners understand the processes by which they come to accept or reject the ideas of others. The position taken in this book is that teachers should empower learners to take responsibility for their decisions rather than blaming empathy or other unidentifiable, hegemonic agents. In this way, unnecessary learner insecurities can be minimised.

As we consider the crucial link between empathy and influence, we can envisage some learners who claim to be influenced, either positively or negatively, through empathy, and others who claim they are not. Those who claim they have been positively influenced may have recognised development of their own viewpoint in response to others, but those who claim they have been negatively influenced may be attributing change in their own ideas in response to others to a lack of confidence in their own ideas, to shock at the ideas of others, or to confusion between self and other. However, those who claim that they are not being influenced through empathy may be suggesting that any development in one's own viewpoint is related to other processes of the mind, and particularly to evaluation, insisting that empathy is what holds one's ideas intact as attention is focused directly on the deployment of specific communication skills to map interlocutor perspectives.

Intellectual empathy, definition and classification

Learners may misunderstand what their interlocutor means by choosing certain words, but start to notice not only that word meaning can differ from person to person, but also that people can be thinking of quite different things during discussion. They can learn what a word means from two cultural perspectives and appreciate how conceptual difference in both concrete and abstract nouns can make it difficult to know what is going on in other people's minds. In the English Japanese Online Dictionary, the Japanese word *yashin* (野心) is defined as 'an ambition' reflecting upon the valencing of the word *yashin* drew learner B6's attention to the fact that her understanding of the word not only differed from one her friends but also from a dictionary definition, which surprised her.

Learner B6: Week 6 Learner Diary

Last E-mail, you wrote 'Ambition is positive in English but *yasshin* is negative in Japanese'. I think it is true. However, one of my friends said *yasshin* has positive meaning. So I bothered about it. And I looked it up in Japanese dictionary. There is a surprising fact! *Yasshin* has both meaning, positive and negative. So, I can't say simply, '*yasshin* is negative in Japanese'. But generally Japanese people feel negative meaning about *yasshin*, I think. How difficult to understand the meaning of words!

In the process of comparing one person's definition against another person's, or against the overarching conceptual structure provided by a value taxonomy, learners may notice various kinds of conceptual discrepancy as learners classify certain aspects of their lives differently within the conceptual framework provided for self-reference. As learners notice similarities and differences between speaker values and concepts, they may focus on particular words to clarify what they mean to the speaker, but this may have a washback effect if speakers reconsider their positions and start to reclassify certain elements differently within the given conceptual framework, perhaps revising the relative prioritisation of values in the process. Conceptual clash between learner and perhaps teacher classification systems may cause speakers to revise their positions, but this very process can alert learners to the existence of difference in values and concepts, stimulating the development of meta-cognitive awareness.

Learner A10: Week 6 Learner Diary

In class, some people had speech about their value. I found each people has own value. It is very natural, but on some point, it was very similar to each other. For example, on point of value achievement and hedonism. Almost of speaker value these strongly. In my speech, I said 'Blood donation is part of value benevolence', but learner A9 suggested that donated blood is needed and took for people in all over the world (among same blood type), so it is value universalism. Then, I reconsider my opinion and I agree with her.

As we look ahead to stage 4 of the ID Model, which involves critical evaluation, it is important to remember that intellectually empathising with others can have an impact upon the conceptual systems of self and other at the levels of word definition and conceptual classification of elements. Indeed, conceptual classification underpins evaluative processes insofar as conceptual components can each be split into sub-components and evaluated separately. So any learners who claim they cannot evaluate a particular concept because they can see both good and bad points may find later that they can evaluate quite clearly if they break down the concept into its constituent parts. The data extract below highlights the importance of pre-evaluation analysis.

Learner A5: Week 24 Learner Diary

I learned from my speech today. I said I cannot judge or cannot say good or bad about universalism first. But After finishing my speech, by being asked about it, I could make my idea and judge very clearly. However I use 'cannot judge good or bad' in the mean which I said after my speech so I just didn't write it down. That's why I think this is not unconscious value. I was aware of it before ... I admit that there are two kinds of definition in the word. One is rough definition and another is precise definition. So, as you wrote, we should select them depends on situations. Precise definition was used in our class, as you said, we should split words into small parts to judge. So, I think this is precise definition. Rough definition is general way of use. I mean, in our daily life, we use words without thinking its definition well.

Intellectual empathy and contradiction

As learners listen to other learners describe their values and attempt to make sense of their positions, they may start to connect pieces of information about different aspects of different values, or identify links between particular values, their sources or functions and relative prioritisation in the process. Influence seems to be sparked primarily by the identification of contradiction between such elements at different levels. Learners may identify discrepancies in what speakers claim to value and what they seem to do in practice. While concepts may seem reasonable when focused on separately, focusing on the relations between them may reveal contradictions, and learners may reflectively notice contradictions in their own positions too.

Learner B10: Week 6 Learner Diary

We listened to other learners' speeches and learned what to do to understand their ideas better. Taking notes while listening to speeches was very difficult for me. I can't concentrate on two things at the same time. When I was writing words down, I was not paying enough attention to the speech. I found that 'to value something' is one thing and 'to take action for it' is another. Many learners value universalism, but few of them actually do something for it.

Learner B10: Week 8 Learner Diary

I finally finished my speech. Looking back all the questions I got from other learners, my speech was not good enough. I didn't think about all aspect of one value. .... It's difficult to mention every value, every aspect of it. Moreover, even if I think that 'I don't want Power', I might value it deep in side of my mind.

Having attempted to intellectually empathise with someone from a different country by interviewing them about their values, and having presented their descriptions to their peers, learners may feel motivated to discuss points that arose with other learners. Even learners who appear to have succeeded in suspending their own values and concepts by writing non-evaluative descriptions of their interviewee's values in their essays may do this. And learners may start to change in response to others as they consider the impact of intellectual empathy upon themselves and others, developing not only meta-cognitive awareness but also their own terminology to discuss complicated ideas in the process.

Learner B8: Summer Assignment

Finally, I'd like to say what point was changed by talking with (my foreign interviewee). Thanks to her, my thinking about TRADITION was changed. I have lived in Japan for 20 years, but I don't know Japan well. If I went to abroad, I will not be able to tell Japanese history and culture to foreigners. But, she knows about her country's history and culture. And she has her own opinions about them. I think that her diligence is a good example for us to follow. Then, I want to ask you 'Do you know about your country well?' Please discuss about it!

Learner B11: Week 24 Learner Diary

Learner B3 became curious after the interview. She wants to know about the partner more. Learner B6's value about achievement was grown up. She was motivated by her partner. She changed in positive way. Learner B7's stereotype that Americans have a strong opinion was broken. And learner B8's partner made her to think she has to know about Japan more.

As they discuss the impact of intellectual empathy, some learners may insist on the need to value one's own culture, mind, values, nationality and belief before empathising, or to know one's own mind clearly to avoid being negatively influenced as they consider other viewpoints. Learners may feel afraid of confusing their opinions with those of others as they attempt to empathise intellectually with them, anticipating shock at new ways of thinking, especially if they lack confidence in their own opinions.

Learner B9: Week 23 Homework

We learned about to empathize to understand other's opinion and value. We try to understand other's opinion with using empathy. This act is very important I think. But if I have a vague opinion, my opinion may change. So if people who give priority empathy change their opinion and sink in a strong people who have a big influence, we should cut off all concepts and values including my own. When we use empathy, we should be careful like learner B1 said 'Before we use empathy, we have to treasure our culture, mind, value, nationality and belief'.

Other learners may claim that intellectual empathy holds their own ideas intact by holding them in suspension as they direct attention onto the active and conscious deployment of communication skills and perspective-mapping. Such learners may claim that evaluation and empathy constitute two separate mental processes, and that evaluation *follows* empathy and involves influence, suggesting that learners who find themselves being influenced by others have failed to empathise properly.

Learner B7: Week 23 Homework

When we talk to other person, firstly we empathise their opinion; next we judge it in our mind using our perspective and others perspective. Then it leads new opinion. So I think to treasure a lot of culture and mind and so on is useful for empathy, but to change our opinion and sink is a strong people who have to a big influence is related other process of our mind.

But even learners who struggle to empathise intellectually may recognise the potential for positive development of their own ideas in response to others as new concepts are added to their own, broadening their viewpoint in the process. The separation of empathy and evaluation may seem like an ideal way of thinking, insofar as it flexibly allows evaluations to change in response to new information. They may recognise the need to evaluate based on detailed information rather than on stereotypes.

Understanding the impact of intellectual empathy

How can the impact of intellectual empathy be explained? Ruben and Kealey (1979) linked empathy with influence by suggesting that those who are most non-judgmental in interaction and relativistic in their orientation towards knowledge seem to experience the greatest culture shock. They speculated that receptivity towards other life orientations and viewpoints may lead to intra-personal turmoil as people seek to resolve value contradictions and discrepancies.

The undermining of identity through intercultural interaction is addressed from a theoretical standpoint by Kim (2009) in relation to *identity security*, and from a practical standpoint by Holmes and O'Neill (2010) in relation to *the vulnerable self.* Cultural factors may also play a part. For example, Lebra (cited in Rosenberger, 1992: 109) describes the Japanese empathetic self in terms of the fusion, synergy or interchangeability between self and other, such that the self and other become loaded with each other. This possible Japanese tendency to fuse self and other through empathy may explain why some Japanese learners may feel threatened by empathy, but the kind of intellectual empathy required in the ID Model must be firmly distinguished from the kind of empathy described by Lebra. The definition of empathy in the ID Model is the critical thinking skill of intellectual empathy defined by Paul and Elder (2002) as the accurate reconstruction of another person's point of view free from one's own biases.

Thus, cultural tendencies to fuse self and other may thwart intellectual empathy but also, such fusion may be expected within the rather limited confines of the foreign language classroom as learners of similar ages (and perhaps the same gender) focus intensively on each other in a primarily local context. Barnett (1997) highlights Habermas' point that constituting the self through the particular renders the self liable to ideological take-over. This further highlights the need to offset the dangers of focusing attention strictly upon ascertaining the perspective of one other individual, in all their particularity within the local context, by referring to larger frameworks reaching outside the immediate context to introduce cross-boundary forms of communication. This constitutes yet another argument in favour of introducing external abstract frameworks for self-reference from outside the immediate context.

Indeed, Barnett places equal emphasis upon the local and the cosmopolitan, taking the view that we can be attached to a larger reference group in addition to our immediate reference group. This implies that learners should be able to refer themselves both to immediate reference groups and to those that lie beyond, which implies that self-referencing during self-analysis should be controlled by the teacher via value taxonomies, for example, that reach beyond the immediate environment.

The inner dynamics of value and conceptual change in response to others need to be taken into consideration in foreign language education in relation to the dynamics of internalisation. Simon *et al.* (1995) identify inculcation and modelling as the two processes through which values are formed, the former resembling introjections and the latter resembling memetics since it involves imitation of others. The core concept of memetics, the meme as cultural replicator, was coined by Dawkins (1989) as the cultural equivalent of the gene. Dawkins' book, entitled *The Selfish Gene* was later followed, amongst others, by Distin's (2005) book entitled *The Selfish Meme.* Ideas generated in this field can be used as a lens through which to view cultural evolution which necessarily implies evolution of the self.

According to Dawkins, cultural transmission is analogous to genetic transmission in that it can give rise to a form of evolution. Cultural evolution is unrelated to genetic evolution but in both, the change may be progressive and like genes, memes are replicators in that they are cultural units transmitted as ideas that propagate by spreading from brain to brain through imitation. Like genes, memes also have survival value as they penetrate and stabilise in the cultural environment with some memes surviving longer than others. This is the analogy Dawkins draws with the principle of natural selection with longevity, fecundity and copying-fidelity being three qualities that increase the chances of meme survival in the cultural pool. Of particular relevance is the quality of copying-fidelity, which involves memes being passed on in altered form as people blend the ideas of others with their own, which in turn relates to conceptual blending.

Viewing conceptual development in evolutionary terms, Fauconnier and Turner (2002) claim that the development of the blending capacity was adaptive, insofar as it increased the human cognitive ability to compress, remember, reason, categorise and analogise. They suggest that in language, double-scope blending in particular is indispensable. Fauconnier and Turner define double-scope blending in terms of conceptual networks that have inputs with different (and often clashing) organising frames, as well as organising frames for the blend that includes part of each of those frames, and have emergent structures of their own. Both organising frames make central contributions to the blend and their differences carry the potential for rich clashes stimulating the imagination giving rise to highly creative new blends.

Returning to memetics, Dawkins claims that as with gene complexes, meme complexes can be divided into large and small memetic units, and units within units, which fits the picture of value and concept system presented in the ID Model. Further, memes are necessarily placed into competition with each other, since time and storage space, in attention and memory respectively, are limiting factors. But Dawkins claims that while human beings are endowed with foresight, genes and memes are not, which means that human beings are capable of overcoming their own indoctrination, rooted in memes unconsciously copied from others, with conscious deliberation. The enhancement of conscious deliberation is one of the primary aims of the ID Model.

The issue, however, roots itself in debates about the existence of free will. Blackmore (1999), for example, argues that memetic evolution cannot be influenced by human intervention since the self itself amounts to nothing more than a complex of self-replicating memes, whilst Distin (2005) argues that people can influence the process. Of these, the ID Model aligns itself with the ideas of Dawkins and Distin, insofar as it presupposes that learners can engage in autonomous self-reconstruction, and the later stages of the model take the enhancement of such processes as their main aim.

Stage 3: Comparing and Contrasting Self and Other

The next stage of the ID Model engages learners in the conscious and systematic comparison and contrast of the values of self and other. We can envisage learners who, having analysed their own values and those of another person in stages 1 and 2 of the model, have now produced two separate written documents that each describe their own and their interlocutor's values in essay form. The limitations placed upon the essay length close the information to be analysed into two discrete units that can be juxtaposed and analysed. In this process, learners can be encouraged to monitor and track their own reactions and tendencies in response to the experience.

As learners analyse, they are actively seeking and finding similarities and differences between the two descriptions. As they monitor their own reactions, they are also noticing that they tend to seek, or expect to find, either similarities or differences and perhaps tend to react to them in particular ways, all of which may draw their attention to their own biases and tendencies, developing meta-cognitive and meta-affective awareness in the process. Learners who notice their own responses and tendencies may start to describe them, but they may change over time. Learners may notice this and be able to describe this change, a process that requires the adoption of critical standpoints as learners reflect upon themselves.

We can link this stage of the ID Model to level 2 of Barnett's critical reflection in that careful analysis is required to understand perspectives of others as they are considered separately from one's own. It also relates to Byram's notion of *savoir s'engager*, which includes not only the ability to evaluate, but also to compare and contrast the systems and origins of values, and mediation between the two. This slightly differs from the ID Model because it devotes an entire stage to the comparison and contrast of knowledge-laden documents, separate from and prior to, the evaluation stage in Stage 4 (Table 6.5).

A positive effect of consciously comparing and contrasting self and other is the development of meta-cognitive and meta-affective awareness, as learners monitor and note their own tendencies and reactions to others, which can be considered a by-product of analysis. Some learners may simply consider both similarities and differences to be natural or find them interesting. They may expect to find similarities between people, but be surprised

Table 6.5 Conceptual links between Stage 3 of Houghton's (2007, 2009a, 2010) Intercultural Dialogue Model, Byram's (1997) Model of Intercultural Communicative Competence and Barnett's (1997) levels of critical reflection

	Houghton: ID Model: Stage 3	Byram: Model of ICC	Barnett: Levels of critical reflection
3	Compare and contrast the perspectives of self and other	*Savoir s'engager* Compare and contrast the perspectives of self and other	Educational dispositions/Stance: (1) Determination to search deeper and seek breadth not resting on current understandings (2) Willingness to step outside own perspective to appreciate others (3) Concern for truth and precision in communication and analysis

at the degree of value difference they find or even disagree about the degree of similarity they find between them, which forces them question their own analytical processes. Learners may notice that they feel comfortable when they identify similarities but uncomfortable when they identify difference if it causes self-doubt or undermines their self-confidence.

Other learners may initially feel uneasy about revealing their opinion to others, but later enjoy finding differences and recognising their importance. They may start noticing their tendencies to either seek differences or similarities, and they may think that identifying differences highlights particular aspects of their own distinct character. Others may claim that identifying difference helps develop their point of view and that they enjoy talking to different others. Some may even start to enjoy finding unacceptable aspects in the positions of others or recognise the importance of honestly addressing difference as an important part of relationship development. The identification of difference may even help some learners identify special aspects of their own character and help to develop their viewpoint as they notice new points reinforcing both personal identity and opinion.

Learner A1: Week 15 Homework

First, about comparing and contrasting values, I practiced a lot in the classes. I think I have to compare with others to know myself well. If I try to know about myself by just self-examination, there is a limitation. The standard for comparing and contrasting was same or different. I tried to find similarities and differences, and I recognised the differences as my special character. The sense helps me, because I could feel that everyone is different and everyone is special and important.

This discussion of meta-cognitive awareness and control clearly underpins critical thinking. In particular, it underpins the definition of critical thinking as the development of discerning judgment based on standards, and the general push in the critical thinking movement towards self-governance through the development of second-order thinking.

7 Critically Evaluating Self and Other

Stage 4: Evaluating Self and Other

In this stage of the ID Model, we can envisage learners consciously evaluating self and other having analysed, compared and contrasted their own values with their interlocutor's, perhaps reacting positively and/or negatively to the process as it unfolds, but monitoring the reactions as they occur. They may find that the process of evaluation opens up opportunities for selection between alternatives, which perhaps causes confusion but holds the potential for change. Within the ID Model, this includes selecting from among the many cognitive and affective tendencies identified through self-reflection over time, and through a discussion of those tendencies with others who have, in turn, been reflecting upon their own tendencies during the same course of study. In this way, orientation to otherness can be selected by learners as a process of self-definition or *self-authoring* (Kramsch, 1993). This factor characterises level 6 of Barnett's concept of critical reflection.

Stage 4 of the ID Model cannot only be linked with the part of Byram's (1997) dimension of *savoir être* that focuses learner attention on their own tendencies as opposed to the internal structures of their concept of self, but also with the evaluative dimension of Byram's *savoir s'engager* and with level 5 of Barnett's (1997) critical reflection, which involves the evaluation of multiple options, the selection of some options and rejection of others, and general attempts to bring order to chaos as key aspects of the decision-making process. Barnett frames this in terms of action, insofar as choice and implementation of action puts into practice decisions that have already been made reflectively.

Such connections refer us back to the overarching theme of reconstruction of the self as learners start to exert selective control over their own identity development orienting themselves to otherness in the process. To take account of this extra dimension, *savoir se transformer*, or knowing how to become through interaction with others has been added by Houghton to Byram's model to complete the picture (Table 7.1) (It is underlined for emphasis).

In this section, an overview will be presented of the patterns that emerged at this stage with Japanese learners to exemplify the ways in which the dynamics described can play out in a particular cultural context, before an attempt is made in the section that follows to recognise the cultural aspects themselves. When learners are asked to evaluate self and other in public on a point-by-point basis, they may experience a range of negative reactions if they feel like they are being rude, or if they feel guilty or uncomfortable, perhaps due to lack of self-confidence. Learners may even feel quite

Table 7.1 Conceptual links between Stages 4 and 6 of Houghton's (2007, 2009a, 2010) Intercultural Dialogue Model, Byram's (1997) Model of Intercultural Communicative Competence (with *savoir se transformer* added by Houghton) and Barnett's (1997) levels of critical reflection

	Houghton: ID Model: Stage 1	Byram: Model of ICC	Barnett: Levels of critical reflection
4	Evaluate the perspectives of self and other	*Savoir s'engager* Evaluate the perspectives of self and other	Action Aspects of decision-making: (1) Evaluation of multiple options
5	Selection between alternatives/self-reconstruction	*Savoir être* Selecting tendencies and future orientations to otherness from a possible range	(2) Selection of some and rejection of others (3) General attempt to bring order to chaos Self-realisation
6	Orient self to other		Reflect upon personal experience defining the self through personal projects seeing attempts to understand the world as projects of self-discovery using education as a vehicle for realising one's own projects.
		Savoir se transformer Knowing how to become through interaction with others	

shocked after critically evaluating other learners openly in class, even if they accept the value of the process in principle.

Learner A8: Week 24 Learner Diary

I took my speech and listened to other speech. And we discussed each critical evaluation. After my speech, I was so upset and fell into sink actually. I had a kind of confidences for what I decided to judge my interviewee's opinion and describe my feeling about it clearly. I even know that in Japan to express something bad to someone is not so good, but I realized I need to do so. I want everyone to think about to judge. In this sense, it succeeded. However, I hadn't expect that I shocked and fell into sink so terribly.

When proceeding through stage 4 of the ID Model, then, teachers should minimise unnecessary negative reactions to critical evaluation by clearly defining it in terms the learners can understand, and justifying its practice in the classroom. Evaluation can be defined as consciously evaluating similarities and differences between self and other, either positively or negatively, with conscious reference to a clear and explicit standard. To justify its practice in the foreign language classroom, critical evaluation can be justified in terms of the need for self-monitoring, consciousness-raising and the development of meta-cognitive and meta-affective awareness, and control in intercultural communication.

In particular, the meaning of critical evaluation should be distinguished from *criticism*, which can often be taken to mean negative evaluation only or speaking ill of others without good reason (i.e. the expression of prejudice). If critical evaluation is not defined carefully enough, some learners may reject the process itself as the active promotion of prejudice by the teacher. So, the terms themselves should be clearly defined and distinguished in the first place to avoid misunderstandings on the part of learners. In addition, it is important to ensure that learners have gathered sufficient information in earlier stages of the ID Model to use as a sound basis for evaluation. Without that, some learners may not want to evaluate their peers based on the rather limited information presented in their speeches in class, for example, especially if they know they failed to make notes on some important points and cannot remember them later.

Learner A3: Week 15 Homework

About judge, I think it is danger. Because we heard only a little bit of each speech. Can we judge other people with not enough to resources? Value speech is very limited information. If we judge without enough information, we might be misunderstanding.

Some learners may claim that they simply dislike critically evaluating self and other, refuse to evaluate or claim they cannot evaluate because they think that people's opinions can always be expected to differ depending on personal background. They may even choose to deliberately focus their attention only on what they see as being the positive aspects of other people's positions, as a matter of principle, as a systematic way of consciously trying to accept and understand others, even though they may also admit that they may make negative evaluations briefly along the way.

Learner A10: Week 15 Homework

I had negative image for 'Judge' because I think judging lead to prejudice. Therefore in the interview and reply for my diary, (The teacher) explained for me that prejudice means pre-judge. I could learn about connection between judging and prejudice. However, still now I have negative image for 'Judge' and I'm hard to judge clearly. Also, I have questioned when we have to judge something, why aren't there choice of 'middle'. I think things have both advantage and disadvantage, so I often wondered. Learner A1 tends to judge similarity positively and differences negatively. I think her tendency is normal when compare own value with others. Also, my tendency of judgment is to judge positively. Though, in the interview, learner A7 said to me that I might have judged negatively for differences in my mind at least a moment. I might have negative image quickly, but thinking deeply, then I gradually tend to accept.

Apparent refusal to evaluate may, however, be little more than the refusal to *verbalise* evaluation rather than to *think* it, perhaps because learners do not want others to think badly of them, or to point out the faults of others. Also, refusal to evaluate may also manifest itself as inconsistent evaluation across situations for various reasons; however, once learners notice this tendency, they may reject it and resolve to improve their evaluative processes in the future. But, they may explain the reasons why inconsistent evaluation happened in the first place in terms of trying to accept all values by judging positively or feeling guilty at evaluating others negatively. Other possible reasons for inconsistent evaluation across situations are listed in Tables 7.2 and 7.3. Learner resistance to evaluation may be rooted in their own initially negative reactions to being evaluated by others.

Table 7.2 Possible reasons for inconsistent evaluations across situations

We learned that	judging is not negative but still tend to take a negative view of it	perhaps out of prejudice against the word itself and avoid judging	But even so, we still judge people unconsciously sometimes, so we should reflect on what is really going on in our minds
	critical evaluation does not mean to speak badly of others or to hurt them but making negative comments about other people's values is still not easy	I tend to accept other people's value but is this wrong? Do I just try to avoid criticising others? I don't think so	Judging people publicly makes us feel uncomfortable
Whether or not I can judge depends on whether the person is real or unreal. It is easier to		criticise fictional characters than real people	because we worry about how they will react and do not want to hurt them
		judge in fictional situations than real ones	
		judge people you don't know than people you know	
It is easier to judge people		positively not negatively	
		when I have a clear or strong opinion	
It is difficult to judge people when I see both good and bad points or when I am neutral			

Table 7.3 Range of reactions to criticism

If I were being constantly judged, I would not know how to cope. I would feel so bad. I am not that strong.		
I would not feel sad if I were criticised because I do not change my ideas so easily but basically I dislike it.		
At first, I might have a negative reaction or feel sad	but it may even consolidate our relationship if I understand and the person is a good friend. It would be harder to change my norms than my values. It would be easier to change my values than my beliefs	
	but may be able to accept it later or try to improve myself depending on	the nature of the criticism, how it is expressed, their relationship and the degree of trust
		the reason
		whether or not I can understand their position
		how persuasive the person is
		whether or not the person is trying to hurt me
		how well the person knows me
		the character of the person more than the reason
		how the point is communicated

But even learners who accept the process in principle, and perform it well, may feel quite shocked after evaluating another person publicly. Learner resistance to evaluation may run deep with some reservations persisting over time. Some learners may simply refuse to do it because they dislike it, questioning why they are not allowed to adopt a middle position. Even learners who recognise they evaluate unconsciously may still refuse to evaluate consciously, even if it results in inconsistent evaluation across situations and even when they recognise this as being problematic.

Other learners, however, may come to recognise the importance of critically evaluating self and other as they get used to analysing their own evaluative tendencies and identifying their standards. They might perhaps, develop better evaluation strategies by taking ideals as guiding principles, for example. They may slowly refine the definition and purpose of critical evaluation in their own minds, perhaps seeing it as an unpleasant but necessary step towards mutual understanding between people from different cultures, identifying the key point as being to explore why people react in certain ways to prevent barriers from forming.

Critical evaluations may still be left incomplete if learners continue to avoid evaluating, perhaps even hiding, as they attempt to critically evaluate others. They may need pushing to complete the process from time to time. Hidden values may have simply been previously unnoticed values, but other possible factors may have included lack of preparation time or reluctance to reveal points of uncertainty, possibly depending partly on the situation, the relationship, the desire to present themselves as an ideal person by hiding their bad points or the desire to protect themselves when interacting by not expressing their own ideas.

Learner A12: Week 25 Learner Diary

I have a tendency that I don't want to show or try to hide things, which I don't have self-confidence or didn't do well. That depends on situation or relationships that we have, but this tendency may comes from my inner feeling that I want to be an ideal person or I don't want to show my bad points. Maybe I want to protect myself, and this feeling can be strong when I see or talk with people I don't know well or don't have good relationships with them.

Despite possible learner resistance to the critical evaluation process, the ability to evaluate can be developed by splitting values and their associated concepts down into component parts to be evaluated separately. Since any given value contains sub-components, value difference may exist despite the appearance of similarity if some sub-components are selectively considered to the exclusion of others. Such hidden sub-structures not only conceal learners' differing foundations for evaluation, but also underpin influence dynamics, that may be triggered as learner attention is drawn to hidden or neglected sub-components of values, or associated concepts, which they had not previously considered in their analysis.

Insofar as conceptual detail influences evaluation, prior knowledge of the interlocutor may come into play as the critical evaluation process unfolds, enabling learners to identify discrepancy between interviewee actual and stated values, for example. Analytical complexity seems to be an important factor. Learners who appreciate the complexity and inherent contradiction of value systems with their alternative underlying classifications may have difficulty evaluating if they claim to see good and bad in everything, preferring to focus instead on information gathering, not wanting to miss important points or evaluate based on limited information.

Learners may encounter analytical difficulty arising from a selective focus upon different elements of particular values in the speeches of other learners, which they realise may be masking differing underlying foundations for evaluation that can prove hard to identify. Analytical complexity arising from the fact that there is good and bad in everything may also be cited as a problem, insofar as it clouds objective evaluation. While some learners may simply recognise the importance of critical evaluation, and its inevitability at least on an unconscious level, others may note how it helps them spot connections between the speaker's thoughts and feelings. In particular, comparison between self and other seemed to help learners get to know themselves better.

Learner A1: Week 15 Homework

About classes, I was interested in talking about values. I liked speeches about 10 values, because I could know how difference our values were, regardless we were brought up in same country. In addition, thanks to evaluate them critically, I could know the details of values. In other word, I could know that how connect between the value and their feeling in the speaker's mind.

Others may claim that evaluation helps them see how values and feelings connect in the mind of the speaker, and can enhance both self-knowledge and relationship management. When learners critically evaluate their own values, they may identify self-discrepancy through reflective self-analysis, be open to influence by others and start analysing the effects of the process.

Learner A11: Week 10 Homework

Next I effected by her on stimulation, too. I think I don't value it in the first time, because I don't like roller coaster, I don't tend to challenge new things. However, she said 'some stimulation can make me achieved'. I've not hit on such an idea before and I could agree with it. If I must do presentation, I feel nervous very much, but because of the nervous, I'll make efforts to succeed it. So stimulation is important for me to achieve or grow.

Influence seems to be a common effect of critical evaluation and a dynamic zone seems to emerge in which learners may push, shift position, agree, disagree and evaluate self and other, sometimes expressing the desire to change in response to the other, perhaps because they notice new parts of themselves as they compare and contrast self and other. Some of these

Table 7.4 Reflections on change during the course

I influenced others
I can not only express myself better than before but can resist and even persuade others
I was influenced by others
My point of view changed
My way of dealing with stereotypes changed
My values were clarified and changed
My values were clarified but did not change
My value change may or may not have been because of the course
I learned that studying English is not about talking with westerners but exchanging ways of thinking and understanding each other
Listening to others triggered memories I had forgotten
Identifying self-discrepancy motivated me to reconsider or develop my position
I still have unresolved discrepancies at the end of the course
I am more comfortable about living in Japan than before and can appreciate its good points and bad points
I am not so prepossessed with western values. There is good and bad in everything.

dynamics are reviewed in the data extract below, and wide-ranging learner reflections on change are listed in Table 7.4.

Learner A1: Winter Assignment

Let me review about the conversation with learner A9, I was pushed by her. I didn't know the reason then, but now I can explain it. At that time, learner A9 had a vision, which she wanted to be a captain in order to win her volleyball team. On the other hand, I didn't have such vision, and tell her not to be a captain with a selfish reason, which I wanted to avoid responsibility. However she had ideal self, and I didn't. Therefore my value became week. In the case of universalism, I push learner A10, because I had clear vision to protect nature, but learner A10 didn't. I cared about ideal-society, so my value was strong. I think the difference between strong value and week value is whether having ideal vision or selfish vision. Negative judgments let me know which aspect has a problem, and how to develop the point, because the opposite value is often a good model. That means to learn from others. To do so, I have to be flexible to receive them, at the same time I have to be enough clever to analyze them. That means I have to evaluate critically.

Learners may evaluate one aspect of another person's values positively, framing negative self-evaluation positively by stating how they want to be. This could either indicate value change or selection between one's own conflicting values, which may only come to light when responding to others. Learners may claim their own values have not changed if they recognise positive aspects in those of others, but recognise the contradictory nature of that position. Some learners may find that they use self-evaluation to develop self-knowledge, confirm identity or identify their evaluative standards. They may find that whereas positive self-evaluation underpins self-confidence, negative self-evaluation underpins the desire for self-enhancement. Some learners may think self-evaluation can improve society as a whole, helping them to see both good and bad points about their own society, but others may not.

Connections may be found between self-evaluation and the evaluation of others if learners evaluate others negatively as they evaluate themselves positively and vice versa, but negative self-evaluation combined with positive other-evaluation, in particular, seems to motivate change. As they consider conceptual consistency, learners may allow the concepts of others to impact upon their own, selecting and rejecting at will, as contradiction between elements surfaces.

Learner A1: Week 25 Learner Diary

Judging myself positively is related on confidence or proud. Judging myself negatively is related on enhancement or loosing identity. I should separate between personal feeling and value evaluation, then I have to focus on what I should do and our society should be. That point will give me the hint how to live. The best thinking chance is when I encounter the person who has difference values. I noticed that today, learner A12 evaluated her interviewee well when she found out any similarities, but she seemed to avoid evaluation when she faced on differences. This tendency applys to me! From now on I have to try not to miss such chances.

The critical evaluation of self and other can stimulate the development of meta-cognitive awareness to the point that learners can start to identify, describe and verbalise their own evaluative patterns and tendencies, and those of others. The identification of evaluative standards is thus a key concern in this stage of the ID Model. As learners make positive and negative evaluations of self and other, they may direct their attention not only to what is happening in their mind, but also to their positive and negative emotions. They may identify and label specific emotions, recognising the impact

of emotion upon evaluation. Both meta-cognitive and meta-affective awareness and control may be indicated by this kind of discussion as learners pay
conscious attention to, and develop their own terminology to discuss, subtle
cognitive and affective distinctions and dynamics within themselves and
others. As learners became familiar with the evaluative tendencies of others
through ongoing discussion, personal approaches towards critical evaluation
gradually surface, although discussion of this kind may require higher levels
of English language ability at which abstract thought can be expressed and
discussed. Such patterns are presented in Tables 7.5 and 7.6.

Teachers should thus be aware that a wide range of tendencies may come
to light. When evaluating others, some learners may find they tend to evaluate either positively or negatively, perhaps evaluating everything positively
hiding negative evaluations in the process. Learners may recognise not only

Table 7.5 Meta-cognitive awareness of own evaluative patterns

Evaluate similarities	negatively
	positively
Evaluate differences	negatively
	positively
Judge everything	positively
Hide negative evaluation and focus on positive evaluation	
Recognition of own bias	and its underpinning value
Recognition that one's evaluation is becoming less stereotyped	focusing on information-gathering and taking responsibility for own opinion
Positive evaluation of others may indicate positive self-evaluation	
Recognition that one is making surface evaluations less than before	

Table 7.6 Perceived evaluative patterns of others

Verbalise	positive evaluation	as Japanese tendency
Hide	negative evaluation	
Evaluate similarities	positively	
Evaluate differences	negatively	
Evaluate	positively	if they share either a positive or a negative value, regardless of strength even if the value difference is great.
	negatively	if they have an opposite value
Non-evaluative stance		because evaluation is biased by one's own values

their own bias but also see connections between their evaluations of self and other, possibly tracking change in their evaluative tendency over time. Possible links between the evaluation of others and self-evaluation may emerge, with self-evaluation indicating whether learners are likely to change position. Learners may evaluate others negatively when they evaluate themselves positively and vice versa. Negative self-evaluation and positive other-evaluation may be accompanied by the desire to change.

As learners discuss their reactions to being criticised by others, meta-affective awareness may also develop as they reflect upon their emotional reactions. Learners can be expected to go beyond simply performing critical evaluation to reflecting upon and discussing its effects in direct relation to their own tendencies and preferences. If learners find it difficult to evaluate, they may be able to explain why, perhaps identifying their own evaluative tendencies and biases (such as their tendency to evaluate positively or negatively, if any), and reflecting on value change more generally. As learners discuss the role of self-evaluation in critical evaluation, and what it means to them personally, they may consider their ideal way of evaluating, moving beyond performing the task itself to reflecting on its meaning and value.

Learner A5: Week 26 Homework 1

Role of self-judgment play in critical evaluation is to understand or find myself. For instance, character, what I like, what I feel, or what I think, etc. also, hearing other people's self-judgment, I could see some point of the person which I had never seen. And it makes broaden our view or idea.

Critical evaluation and cultural tendencies

It was noted above that learner critical evaluations of others may be left incomplete if, having compared and contrasted their own values with those of their interlocutor, learners stop short of evaluating and justifying, perhaps refusing to evaluate. Indeed, learners may seem to be hiding as they performed the critical evaluation. But to what extent can such tendencies, if any, be considered cultural in nature?

Learner A8: Week 25 Learner Diary

In this class, I wondered that what they say is not always truth. Of cause, I think I always don't say what I think about. It's not so unusual thing, but why sometimes do we hide our actual feelings in case?

Two factors influencing the evaluative dynamics outlined in the previous section include possible Japanese cultural preferences for indirectness and ambiguity. Japanese people tend to understand each other even when they use indirect and ambiguous language, but when Japanese learners make critical evaluations, their underlying cultural tendencies towards indirectness and ambiguity may manifest themselves in language patterns that render the critical evaluation rather unclear *in English*, so teachers may need to clarify the kinds of sentence patterns that they want. Some learners may not have wanted to express their negative feelings directly (i.e. hide them) noting that *criticism* is disliked in Japan. In this sense, the teacher's requirement for *directness* during critical evaluation may also conflict with the Japanese value of harmony, or *wa* (和), in the study described in this book. This point will be returned to below.

Data G9: Learner A3: End-of-Course Interview

Japanese don't like break harmony and community but I like this custom, so … because sometime I want to say about me very directly or straight, but almost all time, I don't want to straight comment. So … nn … in my case, if I want to say straightly, I say people please … please comment straightly.

Asking learners to express their own true feelings also seems to conflict with the Japanese concepts of *honne* (本音) and *tatemae* (建前). *Tatemae/honne* distinguish between the world of social relations (surface reality) and the world of feelings (inner reality). *Tatemae* refers to formal principles or rules to which one is at least outwardly constrained, while *honne* conveys personal feelings or motives, which cannot be openly expressed due to *tatemae* (Bachnik, 2007). Japanese learners may initially not want to use *honne* to avoid being considered rude but start to use it naturally as they get to know each other better. They may feel uncomfortable about being direct at first, or perhaps just need time to organise their feelings before describing them to others. They may open up and be more honest with each other as they get to know each other better over time.

Learner C5: Winter Assignment

In April, we didn't know well each other, so I couldn't use *hone*, because there was a possibility that I said rude things to other learners. Some weeks have passed, and we were using *hone* without notice. I think that's evidence which we understand each other.

If learners appear to hide when asked to evaluate, other learners may doubt the truth of learner assertions, including their own, wondering whether this apparent tendency to hide may be cultural, claiming that Japanese people tend not to express negative feelings directly because they dislike criticism. The desire to preserve *wa* may cause Japanese people to hide their true thoughts and feelings, speak indirectly or say things they do not mean perhaps to avoid hurting others or being hurt themselves. Japanese people may tend to prefer to hide their opinion or agree with others to avoid causing trouble, although this may depend on how important the issue is to them.

Data T29: Learner C5: Week 15 Homework

I think that Japanese don't try to state their opinions even if there were appropriate, because we hate being denied by others, and disturbing harmony. Learner C7 said that she tends to agree with other's opinions to avoid conflict. This tendency is often seen in our daily life. When we do something, we try to wait for someone's suggestion at first without stating own opinion. It's hard for me to judge other people's opinions. When I deny other's opinion, I feel small. I'm Japanese, so I'm accustomed to adapt to people's opinions. I fear some troubles happening by asserting myself.

The teacher's requirement for directness, which includes making negative evaluations of others during critical evaluation, seems to conflict with the Japanese value of *wa*. The desire to preserve *wa* may be defended against Westerners on the basis that even internationally-minded Japanese people should not have to go through the agony of denying something as precious as *wa* that has been cultivated in Japan over time.

Learner A3: End-of-Course Interview

Japanese don't like break harmony and community but I like this custom, so . . . because sometime I want to say about me very directly or straight, but almost all time, I don't want to straight comment. So . . . nn . . . in my case, if I want to say straightly, I say people please . . . please comment straightly.

Learner C3: End-of-Course Interview

I am not going to judge eternally, even though I learned the way to judge through this course. I'm not good at judging anything anyway. Especially I'd not like to judge whether it is good or bad toward culture, people, and historical things in my life although I sometimes need to judge. In fact, those who felt painful dropped out of this course. The Japanese conception, *wa*, in other word, 'harmony' is indeed beautiful. We don't have to be westernized by denying such a beautiful conception. The point is that even though we try to become cosmopolitans, it is wrong to deny the way with agony, which Japanese have cultivated so far. I am not going to introduce the way to judge everything into my life. All of things have both good and bad elements. We can argue a lot against Westerns who judge such Japanese as indecisive people.

Let us recap some points made earlier in the book in relation to harmony. The concept of harmony was referred to in Guilherme's rejection of Robinson's conceptualisation of culture learning for its underlying harmonious and consensus-driven idea of intercultural relations. Also, the implication that harmony-based social systems are at a lower stage of moral development than rationality-based democratic ones opened Kohlberg's stages of Moral Development up to criticism for being too western in its approach. As we have seen, Heine, Markus and Kitayama suggest that interdependent relational selves in East Asia may prioritise harmony between self and other. This can be linked to Lee's concept of *relational being* through which it is suggested that East Asians may prioritise the maintenance of harmonious human relationships over working towards an ideal state.

The desire for self-protection from the potential negative evaluations of others may cause problems for Japanese learners, who respond by avoiding or refusing to evaluate as they tried to hide their true thoughts and feelings. Out of the following possible evaluative flows, F seems to present itself as a problem when learners are asked to do C and D.

A: Self evaluates self (positive)
B: Self evaluates self (negative)
C: Self evaluates other (positive)
D: Self evaluates other (negative)
E: Self is evaluated by other (positive)
F: Self is evaluated by other (negative)

But looking to the academic literature at large, B seems to attract the research attention of cross-cultural researchers seeking to account for the apparent East Asian tendency towards self-criticism over self-enhancement (Heine, 2001). Whereas North Americans seem to respond to negative input by employing various self-enhancement biases (Heine, 2001), Japanese learners may avoid triggering negative input by hiding their honest evaluations of others. But Heine also suggests that concern for evaluations by others may be worth exploring in relation to Japanese self-criticism, an issue considered by Miyahara *et al.* (1998), who suggest that what appears to be other-centred styles of communication in young Japanese may actually be ego-maintenance and face-saving strategies, rather than genuine concern for others feelings. But concern for others feelings may be another reason why some Japanese people are reluctant to state their opinions (Naotsuka, 1981).

In addition to sensitivity to potential negative evaluation and consideration for others, other pivotal issues appear to be honesty and directness. Japanese people may speak directly with people they trust precisely because they trust them, but need time to establish that trust. This may affect both inter-learner and teacher–learner relations and highlights the relevance of closeness of relationship to honest self-expression in Japan, which may in turn relate to the Japanese concepts of *uchi* (内) and *soto* (外). Maynard defines *uchi* in terms of 'in, inside, internal, private, hidden'. *Uchi* persons belong to the same group, whereas those outside the group are referred to as *soto* persons, meaning 'out, outside, external, public, exposed' (Maynard, 1997: 156–179).

Maynard (1997) also contrasts Americans and Japanese on this point. Whereas the former seem less threatened or hurt by residual difference of opinion, the latter remain relationally vulnerable feeling psychologically or emotionally stressed by unplanned conflicts in the *soto* relationship. Maynard (1997) notes that among Japanese, direct exchanges occur most frequently between *uchi* members regarded as close friends where the *amae* (甘え) relationship is well established, and hurt feelings are likely to heal easily.

Maynard (1997) draws upon Doi to define the Japanese concept of *amae* in terms of the need for psychological and emotional dependence, imbued with sweet, all-embracing love and care that motivates Japanese people to unify in groups where they can feel secure. *Amae* releases Japanese people from the potential social injury caused by interaction with unknown others. From this, we can speculate that asking Japanese learners to critically evaluate foreign strangers, and (initially) *soto* Japanese peers, may cause them to resist evaluation. It would also explain why some learners find critical evaluation easier over time as they developed more *uchi* relationships with their peers.

However, even Japanese people who do hide their feelings can imply what they really mean, or express negative feelings indirectly, knowing the other Japanese person will understand. This relates to Hall's (1976) notion of high context culture of which Japan is but one of the many examples. Hall describes high-context communication as 'one in which most of the information is either in the physical context or internalized in the person, while very little is in the coded, explicit, transmitted parts of the message' (Hall, 1976: 79). Tobin relates this in turn to the Japanese concepts of *honne* (本音) and *tatemae* (建前) (Rosenberger, 1992). The fact that Japan tends to be a high-context culture may explain why Japanese learners may use vague language patterns that seem to obscure critical evaluation made in English.

Thus, critical evaluation needs to be considered in relation to cultural tendencies that may be related to underlying Japanese communicative patterns and cultural tendencies that equip Japanese people to get along with *uchi* people in high-context culture. Rephrased in those terms, the common aim of the ID Model when used in the Japanese cultural context is to help Japanese learners improve their communication with *soto* members, especially foreigners, in intercultural communication. The challenge is not, and could never be, to help Japanese learners transfer *uchi* oriented high-context communication patterns automatically to *soto* relations in intercultural communication. But clearly, being asked to critically evaluate *soto* members may make Japanese learners feel uncomfortable.

The critical evaluation of self and other thus needs to be considered in relation to communicative patterns and cultural tendencies. This relates back to the distinction made earlier in the book with regard to self-development between intra-individual and extra-individual focus. In the latter, non-verbal communication can play a particularly important role as verbal communication is downplayed as contextual factors are relied upon more instead. Interesting parallels may be drawn between Japanese and other cultures as diverse as the Arab world (Zaharna, 2009) and Africa (Nwosu, 2009) through the unifying cultural lens of *the interdependent self*. However, while giving due recognition to such cultural specificities, it is also important to keep in mind Kim's reminder that intercultural competence involves engaging in behaviours that 'foster cooperative relationships in all types of social and cultural contexts in which culturally or ethnically dissimilar others interface' (Kim, 2009: 62).

Stage 5: Selecting between Alternatives

Selecting evaluative tendency

Identifying their own tendencies, and a range of possible other tendencies generated by others, places learners in a position to make conscious selection between them; consequently a wide range of options may arise. For example, positivity may emerge as a selected tendency, a target value, a form of relationship maintenance, an orientation towards attempting rather than denying others and a generally desired internal state, though despite good intentions, positivity bias remains a form of prejudiced evaluation.

Learner C1: Week 15 Homework

Next I will talk about importance of being positive. I said that I tried to be positive. Sometimes, I can not think positively but I think that I want to have positive thinking as long as I can. Because positive thinking gives me courage to do anything and it cheers me up. As for me, not every time but almost when I am in low tension, my ways of thinking is negative. It is hard to stop negative thinking once starting to think about it so I try to be positive. If I cannot think positively, I ask for my friend who is expected to have positive thinking. For enjoying own my life which I cannot live just one time, it is important to be positive, I think.

Learners may consciously decide to make both positive and negative evaluations in recognition of the fact that they are not always right. They may constructively associate negative self-evaluation with self-enhancement, and perhaps attempt to increase honesty, fairness, self-knowledge or bias-reduction by considering both positive and negative aspects before reconsidering their position while rejecting emotional evaluation.

Learner A7: Week 27 Learner Diary

The approach to critical evaluation was interesting for me. I chose 2, because it seems to be more unbiased than others. Also, my idea is that when we 'feel' something positive or negative, I always reconsider why I felt in that way. It sometimes helps me to clear my values and how I think about. I found it through the classes.

Learners may prioritise flexibility over taking a fixed position as required in critical evaluation if they are unable to select between two contradictory values, able to understand both sides despite holding a clear opinion, or if they opt to remain neutral (i.e. choose not to evaluate). Learners may recognise that their ideas can develop through discussion with others, but being pushed to take a clear position may cause problems if it conflicts with notions of flexibility, perhaps because learners want to protect dual or multiple sets of values developed in different cultures that they want to deploy flexibly by choice. But even learners who claim to be stubborn may learn to consider the opinions of others and develop their own way of thinking through discussion, perhaps changing their mind frequently as they develop their viewpoint.

Learner C12: Winter Assignment

The most impressed thing is the idea, 'flexibility'. Before taking this class, I thought I shouldn't change my idea easily through listening other people's opinions. I also have stereotype of my belief, so I thought 'I have to be like my stereotype' But when we discuss understanding different cultural values, I was taught the flexible view is important in intercultural communication. Firstly, it was difficult to accept other's idea, but when I tried to understand about the view of other position, my view became wider and deeper than before.

Through flexible thinking, learners may actively be developing their own identities and opinions through others. From this standpoint, evaluation can be flexibly revised, given the possibly endless flow of incoming information. The flexible revision of evaluation in response to new information characterises unprejudiced evaluation, the flexible revision of stereotypes and open-mindedness. Other learners who select flexibility may, however, be using the word rather differently to mean understanding and appreciating situations from more than one standpoint, not only recognising the value of both, but prioritising this kind of flexibility over taking a clear position, perhaps being unable to select between what they perceive to be contradictory yet equal values. This may be found in learners who have spent an extended period of time abroad who claim they have internalised a dual set of differing cultural values that they can deploy at will.

Flexibility is an important factor in intercultural communication that is often discussed in relation to stereotypes, and it comes into play during empathy and critical evaluation. Just as the *flexible* revision of stereotypes should be encouraged, critical evaluation can and should be revised *flexibly* given the possibly endless flow of incoming information. Learners can be encouraged to look at their current configurations of values, explore those of others and develop *flexible*, open minds that would allow them to change freely, through conscious choice, in response to others.

Similarly, if prejudice involves evaluating before receiving all the relevant information, there must also be a pre-evaluation information-gathering stage, without which evaluation would be prejudiced. Two possible approaches suggest that empathy can be considered a pre-evaluation information-gathering phase that requires good communication skills. Insofar as we sometimes evaluate automatically without having enough information, we should gather information prior to evaluating to make more informed evaluations.

Thus, flexibility may be selected by learners as a tendency, but two competing definitions of the concept need to be distinguished. First, flexibility may be taken to involve cognitive shift through intellectual empathy to evaluate phenomena from different cultural standpoints. Second, it may be taken to mean the flexible revision of one's own point of view in response to another, which suggests that other perspectives are consciously being considered and integrated into existing conceptual systems. In this sense, information processing should be considered a never-ending process that requires the constant revision of existing information in the light of old, despite the adoption of clear, evaluative positions at any one time. This kind of flexibility should, in my view, be encouraged instead of insisting that learners adopt clear, evaluative positions that are fixed. Learners may decide to make both positive and negative evaluations systematically in the name of fairness, others may consciously select non-judgmental stance as a more general disposition in a conscious attempt to accept otherness. They may make this decision having considered, and rejected, the claim that non-evaluative stance is impossible, and having passed through all the earlier stages of the ID Model.

As we saw in Part 1 of the book, differences of opinion on this matter were identified between authors such as Byram and Guilherme who rejected non-judgmental stance, and Bennett, de Bono, Paul and Elder who argued in its favour. In the end, the same difference of opinion that is found in the academic literature may be found among both teachers and learners. Thus, while both evaluation and its suspension find their place in the ID Model at different stages, the ultimate decision-making power over which to employ in the future is left to learners themselves. Having passed through the various stages of the ID Model, they should be better equipped to make informed decisions as an act of free will. The onus is thus placed upon the teachers to maximise the learning experience at every stage to genuinely place learners in a position to orient themselves to others in the future. To that end, let us consider the following options that may present themselves, related to the selection of standards from learners' own alternatives, including ideals, and from teacher selections.

Selection of standards

Selection of standards from own alternatives

Focusing on the positive aspects of the critical evaluation process, learners may select from alternatives that already reside within them in the form of identifiable cognitive, affective or behavioural tendencies, discrepant components within their own value and conceptual systems, and visions of their current or future selves. Given that each learner holds within them a particular configuration of alternatives, further alternatives can be generated through discussion with others from which learner selections can be made. Other alternatives also can be suggested by the teacher in the form of particular content, or external standards, all of which may generate further alternatives, partly by inducing discrepancy with learner internal systems. In sum, learners may identify their own and other possible evaluative tendencies through discussion with others, which then places them in a position to make informed and conscious selections as they orient themselves to others in the future.

Perhaps the most important factor regarding evaluation is the selection of standards to apply when critically evaluating self and other, which is the key concern in this final stage of the ID Model, as learners consider how to develop themselves in response to others and how to orient themselves to others in future. Let us recall that identities were described in earlier stages of the ID Model as comprising components and sub-components that can each be evaluated separately, either positively or negatively, in ways that can highlight discrepancy between the parts, such as between real and ideal values.

Learner A3: Week 26 (Hmk) 1

After read learner A1's diary, I think learner A1's discussion points is very right. Judging myself positively is related on confidence or proud and judging myself negatively is related on enhancement or loosing identity. I think look each's value and each's judge very carefully, we can discover each person's way of life and personal charactar. But I think loosing identity is not related on judge myself negatively so well. Because how can I say … I think identity is made of positive parts and negative parts. And I agree with her the point that I have to focus on what I should do and our society should be.

Cultural preferences notwithstanding, an important positive effect of asking learners to critically evaluate self and other is the emergence of a range of possible reactions and tendencies that may then be consciously selected by learners. Attaining discussion of this kind, however, may require higher levels of English language ability at which abstract thought can be expressed and discussed. Learners need to identify their own evaluative standards before considering other options, but a range of options is likely to already reside within them.

Recalling that value systems contain both positive and negative, possibly discrepant parts, learners can move from a position of not knowing their own standards to identifying them, before being able to choose from among their own alternatives. Some learners may recognise the role of personal emotions in evaluation, perhaps not being able to extract emotion from evaluation without knowing what they want, or not wanting to separate them

Table 7.7 Views on the emotion/evaluation connection

Extracting emotion from evaluation is	ideal but difficult if not impossible	
	probably impossible	
	not necessarily desirable	values are deeply related to personal feelings. Separating them may render communication rather superficial. I don't want people to hide their feelings because I want to consider them. I don't want to limit people's feelings. I want us to understand each other
Ideal and emotional standards are connected and sometimes the same	head and heart are equal. I do not need one to rule the other but can select according to the situation. I usually follow my feelings but I sometimes need to follow my head (ideal)	

because neither can be ignored. They may reject emotional evaluation as an inferior standard and reflect generally on the viability of separating the two (see Table 7.7).

As meta-affective awareness develops over time, learners may start labelling and discussing emotional reactions, and reflecting upon the nature of ideals, the link between emotion and ideals, and the role of feelings in evaluation. Learners can learn not only to identify and describe their own personal approach to critical evaluation, but also to compare and contrast their approach with others and identify patterns within the group, which can generate new options for selection and thus new directions for learners. Some learners may want to make positive evaluations only while others wanted to make both positive and negative evaluations, for example. The role of ideals in evaluation may also be considered in some depth if learners start discussing which ideals should be set as new standards for evaluation, perhaps rejecting emotion as a base.

Learner A1: Week 15 Homework

Second, about judge, at the beginning, I don't like judging, because I felt that I was a rude person by deciding others good or bad. However after I analyzed my judging tendency, I could be getting used to it little by little. In first semester, I hadn't found my standard for judging yet, so my judging depended on my feeling, whether I felt good or bad. It was so simple. However I think the hint to get the standard for judging was hiding, because I wrote in my diary 'I judged differences positively if I can agree with them.' It means if the differences are reasonable or good, I can accept them. In 2nd semester, thanks to (the teacher), I could get the word of 'ideal' as my key word for judging.

Some learners may choose to base their evaluations upon their ideal future selves, focusing on what they should do or what society should be, setting their ideal values for self or society as new target values for the future. They may make selections in the present based on visions of their ideal future selves, considering failure to consider the gap between real and ideal as a possible cause of identity loss, highlighting the need to prioritise careful critical evaluation over ill-considered evaluation. Other points related to self-evaluation are listed in Table 7.8.

Learner A1: Week 26 (Hmk) 1

I think self-judgment needs to find more ideal self and society. For example, when I made New Years Resolution, I judged myself negatively and tried to improve myself. Last year I thought everything too much to carry out. Therefore I decide that I don't worry and I don't be so serious, and try to do before heavy thinking. The key sentence in this year is 'Fear is often worse than the danger itself.' I will have courage to carry out what I want to do. On the other hand, in case that self-judgment leads to loosing identity, the cause is not to consider the distance between ideal one and current situation. I think I should not judge myself negatively without considering myself and others deeply. That means without critical evaluation we should not judge negatively toward ourselves and others.

Language and values may evolve if learners start to change in line with their ideals. Others may not, however, seem so ideal-driven preferring to root their decisions in reality, perhaps not wanting to set limitations upon feelings for fear of rendering communication superficial. They may prioritise instead the expression of true thoughts and feelings to enhance genuine self-expression and mutual understanding. Other tendencies may be selected by learners regardless of teacher recommendation. The main point to emphasise here is the need for learners to identify distinctions and dynamics within themselves, developing their own terminology if necessary. But clearly, teachers who are aware of the various kinds of tendencies that can arise will be able to support the identification process by guiding learner attention and

Table 7.8   Views on self-evaluation

Self-evaluation	helps me notice new parts about myself		If I noticed any bad points about myself, I would try to change in line with my ideals
	confirms identity	Judging oneself positively relates to confidence and means that part will be kept and developed	Judging oneself negatively is also related to the desire to change and improve
		I don't understand why we should focus on what we should do or what our society should be	
	reflects our standards and hidden self-judgment helping us to identify ourselves and reduce our hidden stereotypes	It can also improve society	In Japan, we tend not to say what we think even if it negative although people may try to change or hide, which can support cooperation but impede achievement
	helps with consciousness-raising and contains both self-concept and self-evaluation. It helps us notice our hidden values	It is a kind of self-review that people should engage in to develop self-awareness especially in conflict-situations	It can help us reflect on Japanese culture more objectively paying attention to both good and bad points
Even if I agree with someone, our positions still differ because we have different foundations of evaluation	If I am influenced by another person's value, I just accept some parts of their ideas as part of my own	Positive self-judgment may relate to confidence because without it, I may simply follow others	Negative self-judgment is unrelated to self-enhancement or identity loss

providing suitable language for learners to describe it. Given that a particular configuration of alternatives resides within each learner, further alternatives may be generated through discussion with others from which learner selections can be made. This implies that discussion of distinctions and dynamics within the self should be included in course content. Examples of possible tendencies, some of which will be considered in more detail below, include:

- Tendency to evaluate positively, negatively or both.
- Tendency to hide negative evaluation of others.
- Being able to evaluate the same phenomenon from different cultural perspectives.
- Links between evaluations of self and other (e.g. negative self-evaluation/ positive other-evaluation leading to change or framing negative self-evaluation in terms of positive other-evaluation).
- Links between evaluation and other aspects of the self (e.g. negative self-evaluation can be linked with either self-enhancement or identity loss. Conflicting evaluations of different parts of the self leading to confusion).
- Links between being the subject and object of evaluation (e.g. not wanting to evaluate others negatively because of personal dislike of being evaluated negatively).

We can consider this in terms of the development of second-order thinking as described in relation to critical thinking and Byram's notion of *savoir être*, insofar as learners become aware of their own tendencies. Socrates' injunction *Know thyself* captures the priority at this stage, as learners are asked to describe distinctions and dynamics within the self in increasingly fine detail. As first-order thinking is raised to the conscious level and second-order thinking starts to emerge, learners can be encouraged to govern their thoughts. In part, this involves exposing inappropriate standards and replacing them with sound ones, which in turn relates to the point that lower-prejudice people may have personal standards that allow them to control prejudicial thought as it arises.

An aim of this stage of the ID Model is to encourage learners to consciously select and apply their own evaluative standards. This is consistent both with Bennett's description of integrated people as 'choosers of alternatives' (Bennett, 1993: 62) who are able to draw upon multiple-frames of reference as they consider selections. It is also consistent with de Bono's suggestion in his description of lateral thinking that people can restructure their own thought patterns through conscious choice by leaping between patterns, and looking between and around conceptual boundaries, to discover new ways of perceiving the world beyond that which they can already imagine. The question then arising is the range of options learners might be expected to select from, and whether any of these should be prioritised by teachers.

Ideals may present themselves for selection as discrepancies open up within the self during earlier stages of the teaching model. It would seem counter-intuitive to suggest that ideals should *not* be selected, since they carry the potential for shift towards something better than what already exists. Moving gradually towards an ideal-state may even seem like common sense, but Lee's (2001) point that Asian societies may prioritise social harmony over moving towards an ideal state brings ideals this into question.

Nevertheless, the notion of decision-making based on visions of future self and society *does* seem to invoke ideals, as people decide how they want to be in their ideal-state. The claim, for example, in the UNESCO Declaration and Integrated Framework of Action on Education for Peace, Human Rights and Democracy (1995), that education should cultivate in citizens the ability to make informed choices, basing their judgments and actions not only on the analysis of present situations but also on the vision of a preferred future, seems to invoke ideals. Indeed, Donnelly (2003) suggests that the very concept of human rights comprises both utopian ideal and a realistic practice for implementing that ideal, but ideals can also be problematised.

Instability in learner descriptions of their values and those of others may be rooted in their changing perceptions of reality. Their perceptions can shift as their awareness of the ways in which reality can be transformed increases. This gap between what Freire (1990) terms *real consciousness* and *potential consciousness* implies an internal gap between conceptualisations of *what is* in the present and *what can be* in the future. Freire's singling out of aspirations, motives and objectives all connect to the idea of the future. They resonate with the view of human beings transforming what is in the present into something different in the future, rather than simply adapting to what is in the present. While the gap between the real and the ideal within the self can thus be a powerful motor of change, ideals are also a double-edged sword.

An example of the way in which ideals can cause problems in foreign language education in relation to intergroup dynamics, stereotyping tendencies and prototypes, is provided by Rivers (2011: 844) who suggests that 'if the native-speaker English teacher within Japan is idealized and evaluated in a manner consistent with the prototypical exemplar model ..., then those English teachers who deviate from such norms pose a greater threat to the vitality of the in-group, and are therefore theoretically more likely to be evaluated in a negative manner as a means to maintain the valence of the accepted in-group'. The prototypical exemplar model mentioned above is considered to comprise linguistic, racial, behavioural and cultural dimensions examples of which, drawn from Rivers (2011), are listed below:

- Linguistic: The ideal 'native-speaker' English teacher should be monolingual to maintain a perception of purity and authenticity.
- Racial: The ideal 'native-speaker' English teacher should originate from an inner circle (Kachru, 1985) country and be of Caucasian origin.
- Behavioural: The ideal 'native-speaker' English teacher should be a charismatic, outgoing person who is talkative, enthusiastic and entertaining.
- Cultural: The ideal 'native-speaker' English teacher should embrace events such as Halloween, Christmas, Easter and Valentine's Day in a manner consistent with Japanese stereotypical images of tradition within the 'native-speakers' single country of origin.

Freire also frames ideals negatively, in terms of oppressed people 'hosting the oppressor' (Freire, 1990: 27) by internalising oppressor models before going on to set oppressor ideals as their own. In this regard, Guilherme (2002) highlights Gramsci's view that domination may rely upon persuasion and consent through ideological hegemony.

In sum, 'hegemony is primarily a strategy for the gaining of the active consent of the masses' (Buci-Glucksmann, 1982: 119), that is, by universalising ideological assumptions it also generalises predispositions, interest and needs. (Guilherme, 2002: 87)

Freire argues that because the oppressed host the oppressor, the oppressed are highly likely to become oppressors themselves when power is placed in their hands, unless they can free themselves conceptually from the inherent contradiction bound up in this dialectical conflict between opposing social forces. Freire also identifies prescription as a basic element in the relationship between oppressed and oppressor, which involves the imposition of the choices of the former upon the latter. This process is further compounded by fear, which blocks the ejection of the oppressor image and its replacement with autonomy and responsibility. Introjection is as a core concept of internalisation through which characteristics of a person or an object are unconsciously incorporated into the psyche (Wallis & Poulton, 2001).

This thread echoes Kramsch's (1993) point that conflicting self-accounts can also be interpreted in terms of power, through the notion of *double-voiced discourse*. From this standpoint, learner utterances naturally conflict since their language is populated by the intentions of others that they cannot easily differentiate from their own meaning. This means that the conflicting values and concepts of learners may originate in the views of others. To overcome this, Kramsch highlights the need for self-authoring through language education to help learners become authors of their own words. Foreign language teachers should thus help learners distinguish their own ideas from those of others.

Notwithstanding the separation made between the analysis of self and other in the ID Model, it is worth noting that the notion of double-voiced discourse highlights how difficult it can be to distinguish self from other, which explains why critical discourse analysis is relational in orientation 'in the sense that its primary focus is not in entities or individuals ... but on social relations' (Fairclough, 2010: 3), which are also dialectical insofar as they revolve around, and are both generated and influenced by, dialogue: 'Dialectical relations are relations between objects which are different from one another but not ... "discrete", not fully separate in the sense that one excludes the other' (Fairclough, 2010: 3).

Foreign language teachers can thus help learners distinguish their own ideas from those of others through intercultural dialogue that acknowledges the dynamic and dialectical relationship between self and other, which also involves power relations. Guilherme endorses Foucault's description of power relations as enabling and generative of cultural production, and Canagarajah calls for the integration of critical pedagogy with English language education to overcome the imperialist forces at work in English language education. Indeed, the main challenge of education according to Freire is to resolve the fundamental oppressor–oppressed contradiction, by fostering the development of individuals who not only free themselves from its trappings but who also replace it with autonomy and responsibility partly through the interrogation of ideals (Holliday, 2011). Into the mix, we can add another issue identified by Rogers (1951), namely, discrepancy can open up between the self and the world if one's values are based not upon first-hand experience but upon hearsay, which causes tension. To overcome this, Rogers suggests that integration should be promoted whereby all experience is made admissible to awareness, accurately symbolised and organised into one internally consistent system which is related to the structure of self, thus promoting growth.

In this way, the basic similarities in all human experience can be foregrounded, stimulating self-enhancement as all experiences and attitudes are permitted conscious symbolisation, and behaviour becomes the meaningful and balanced satisfaction of all needs, these needs being available to consciousness. Rogers claims that while individual formulation of value systems based upon direct experience is likely to stimulate the emergence of personal value systems unique to the individual, anarchy would *not* be the likely result because, counter-intuitive as it might seem, the basic needs shared by all human beings will ultimately stimulate the development of individual value systems that possess a high degree of similarity in their essentials. This would be rooted, in turn, in autonomy. Similarly, Simon *et al.* (1995) emphasise the need to foster the ability to select between the bewildering arrays of alternatives presenting themselves for selection in everyday life, which involves selection and rejection of elements free from peer pressure, unthinking submission to authority or the power of the mass media.

Selection of standards from teacher selections

Teachers may recommend or enforce external evaluative standards for particular pedagogical purposes in the hope of influencing learner orientation to others and the future. Prescriptive ideals and standards may be lifted from international human rights law, for example, which may or may not conflict with existing learner value systems, preferences and selections. Inducing discrepancy between internal and external evaluative standards seems to be the most effective way of generating learner change. But change may be happening anyway as a natural part of the analytical consciousness-raising process regardless of teacher approach, which implies that selection of conceptual content itself also plays a role.

Learner C6: Week 10 Homework 1

I'm not weak to go around with strange people, but I don't like to do and I don't care about them. But this attitude is disadvantage for intercultural communication, I think. When I talked with other learners, I noticed that I only see small world. I talked about benevolence with learner C12, and she said 'When I help people, it's not concerned with the people whether I know them or not.' Next, I talked about tradition with learner C3, and then I said 'I think we don't have to protect it,' but she said, 'If we don't know Japanese tradition, we can't absorb foreign culture.' I have never thought like them. And their opinion made me think about my value sense. I hope to challenge new things on the other hand I'm afraid to meet new things. I don't think my opinion is bad, but I should have a bigger view. I think it helps me to communicate with strange people.

Confusion may be a common product not only of the clash of classification systems, but also of the clash of teacher and learner logics if the teacher draws learner attention to inconsistencies in their lines of reasoning. Teachers may actively and consciously try to change learner values, sometimes apparently succeeding. In the data extract below, for example, democratic awareness may have been raised. The discussion below took place between the teacher and learner C9 in response to a task about voting rights that took place in week 19 of the course that aimed to nurture the development of learner values supportive of democracy and human rights. A general election had taken place a few days earlier but learners aged 18 or 19 were not allowed to vote. Suffrage is not awarded to Japanese citizens until the age of 20, despite the ratification by the Japanese government in 1994 of the Convention on the Rights of the Child, an international human rights treaty that states in article 1 that 'a child means every human being below the age of eighteen years unless under the law applicable to the child, majority is attained earlier'.

Task 19.4

Democracy: The Right to Vote

Read article 1 of the Convention on the Rights of the Child. This is a United Nations Human Rights Treaty, which Japan ratified in 1994. Answer the questions below.

Article 1

For the purposes of the present Convention, a child means every human being below the age of eighteen years unless under the law applicable to the child, majority is attained earlier.

See: http://www.bayefsky.com/treaties/crc.php

(1) How old are you?
(2) Under international law, are you an adult?
(3) Under Japanese law, are you an adult?
(4) Were you eligible to vote in the General Election on Sunday? Why? Why not?
(5) Do you think people aged 18–19 should be eligible to vote?
(6) Why do you think the government does not recognise this right?

The conversation below carried the discussion that had taken place in class further partly by relating it to the Japanese *kohai/senpai* system, which can be considered an institutionalised form of power relation that is based on age. In the Shogakukan Progressive Japanese-English dictionary, *kohai* (後輩) is defined as 'junior, younger learners' and *senpai* (先輩) is defined in terms of having 'more experience' or being 'years ahead in school'. In practice, younger members of society are expected and often required to publicly display respect to older members of society on the basis of age. In the view of the author of this book, young people are not only politically disempowered in Japanese society, but also politically disenfranchised as a result. Further, since they are not expected to vote, they are not expected to pay attention to politics, which disempowers them even further since they often conclude that since they do not understand politics well enough, they should not be given the responsibility to vote until later in life.

Learner C9: Week 19 Learner Diary

I didn't know a child means below the age of eighteen years as United Nations Human Rights Treaty. So I am an adult. But I don't have right to vote. I understand Japanese system (the standard of age of adult is 20) but it's inequality a little in another situations.

Teacher's Reply

Well, I think this is a very bad situation. As far as I know, any international laws Japan has signed/ratified are supposed to override Japanese law. That law clearly says childhood ends at 18, and I think you should have the right to vote. If I were you, I would be very angry. In fact, I'm angry for you. Why do you 'understand it'? The Japanese government should have more respect for the views of young adults. They don't and I think this relates to the *kohai/senpai* mentality. Maybe you 'understand' it because you have been raised with this mentality but I think it undermines democracy.

Teacher's Note

I'm really pushing learner C9 on the political aspects and I'm wondering whether at some point, she'll start resisting me.

Learner C9's Reply

Well ... because the age of 20 is well known standard of adults for Japanese. Drinking, Smoking ... most things are allowed from 20. As you said I educated this mentality from childhood, so it's natural. In addition to this, I am not interested in politics now, so I don't think I want to have the right to vote.

Teacher's Reply

Why not? Are you 100% happy with the way politicians organise and run your country?

Learner C9's Reply

I am not moved or attracted any politicians. Maybe now I don't listen to them carefully, but the image of politicians is not good for me. I think the chance to vote should be given more often for us. So we will get to have interest in politics. For example, about Japanese army, most of Japanese disagree to send them to Iraq. However, the Japanese government tries to send them. I think such a important subject should be voted.

Teacher's Reply

Yes, I read the same thing about the UK just yesterday, Apparently, they are thinking of lowering the voting age from 18 to 16 for that very same reason! Look: http://news.bbc.co.uk/2/hi/uk_news/politics/3297739.stm What do you think?

Learner C9's Reply

I read the article on that webpage. After reading, I'm also not sure whether the age of 16 should be given a right to vote or not. 16 is high school learner. I think that the most high school learners of now, are less interested in politics than me. Of course it is a very good chance to have an interest. However they may not think seriously. I think now (the age of 19) is the term of preparing. I am not interested in politics last week, but now, as I was listened to your opinion, I have gradually started to think.

But teachers aiming to develop democratic awareness by prescribing, perhaps enforcing, certain values or evaluative tendencies need to decide how to rank the following two types of learner, recognising that the distinction between the two may not be clear in practice:

- Learners who cooperatively select teacher-selected values and who are thus conforming to the will of the teacher as authority-figure.
- Learners who forcefully reject teacher-selected values or requirements for social action outside the classroom in the face of authoritarian teacher pressure exerted in the name of human rights and democracy.

Learners may not only be tracking the teacher pressure dynamic, but also recognise that communicating in a foreign language can generate value change in learners. Teachers who are attempting to help learners express themselves more effectively by helping them rephrase in better English may also be seen to be pressuring learners to say things they do not really mean. Some learners may insist upon freedom of choice leaving prescriptive teachers feeling that whereas such learners are standing for the tolerance of difference, they themselves seem to be standing up for the opposite. Learners may make different selections and rejections than the teacher in the same general support of democratic society, perhaps seeming more democratically minded than even the ethically driven prescriptive teacher at times.

Learner C3: End-of-Course Interview (Japanese Interviewer)

We are handicapped to speak English because English is not our mother tongue. (The teacher) led us to what we want to say under real consideration of our situation. But I thought she sometimes led us to what she wanted to listen under expectation. I really appreciate her to cover our language disadvantage. I could learn the phrase and how to construct the sentence. But when I was urged to say something by her under expectation, the opinion strayed a little from what I really wanted to say. And unconsciously I came to admit the other opinion.

Learners may select evaluative standards from those selected by the teacher, but should teachers recommend standards for evaluation? Byram (1997) claims that his model of intercultural communicative competence does not impose or recommend a particular set of values supporting freedom of value choice as part of democracy. This is considered a softer approach to democratic citizenship than theorists such as Guilherme, Osler and Starkey who encourage teachers to deliberately set out to bring learner values into line with what they claim to be *universal* values such as human rights, which may be explicitly set as target values for intercultural communication to nurture what Starkey calls world citizenship. But let us make a clear conceptual distinction between:

- The use of a top-down conceptual framework for self-reference that presents the concepts and values inherent in the notions of democracy and human rights as content to be introjected by learners; and
- The education goal of promoting self-determination by fostering the ability to reconstruct the self free from past introjections, which itself promotes democracy even though that is not the primary aim.

The view that underpins the ID Model is aligned with Rogers' (1951) democratic view of education, which is based partly on Hutchins' claim that universal suffrage, insofar as it makes everyone a ruler, is the foundation of democracy. Rogers presents reconstruction of the self as a democratic goal, describing it in terms of the learning of the self. Willingness to be a process, rather than a product, characterises people who shift the locus of their evaluations from a point external to the self to a point internal to the self (Rogers, 1961, 1980).

From this standpoint, top-down conceptual frameworks should be used to help learners work with multiple mental models, and those promoting democracy can be presented as options for selection from a range of alternatives. The complex of concepts and values that comprise the concept of human rights itself are seen to be no more than just that; conceptual frameworks that are open to criticism and negotiation like any other. They are objects that present themselves for selection from a range of alternatives, which implies they should be presented alongside their opposites as a range of *not-democracy* and *not-human rights* options. Simply from a conceptual point of view, this is necessary to delineate where the boundaries of the concepts lie (Oser, 2005). This, in turn, highlights de Bono's discussion of lateral thinking, whereby people should learn to see around, and between, conceptual boundaries to generate new forms of thought free of the limitations of old categories.

Thus, democracy and human rights are viewed as highly abstract conceptual systems that can be used for self-reference. They not only present opportunities to work within multiple abstract mental models but also present objects for selection. Educational support for the freedom of the selection process is *itself* considered to support democracy, but freedom to select *not-democracy* and *not-human rights* options should be presented as genuine options for selection and opened up to critical evaluation. Equally, the conceptual framework used for self-reference at lower levels could take a more theme-oriented approach, such as that suggested by Simon *et al.* (1995) that covers areas such as family, friends, ageing and death, politics, religion and multicultural issues.

Savoir Se Transformer: Knowing How to Become

Kramsch (1993) highlights the role of dialogue in the production of meaning across cultures that can constitute a third perspective, in which meaning is dialogically created through language in discourse. Indeed, change in perspective is implied, etymologically, by the word dialogue itself:

'Dialogos' is a Greek word widely mistranslated and wrongly understood because of a confusion between 'dyo' et 'dia'. It does not mean a conversation between two people or two groups but an acceptance, by two participants or more, that they will compare and contrast their respective arguments to the very end. Dialogue is accordingly a perilous exercise, for it implies a risk that either participant may find his or her argument transformed, and thus their very identity put to the test. The prefix 'dia' is equivalent to the Latin 'trans' connoting a considerable shift in space, time, substance and thought. (Stenou, 2005: 125)

Here, Stenou claims that challenges to one's perspectives can constitute challenges to one's identity, echoing Byram's discussion of *savoir être* within which identities formed through socialisation are challenged through relativisation of the self, and the valuing of the other, stimulating the development of new, decentred intercultural identities. Similarly, Guilherme's view of citizenship is framed in these terms insofar as individuals and societies are considered culturally complex and essentially fragmented with permeable boundaries, and identities must be constantly deconstructed and reconstructed, giving rise to citizenship as a form of constructed identification.

The ID Model suggests ways in which foreign language teachers can manage value judgment as they guide their learners through the whole encounter with otherness, enabling them to manage changes triggered along the way. In reality, many of the processes described probably take place in split seconds and cannot be clearly distinguished, but key processes can be laid out systematically *for pedagogical purposes*, and careful attention can be devoted to them on a stage-by-stage basis. Thus, the ID Model suggests a practical approach through which teachers can both break apart and steer the basic processes of *learning to be* in relation to the concept of *savoir être*. Ultimately, it constitutes a step-by-step guide to the active development of the self through interaction with others.

The notion of *savoir se transformer* finds itself rooted in the concept of the malleability of the self as described by Heine, insofar as people can and are explicitly encouraged to take control of their own self-development in a rapidly changing multi-cultural world in which intercultural interaction between different social groups is hard to avoid. Yet the notion of *savoir se transformer* does not rest upon the presumption that adapting oneself to the world necessarily implies acceptance of the status quo. In fact, self-development and social development seem to go hand in hand, with self-development preceding social development if anything.

In this respect, the notion of *savoir se transformer* may hold some appeal to people from cultures described earlier in the book as valuing malleability of the self over malleability of the world, such as East Asian, Indian and African cultures. While Heine's rather dichotomous description of the two is rejected in this book, its basic tenets are considered useful lenses through which to compare and contrast seemingly different cultures, and as with any such overarching conceptual frameworks that are used to structure analysis, they themselves need to be opened up to criticism as noted by Barnett. Further, the emphasis upon individuality in the notion of *savoir se transformer* is generally supportive of Kim's (2009) attempt to reclaim the primacy of the individual (vs. group) dimension of identity in intercultural encounters, not-withstanding the importance that also needs to be attached to the importance of relationships and context in current theorising about intercultural communication, in which attempts are actively being made to take greater account of distinctly group-based cultural differences.

> Absent in the group-identity polemics are the supposed ideals behind the concept of intercultural competence itself – that people from different cultural and ethnic roots can coexist and strive for mutuality and coop-eration by looking across and beyond the frontiers of traditional group boundaries with minimum prejudice and illusion. (Kim, 2009: 53)

We can relate this thread of discussion back to Barnett's (1997) concept of critical being with its three sub-concepts of critical thought, critical action and critical-self-reflection. Barnett aims to foster both adaptive and transformative capability, which involves the generation of new orderings, insights and sources of action and knowledge. His conceptualisation of criti-cal self-reflection implies self-development, in that development requires self-referential capacities of a higher order, which includes self-reference to abstract conceptual frameworks or to evaluative standards.

Barnett (1997) splits critical being into domain and level, which contain three and four components, respectively. Knowledge, self and the world com-prise the domains of criticality, each of which comprises six levels of critical thinking skills that include meta-critical capacities, critical thinking, critical thought, philosophical and sociological meta-critique. Generally, however, Barnett frames them in terms of developing the ability to operate with the critical standards of our own local framework of thinking, approaching it from an external vantage point. This gives rise to the notions of critique and meta-critique, both of which involve critiquing whole forms of thought, acti-vating the construction of the self in the process. Thus, in Barnett's view, the reconstruction of a new, improved self is a main aim of higher education.

In the discussion of domains and interfaces earlier in the book, it was noted that the ID Model locates itself primarily in the two domains of self and other, while Barnett prioritises the three domains of self, knowledge and the world. Through Barnett's domains, we can carry our discussion of reconstruction of the self from the level of the learner to the level of society. It is at this point that the active development of an inherently malleable self can trigger the development of an inherently malleable society. Barnett emphasises the role played by higher education in offering society alternative conceptual resources, injecting into it new forms of action and knowing, enabling society to see itself anew. To this end, he suggests that education should promote both intra-learner critical self-reflection and inter-learner critical discourse. Personal dispositions and intersubjective relations should be addressed through discussion extending beyond the cognitive to the essence of being itself.

Thus, Barnett approaches the world, at least in part, by passing through the domains of self and other, as envisaged in the earlier stages of the ID Model, within which both intra-learner critical self-reflection and inter-learner critical discourse are prioritised. In the initial description of the ID Model, it was suggested that the interface between self and world might be addressed at higher levels by taking the world, or selected aspects of it, as alternative objects of analysis to those of self and other. But adopting Barnett's standpoint helps us appreciate that both intra-learner critical self-reflection and inter-learner critical discourse can themselves impact upon society by stimulating the generation of alternative conceptual resources, injecting into society new forms of action and knowing enabling society to see itself anew.

Further, Barnett emphasises the role of reflection in stabilising the educational, personal and cognitive disturbances learners face within the self, as they are pulled in new ways through a range of knowing activities. The ID Model frames this not only in terms of the development of self-awareness, meta-cognitive and meta-awareness within individual learners, but also in terms of the ensuing group discussion generating new alternatives for being that present themselves for conscious selection by learners. In the ID Model, these aspects are conceptualised within the domains of self and other, but from Barnett's standpoint, they also impact upon the domain of the world.

Barnett recognises the role of reflection in the three domains of self, knowledge and the world noting that in the latter two, critical thinking not only involves reflection but also evaluation, analysis, the production of alternatives and ultimately better constructions, including self-reconstruction. The conceptual consistency between Barnett's levels of critical reflection and the various stages of the ID Model is obvious. His concept of critical self-reflection is framed in terms of autonomy, personhood and self-actualisation, and reflection is accompanied by a range of alternatives and self-criticism.

Knowing How to Become and L2 Motivation

To expand the discussion of transformation from this point to include language-learning motivation, let us bring the relationship between self-criticism and self-development into relation by sharpening the focus upon ideals. As we have seen, many learners who took part in the study upon which this book is based, were tempted to set their ideals as standards for evaluation, but Freire (1990) framed them negatively in terms of 'hosting the oppressor' (Freire, 1990: 27) as oppressed people internalise oppressor models before going on to set oppressor ideals as their own. Discussing the politics of self and other, Holliday highlights the contradictory ways in which we as people can attempt to rise above prejudice while 'often unconsciously submit to these forces. In other words, we live and perpetuate the prejudices which we abhor' (Holliday, 2011: 69). One of the most significant features of this dynamic is the idealisation of the self in the face of the other, and as such ideals need to be problematised if the blind perpetuation of prejudice in the name of tolerance is to be arrested.

However, it is often perhaps inadvertently encouraged, especially in relation to research on language learning motivation as the role played by ideals is considered extensively in Dörnyei's (2005, 2009) discussion of the motivational self-system. The theoretical roots of the motivational self-system can be traced partly back to Gardner and Lambert's (1959) concept of integrative motivation, and partly back to research on the self in mainstream psychology on possible selves, a concept through which the link between the self-system and motivated behaviour is explored.

> Over the past two decades, self theorists have become increasingly interested in the active, dynamic nature of the self system, gradually replacing the traditionally static concepts of self-representations with a self-system that mediates and controls ongoing behavior. (Markus & Ruvolo, 1989; for a recent review, see Leary, 2007) (Dörnyei, 2009: 10)

While the rather static traditional view of self-concept as a person's self-knowledge tends to focus upon how a person sees self in the present (Dörnyei, 2009), Higgins' work on self-determination theory in the 1980s started to take a more dynamic and future-oriented view through the dual-conceptual lenses of the ideal self and the ought to self. This led to Markus and Nurius' (1986) tri-partite distinction between the ideal selves that we would like to become (that guide people *towards* something), the selves that we could become and the selves that we are afraid of becoming (that guide people *away from* something).

While the basic notion of the ideal self is based upon the attributes one would ideally like to possess (including one's own hopes, aspirations or wishes), the notion of the ought to self is based upon the attributes one believes one ought to possess (including someone else's sense of duties, obligations or moral responsibilities), although it is not always easy to distinguish the two. Dörnyei (2009) notes that self-determination theory (Higgins, 1987, 1996) suggests that the internalisation of external motives takes place in the four graded stages that range from external regulation as the least self-determined to integrated regulation as the most developmentally advanced, as presented in Table 7.9.

However, while both sets of attributes listed in Table 7.9 are internalised into the ideal and ought to selves over time because 'various reference groups (to which every individual belongs) affect the individual by anticipatory socialisation or value induction, it is not always straightforward at times to decide at times of social pressure whether an ideal-like self state represents one's genuine dreams or whether it has been compromised by the desire for role conformity' (Dörnyei, 2009: 14).

Dörnyei's (2005) primary interest in developing the theoretical construct of the L2 motivational self-system lies in motivating language learners, but his promotion of the Ideal L2 Self was tempered by explicit recognition that realistically, learners are unlikely to generate an ideal self out of nothing and the origins of aspirations, dreams and desires go back to views held by others including peer groups, parents and other authoritative figures. Notwithstanding this reservation, Dörnyei (2009) clearly prioritises the development of the Ideal L2 Self over the ought-to L2 Self, which he claims does not lend itself to obvious motivational practices not only because it is external to the learner but also because it is rooted in duties and obligations imposed by others. All things considered, he recommends teachers to increase learner mindfulness about their ideal selves by

Table 7.9 Stages in the internalisation of external motives, according to self-determination theory

1	External regulation	• Entirely from outside sources (rewards, threats) • Least choiceful/self-determined
2	Introjected regulation	• Rules accepted by the individual
3	Identified regulation	• Individual really values/identifies with the behaviour • Choiceful behaviour
4	Integrated regulation	• Fully assimilated with other values, needs and identity • Most developmentally advanced

Source: Higgins (1987, 1996)

guiding them through ideal selves they have entertained in the past and by presenting them with powerful role models as sources of inspiration for the future.

But as one of the leading drivers in the field of L2 motivation, Dörnyei has collided almost inadvertently with a leading driver in the field of intercultural communication, which brings into question the very aims of foreign language education. As it stands, the choice facing foreign language teachers appears to lie between developing either L2 motivation or intercultural communicative competence, but not both, which is clearly untenable in the long term. Evidence of the contrasting priorities is evident in the quotations presented below, both of which address the way in which learner exoticisation of other cultures should be handled.

While Dörnyei suggests that the exotic nature of encounters with a foreign culture should be emphasised by foreign language teachers who want to stimulate the development of learners' ideal selves, Byram suggests that learner willingness to seek out or take up opportunities to engage with otherness in a relationship of equality, which is an attitudinal component of intercultural communicative competence, should be distinguished from (and implicitly prioritised over) attitudes of seeking out the exotic or of seeking to profit from others. This contrast is clear in the two extracts presented below.

(I)n an era when international holidays are becoming increasingly accessible and cross-cultural communication is a standard part of our existence in the 'global village', it is possible to divide creative ideal-self-generating activities drawing on past adventures, on the *exotic* (emphasis mine) nature of encounters with a foreign culture. (Dörnyei, 2009: 34)

Attitudes

Curiosity and openness, readiness to suspend disbelief about other cultures and belief about one's own.

Objectives include:

Willingness to seek out or take up opportunities to engage with otherness in a relationship of equality; this should be distinguished from attitudes of seeking out the *exotic* (emphasis mine) or of seeking to profit from others. (Byram, 1997: 57)

Behind this differing approach towards learner exoticisation lies an even more basic distinction between the relative roles to be played by criticism and creativity in foreign language education. As we have seen throughout this book, research priorities in the European field of intercultural communicative competence tend to emphasise the role of criticism, as foreign language education comes to be characterised as a form of intercultural citizenship, and the concept of criticality can be traced back to the ancient Greeks, in particular to Socrates, as we have seen. Viewing foreign language learning as a form of citizenship may raise the profile of the ought to self.

By contrast, however, the role of creativity is emphasised in Dörnyei's L2 motivational self-system in relation to imagination, which 'has been known to be related to motivation since the ancient Greeks. Aristotle, for example, defined imagination as 'sensation without matter' and claimed that "There's no desiring without imagination"' (Modell, 2003: 108) (Dörnyei, 2009: 16). Identifying imagination as a central element of possible selves theory, Dörnyei recommends teachers to promote the development of the Ideal L2 Self through 'imagery enhancement' (Dörnyei, 2009: 34).

Another important point made by Dörnyei is that for desired possible selves to be effective, the ideal and ought selves should be in harmony, which highlights the motivational drive for cognitive congruence that was explored earlier in this book in relation to cognitive and moral development, and the development of the self. This provides a signpost back to criticism, which in turn rests upon the self-analysis that can shed light upon discrepant and internally conflicting parts of the self as we have seen. Dörnyei (2009) highlights the role of creativity in the L2 motivational self-system by suggesting that the Ideal L2 Self is 'a powerful motivator to learn the L2 because of the desire to reduce the discrepancy between our actual and ideal selves' (Dörnyei, 2009: 29), but this needs to considered in the light of the ways in which ideals were problematised earlier in this book, especially by Freire.

In fact, however, both Freire and Macedo (1987) recognise the importance of both criticism and creativity in the development of literacy more generally. On balance, it seems that attention needs to be paid to the roles played by both criticism and creativity in foreign language education. On the one hand, it seems that intercultural communication theorists need to give greater recognition to the role of creative thinking in both personal and social development. On the other hand, it seems that L2 motivation theorists need to take on board the social implications of their new theoretical direction from more critical standpoints and socially responsible ways that place L2 motivation into its broader social *context*, although there are indications that this is already underway (Dörnyei & Ushioda, 2009).

> To respect different discourses and to put into practice the understanding of plurality (which necessitates both criticism and creativity (emphasis mine) in the act of saying the word and the act of reading the word) require a political and social transformation. (Freire & Macedo, 1987: 54–55)

8 Shifting the Interface: From Self and Other to Self and Society

Having proceeded through all the stages of the ID Model, it is envisaged that learners should not only be able to systematically reflect upon and describe their values to others to some extent, but also be able to explore and describe the values of others using intellectual empathy. Then, they should be able to consciously compare and contrast the two descriptions before evaluating self and other with conscious reference to clear and explicit standards, meta-cognitively and meta-affectively monitoring their reactions to others and making decisions about self-development along the way.

So far, such activities have been located primarily at the interface between self and other, but they can be located at the interface between self and society too. Just as self and other can be opened up to critical analysis and evaluation, society itself can also be systematically broken into conceptual parts that can be analysed and evaluated with conscious reference to selected standards. One way that learners may be expected to use their intercultural skills in society may be through intercultural mediation, which can take place at different interfaces.

Intercultural Mediation

The concept of intercultural mediation was elaborated in Byram's (1997) Model for Intercultural Communicative Competence in which the intercultural speaker was conceived of being able to interact across cultural frontiers deploying knowledge, attitudes, skills of interpreting and relating, and skills of discovery and interaction to exchange information effectively, establish and maintain relationships. This involves the development of *critical cultural awareness* as learner socialisation is challenged and brought into question through intercultural education. Holmes and O'Neill's (2010) description of what it means to be an intercultural speaker illustrates how the concept of intercultural mediation can be located primarily at the interface between self and other.

(W)e draw on Byram's (1997, 2008, 2009) notion of the intercultural speaker – the person who is 'aware of both their own and others' culturally constructed selves' (quoted in Roberts *et al.*, 2001: 30). This person is able to utilise the skills, tools, and attributes of intercultural competence (the five savoirs) to manage communication and interaction with people from other social/cultural groups in daily experience. In further developing the notion of the intercultural speaker, Byram (2008: 68) includes the idea of mediation, between oneself and others. He describes mediation as 'being able to take an "external" perspective on oneself as one interacts with others and to analyse and, where desirable, adapt one's behaviour and underlying values and beliefs.' He also notes that mediating requires individuals to act interculturally, which requires a 'willingness to suspend those deeper values, at least temporarily, in order to be able to understand and empathise with the values of others that are incompatible with one's own' (69). (Holmes & O'Neill, 2010: 168)

In this sense, intercultural mediation involves the adoption of a critical standpoint within the mind during social interaction, coupled with the monitoring of one's own reactions and the possible adjustment of decision-making processes along the way. In short, it involves the deployment of *critical cultural awareness*. But in the real world, intercultural speakers may also be called upon to mediate between two or more other people of different origins and identities as third parties. Both kinds of intercultural mediation described above may involve working with conceptual difference between languages that can cause misunderstanding, considering words or concepts that exist in one but not both languages in use, and words that exist in each language but have different meanings. The question then arising, from a pedagogical standpoint, is how teachers can nurture intercultural speakers capable of the kinds of intercultural mediation described above.

Let us consider how intercultural mediation skills may be fostered by asking learners to mediate conflict situations by critically analysing and evaluating the positions of the two parties involved, and their own in their capacity as mediator, with conscious reference to a clear and explicit standard (Houghton, 2009b). By way of example, let us label that evaluative standard *democracy and human rights*, and let us consider a case in which such

Table 8.1 Target values for intercultural communication

Benevolence	Stimulation	Universalism	Self-Direction
• Help people close to you • Honesty • True friendship	• Novelty • New challenge	• Welfare of all people • Wisdom • Social justice • World peace • Broad-minded • Equality	• Independence of action, thought and decision-making • Creative • Curious

values are purposefully transmitted to learners as target values. Examples of such values are presented in Table 8.1. The reasons for their selection by the teacher were explained earlier in the book, but here they should be taken to represent *any particular values* that may be selected for special emphasis by the teacher. It should also be remembered that regardless of the particular values set by the teacher, it may be anticipated in advance that gaps may open up in learners' minds between what they value and what their teacher thinks they should value, and it is precisely such discrepancy that is understood to carry the potential to generate change in learners.

In practical terms, mediation activities can be set up in class once the teacher has identified areas of potential value difference between learners. After two learners have been paired up, they can then start to discuss the apparent value different between them before imagining a potential conflict situation that may arise from that value difference. A third learner can then be added to the pair to mediate with reference to the target values set by the teacher. Tradition is not listed in the table as a target value set by the teacher, but learners may naturally value it all the same. In the case that will be described, learners C12, C7 and C5 each claimed that on a scale from −5 to +5, they valued tradition at +4, +3 and 0, respectively. On the surface, at least, learners C12 and C7 appeared to value tradition to a similar degree (at +4 and +3, respectively), whilst learners C12 and C5 appeared more distant by valuing it at +4 and 0, respectively).

Learner C12: Week 4 Homework Paragraph

Tradition (+4)

About tradition in my life, I feel the traditional event on anniversary should keep be following. Actually, my family always follow these customs, for example, the winter solstice, the Star Festival, and the Doll's festival. These customs are the characteristic as Japanese. So I think we have to protest these customs.

Learner C7: Week 4 Homework Paragraph

Tradition (+3)

I value tradition, especially its culture. I respect Japanese picture or object of Buddha. Also, I think it is connect with recent Japanese culture so deeply in heart. I like folding paper, and toss beanbags, this is good example Japanese culture.

Learner C5: Week 4 Homework Paragraph

Tradition (0)

In the near future, I'll work at office after graduation if I'm employed. My parents wish that, too. Then there is conformity (I conform to the company), security (I can get salary) and tradition (the company has history). However I must restrain my idea, be obedient sometimes.

Thus, learners with an apparent value gap such as learners C12 and C5 can be paired up, and a third learner such as C7 can be added to the pair as a third-party mediator. In this way, learners can develop the mental habit of adopting a third standpoint in a situation, at a critical distance from the event itself, with a view to being able to adopt a similar third standpoint *within their own minds* when they themselves are embroiled in similar situations in the future.

In this case, learners C12 and C5 discussed their apparent value difference before imagining and writing a role-play to illustrate a value conflict that may arise because of it. The discussion dialogue and role-play are presented below and as we shall see, the discussion dialogue in particular was to have an impact upon the mediation that followed.

Learners C5 and C12: Discussion about tradition

C12:   Why didn't you value the tradition?
C5:   I like novelty, so I don't want to be prepossessed by old custom.
C12:   But, didn't you think the old custom is also lovely? Because each tradition is the own unique custom in each country. Please imagine the Star festival. We string the Japanese paper that we write our wishes on the bamboo leaf. I don't want these customs that only Japanese follow to die out. What do you think about that?
C5:   I agree with lovely tradition, but there are unlovely that, for example, religions trouble doesn't cease. There isn't big difference of religion in Japan, but sometimes, religious trouble develops the war in all over the world.

C12: I never have thought such thinking because I live in Japan. But even if these problems happened, we could learn many things or different views through the experience of tradition. So tradition is important for our life.

C5: How peaceful you are!!

Learners C5 and C12: Conflict dialogue about tradition

C12: Let's go to the museum to experience the papermaking on this Sunday?

C5: Why will we bother to make paper by ourselves? We can get paper everywhere!

C12: But do you want to make and use paper which old people also used?

C5: I'm not interesting in old customs, and normal paper is easy for us to write.

C12: That's not a problem!! I just want to know old customs, and we must convey it to the young generation.

C5: There is no time for saying papermaking. Now we must be able to use computer. I actually a plan to join the internet class on this weekend.

It is evident in the discussion between learners C5 and C12 above that learner C5's reservation about tradition lay in her associating it with religion and world war, which implied that she valued world peace, which was a sub-concept of universalism set as a target value by the teacher listed in the table above. When considering any possible gaps between her own and the target values, learner C12 had already recognised a possible link between tradition and war before writing the discussion presented above with C5, and she had also recognised that her values seemed to be changing in response to the interaction with C5.

Learner C12: Week 10 Homework

When I talked with learner C5 about tradition, I very valued tradition, but she didn't much. And she explained to me that some traditional things, for example, religion, have possibility to occur serious problem like world war. After listening her thinking, I noticed I only consider about the beautiful point of tradition. As one conclusion, because my values have been changing little by little, these values affected my interaction.

Once learners C5 and C12 had finished writing the discussion and conflict dialogue, learner C7 was assigned to mediate, not with reference to her own values but *with reference to the target values set by the teacher*, using them as a *standard* for evaluation. By analysing the relative positions of learners C5 and C12, the mediator noticed that while both learner C5 and C12 rejected war, they also both liked Japanese traditions such as the Star Festival. In response to this point, learner C12 claimed that she had not noticed this similarity because she had been focusing too much on the conflict with C5 attempting to affirm her commitment to world peace, while recognising the place of many traditions (i.e. not just Japanese traditions) within it.

Learners C5 and C12: Mediation of conflict dialogue about tradition by learner C7

C7: Learner C5 thinks that sometimes traditions cause a war, and learner C12 thinks that tradition tell us solutions of war. It looks in conflict between them at first, but I think they are both thinking that the war shouldn't happen. They don't hope someone is harmed or to be unpeaceful. Also, they both think Japanese lovely tradition (for example Star Festival) is good. Therefore, they are similar with that point. So they both are saying honestly. I think they should more listen each other's opinion, and they should do lovely tradition together.

C12: I concentrated to conflict with learner C5, so I couldn't notice our similar point.

C5: We have to learn many different traditions for world peace from now on.

We can see below how learner C12 seems to be starting to value universalism more than before, recognising how it helped her to 'judge equally'. Notably, equality was also listed as a target value in the table above under universalism. Furthermore, learner C12 was recognising the role of tolerance as a way of respecting traditions within the general value of universalism, which represented development in learner C12's position.

Learner C12: Week 12 Learner Diary

You asked me how tradition and universalism are concerned with. If we consider the tradition with the view of universalism, it sometimes may be dangerous. Because we, I and learner C5, discuss before, religion that is one of the tradition, have possibility to occur the war. So in this case, I thought the view of universalism could help me to judge equally. And today I learned we have to think about value with the view of another difference values. And let me tell you about the felt of this well. The tradition is difference for each person. So we have to accept and understand each thought of tradition in international communication. I think universalism have the characteristic of such tolerance. So I felt that universalism need to avoid bad effect of tradition and to live difference tradition together.

Finally, remembering that learner C7 had been asked to mediate with reference not to her own but to the target values, she made it clear as she reflected upon the mediation process that she had not only identified world peace as a similarity between learners C5 and C12, but that she had also noticed a similarity between her own values and those of learner C12. She claimed that this had not, however, resulted in any apparent bias in favour of C12 during the mediation, and she was pleased to learn in the end that learners C5 and C12 were both satisfied with her mediation approach.

Learner C7: Week 12 Homework

I think doing mediation is very difficult for me. Learner C12 and learner C5 think that there are some important traditions, like a star festival, but they have different thinking about religion. I found that difference in the conversation, and also I found similarity about their thinking of world peace. I think the history have very important meaning although this history is too bad thing. Therefore I'm similar with learner C12 on balance. I'm afraid that they were satisfied about my mediating, but they said that we can satisfy about your mediation, so I'm relieved to hear that.

An example of intercultural mediation was presented above to illustrate some of the ways in which a teacher can attempt to prioritise some values over others to support intercultural communication, but let us now bring that approach into question. In fact, the causal connections between developments in the extracts above cannot be establsihed with any certainty. As learner C7 compared and contrasted the values of learners C5 and C12 during critical evaluation as part of the mediation process, she may still have identified their shared valuing of world peace and positive traditions, even without the teacher transmission of target values. It is possible that critical evaluation, rather than teacher transmission of values, supported the mediation process. Insofar as learner C5 introduced aspects of universalism to challenge learner C12's valuing of tradition in the discussion preceding the development of the conflict dialogue, the target value of universalism appeared to be in play even before the mediator was assigned to the pair. Pre-existing learner values and viewpoints unknown to the teacher may impact upon each other through the kind of tasks described above, regardless of teacher value transmission.

As we saw in relation to cognitive and moral development earlier in the book, exposure to alternative viewpoints may generate perspective shifts as new ways of thinking are considered. Existing viewpoints can be thrown into disarray by the introduction of discrepant information that can gradually be resolved as more coherent and comprehensive positions are sought. This basic cognitive process is thought to be at play in the dialectical process of Socratic teaching, through which learners express a point of view only to be challenged by teachers to formulate more comprehensive positions. Learner C12 in particular seemed to expand her way of thinking as she considered alternative points of view put forward not only by the teacher but by her peers, integrating some of their ideas with her own in new ways. Thus, the impact of unpredictable values and viewpoints other than those put forward by the teacher also deserves consideration.

The intercultural mediation processes described above can be considered not only in relation to the ID Model, but also in relation to Anderson and Krathwohl's (2001) taxonomy of learning objectives, which was based upon those of Bloom *et al.* (1956). In that taxonomy, it is suggested that remembering, understanding, applying, analysing, evaluating and creating are six basic cognitive processes common to all human beings; let us call it the *common cognitive inheritance*. Knowledge can be split into the four main categories of factual, conceptual, procedural and meta-cognitive knowledge that can be distinguished as follows:

- *Factual knowledge* consists of the basic elements students must know to be acquainted with a discipline or solve problems in it such as knowledge of terminology or of specific details or elements.
- *Conceptual knowledge* relates to the interrelationships among the basic elements within a larger structure that enable them to function together such as knowledge of classifications and categories, principles and generalisations, theories, models and structures.
- *Procedural knowledge* includes knowledge about ways of doing something, methods of inquiry, and criteria for using skills, techniques and methods.
- *Meta-cognitive knowledge* includes knowledge of cognition in general as well as awareness and knowledge of one's own cognitions including strategic knowledge, knowledge about cognitive tasks, including appropriate contextual and conditional knowledge and self-knowledge.

Let us review the first stage of the ID Model, which paved the way for the intercultural mediation activities described above, in the light of Anderson and Krathwohl's (2001) taxonomy to highlight some of the interplay between the basic knowledge features and cognitive dynamics. In the first week of the course, the term culture was defined by distinguishing values from beliefs and norms, before 10 particular values were presented and distinguished. This can be considered an attempt to build *factual knowledge* through the provision of discrete and clearly defined terminological items that were primarily treated in isolation at the start. Attention to relationships between these elements was drawn as learners reflected upon themselves with reference to the 10 values. As they differentiated between and interpreted the values by referring to their definitions during self-reflection, learners would recall past events by retrieving relevant knowledge from long-term memory before selecting and classifying certain illustrative experiences to summarise and exemplify their values for others, as well as reflecting upon themselves more generally.

This was an analytical process in which a body of source material (i.e. learners' value-laden conceptual frameworks) was systematically broken into parts, cognitively speaking, through reflective analysis. In this process, the experience of which helped develop *procedural knowledge*, learners were expected to bring selected parts of the whole into relation for the particular purpose of describing their values to others, which was necessarily evaluative as judgments were made based upon specific criteria that led to the relative prioritisation of elements. Monitoring and describing their own cognitive processes with a view to making general statements about their values by monitoring and recognising their evaluative tendencies helps develop *meta-cognitive knowledge*.

Finally, the act of writing a speech to describe one's values with reference to a previously unconsidered conceptual framework is a creative process that involves planning and production, insofar as it involves organising and presenting old information in new ways. When learners reached the point at which they could stand up and present an analytical description of their own values to other people in the form of a speech, they had already developed some of the *conceptual knowledge* they needed to describe some of the broader conceptual constructs that had been evoked through self-reflection with reference to the value taxonomy, also developing self-knowledge as another form of *meta-cognitive knowledge* within Anderson and Krathwohl's (2001) definition in the process.

From that point on, we saw earlier in the book how learners developed their ideas in response to others in various ways that had an impact upon their personal development in many cases. Insofar as self-development was taking place by conscious choice, it can be considered a creative process that underpins the mediation processes described above as learners seek new ways of combining and recombining values and concepts in order to solve the conflict that has arisen. According to Anderson and Krathwohl (2001), the creation stage succeeds the evaluation stage and once judgments have been made based upon criteria, elements can be put together to form a coherent or functional whole, reorganising elements into a new pattern or structure in the process. Intercultural mediation can thus be considered a creative process, the successful completion of which may be predicated upon the previous stages of remembering, understanding, applying, analysing and evaluating. In this process, factual, conceptual, procedural and meta-cognitive knowledge can all be drawn upon.

The description of stage 1 learning activities presented above illustrates some of the ways in which all six of the basic cognitive processes described by Anderson and Krathwohl's (2001) taxonomy can come into play within the first stage of the ID Model alone. While the columns on the left and right in Table 8.2 are therefore not directly equivalent, it also seems clear that all the stages do find their place not only in stage 1 of the ID Model but also in its later stages, all of which share knowledge features and involve similar basic cognitive processes, albeit at higher levels of complexity in which the value-laden conceptual constructs of others are taken into consideration and systematically brought into relation. Placing the focus at this late stage of the book upon particular learning objectives designed specifically to operationalise basic cognitive processes and knowledge features common to all human beings, as part of the common cognitive inheritance, throws a loop back to the start of the book where intercultural dialogue was approached, first and foremost, through consideration of information processing, cognitive, moral and self-development.

Propaganda and Persuasion

Interview with James Glassman: US Under-Secretary of State for Public Diplomacy on Hard Talk, BBC World (11 September 2008)

Interviewer: Do you see yourself as America's chief of propaganda?
Glassman: No, because I don't think propaganda works very well.
               I mean ... what I am is American's chief of public diplomacy ... I'm also the head of the inter-agency on strategic communications, or the war of ideas.

Table 8.2 A comparison of the key components of Houghton's (2007, 2009a, 2010) Intercultural Dialogue Model and Anderson and Krathwohl's (2001) taxonomy of learning objectives

Anderson and Krathwohl's (2001) taxonomy of learning objectives	*Houghton's ID Model*
Cognitive Process Dimension	*Stages in the Course of Learning*
(1) Remember • Retrieve relevant knowledge from long-term memory ○ *Recognise, recall*	(1) Learner analysis of own value system (VS1)
(2) Understand • Construct meaning from messages, including oral, written and graphic communication. ○ *Interpret, exemplify, classify, summarise, infer, compare and explain*	(2) Learner analysis of the value system of another person (VS2) having gathered information through empathy-oriented communication
(3) Apply • Carry out or use a procedure in a given situation. ○ *Execute, implement*	
(4) Analyse • Break material down into constituent parts and determining how parts relate to one another and to an overall structure or purpose. ○ *Differentiate, organise, attribute*	(3) Juxtaposition, comparison and contrast of the two value systems (VS1 and VS2) to identify similarities and differences
(5) Evaluate • Make judgments based on criteria. ○ *Check, critique*	(4) Learner evaluation of the value systems of self and other (VS1 and VS2) with reference to a standard
(6) Create • Put together elements to form a coherent or functional whole, reorganising elements into a new pattern or structure in the process. ○ *Generate, plan, produce*	(5) Learner orientation of self to others by selecting standards and evaluative tendencies
Knowledge Dimension	Meta-levels
Factual	Self-awareness
Conceptual	Meta-cognitive awareness
Procedural	Meta-affective awareness
Meta-cognitive	

| Interviewer: | Yeah, but you said in a recent speech, you said 'We want to influence foreign publics in the achievement of our foreign policy goals'. To me, that sounds like a propaganda objective. |
| Glassman: | Well, that depends on how we define propaganda ... Absolutely we are in the persuasion business. But we actually think it's better to persuade people by being a convener, a facilitator, getting people to talk about issues that they don't necessarily talk about ..... |

There is a fine line between propaganda and persuasion, and the difference between them may not always be apparent as teachers engage actively with their learners, especially if teachers are deliberately transmitting target values to stimulate particular kinds of social development. Pratkanis and Aronson (2001) distinguish propaganda and persuasion in terms of moving the masses toward a desired position or point of view on the one hand, and informing and enlightening people on the other. Propaganda involves mass suggestion or influence through the manipulation of symbols and the psychology of the individual, the dextrous use of images, slogans and symbols that play on prejudices and emotions, and can be considered the communication of a point of view that has the ultimate goal of getting people to *voluntarily* adopt the position as their own. Persuasion, however, aims to create a discourse that can illuminate the issues at hand through argument, debate, discussion or well-argued speech, presenting the case for or against a given proposition, to *educate* both audience and speakers. So, propaganda also needs to be distinguished from education.

Pratkanis and Aronson (2001) contrast the two by highlighting Wertheimer's point that while propaganda tries to keep people from thinking and acting as humans with rights, manipulating prejudice and emotion to impose the propagandists' will on others, education tries to equip people to make their own decisions by encouraging critical thinking through which multiple perspectives can be explored through debate and discussion. This echoes the discussion of critical approaches to education presented earlier in the book. Let us now relate the points made in relation to propaganda above to democratic citizenship as a critical approach to foreign language education as we continue to explore ways in which the interface between self and society can be addressed within the ID Model.

Democratic Citizenship

According to Freire (1990), the oppressed are likely to become oppressors themselves when power is placed in their hands, unless they can free themselves conceptually from the inherent contradiction bound up in this dialectical conflict between opposing social forces, a point echoed by Holliday (2011) in relation to ideology. A basic element in the relationship between oppressed and oppressor involves the imposition of the choices of the former upon the latter. This process is further compounded by fear, which blocks the ejection of the oppressor image and its replacement with autonomy and responsibility. Such concepts form the basic building blocks for democratic citizenship.

According to Sumner (1906), bias can be overcome through the development of the critical faculty, and Freire (1990) highlights the emergence through dialogue of nuclei of contradictions that can facilitate the meaningful structuring of content, since they represent situations that have trapped learners. The traps inherent in contradiction open up new possible courses of action in the future, promising liberation from the traps as selections are made and learners move out of, and push people out of, contradictory states by choice. Freire's view of personal history developing through the dialectical interaction of ideas, concepts, hopes, doubts and values accords with the picture of value built up in the study upon which this book is based, in which internal components were often seen to come into conflict within the same individual, generating change in that individual, as previously unnoticed discrepancies and contradictions were consciously attended to.

At the very least, this involves grasping and taking seriously the opinions and arguments of others, according personal recognition to people of other opinions and putting oneself into the situation of others, even if one disagrees in the end. These are some of the basic communicative activities and skills needed by democratic citizens that reflect an *action orientation* (Byram *et al.*, 2009) to intercultural communication that is supportive of democratic society. The ID Model aims to focus learner attention upon such dynamics with a view to taking increased conscious control to enhance personal and social development.

With regard to social development, society itself can be critically analysed and evaluated with reference to a clear and conscious standard, and this includes the media. Contradiction can be found, for example, between articles from different news sources reporting upon the same issue. This is exemplified the two extracts below, both of which reported on the apparent increase in the crime rates of foreigners in Japan that was reported by the National Police Agency in 2003. However, a close reading of both the titles and the extracts reveals something about the political positioning of each of the news sources concerned. While the *Asia Times* online chose to focus on the fear of foreign crime in Japan, *The Japan Times* online chose to focus instead on the rate of Japanese opposition to foreign crime. The identification of discrepancies between sources of information about society can spark discussion that can relate back to the learners themselves. In this case, the examples were provided by the teacher but learners can be encouraged to seek them out independently.

Title: Japan's foreigner crime fears

The National Police Agency recently published a report on foreign crime in Japan, which admitted that foreign crime had fallen in 2000 and 2001. After that, the number did increase but this is natural since the numbers of foreigners in Japan has also increased greatly. (Khan, 2003)

Title: 32.4% of Japanese oppose increase in foreign tourists

The National Police Agency said that last year a record 16,212 foreign nationals were arrested or prosecuted for breaking the law. This showed an increase of 10.6 percent from 2001, according to the report. (*The Japan Times*, 2003)

Recognition and discussion of this particular contradiction prompted learner C9 to recognise the impact of her own fears upon her communication with foreigners. By claiming that she no longer wanted to be driven by her fear, she seemed to not only be rejecting her fear but attempting to take control of it, which seemed, in turn, to be enhancing both meta-affective awareness and meta-affective control.

Learner C9: Week 25 Learner Diary

This week we discussed whether it's good or bad to have a fear in case of intercultural communication. I think I have fear. Of course we had not better have such a fear. I understand. But ... I have. Because when I meet foreign people, I get nervous. I have fear which I can't express and tell what I want to say. However except this fear, I don't think it's bad to have a fear. A fear is also part of me. I don't want to be driven by fear. But I think to know what is my fear is important. And also to think the reason. If I have a fear and I always care its fear, I can't get something new. I have already told you that especially, the new thing is scary for me. But I don't want to be driven by the fear.

Learner C9: Week 26 Homework

I have already told you that we had not better have fear in case of intercultural communication but I have. Honestly to say, maybe I had a fear to you in spring. In my case, I am shy even to the Japanese. I need time to accustom to unknown people. But my fear will be a barrier in case of intercultural communication. As a foreign person, she/he doesn't know whether I have a fear or not. It is regret to spend time to break such a barrier. However, we have fear. Only I can do with fear is to pretend not to have fear. And try to forget the fear during the conversation.

As we have seen, the concept of citizenship addresses what it means for an individual to be a member of society, but what does it mean to be a good citizen? Being asked this question directly by the teacher may encourage learners to take an interest in social development, and to consider their potential role within it, perhaps openly rejecting their parents' and their own prejudices towards a certain minority group. A description of the main minority groups in Japan can be found in the State Seport submitted by the Japanese government to the Committee on the Elimination of Racial Discrimination (CERD) on 19th August 2008, a report that contained 'the third, fourth, fifth and sixth periodic reports of Japan, due on 14 January 2003, 2005 and 2007, submitted in one document' (United Nations Committee on the Elimination of Discrimination, 2009: 1). In that report, Korean residents and the Ainu are two of the main minority groups in Japan, in addition to foreign residents and refugees. Korean residents are thus distinguished from foreign residents in the Japanese context. According to the Japanese government, Korean residents in Japan can be described as follows:

Korean residents in Japan

21. The majority of Korean residents, who constitute about one-fourths of the foreign population in Japan, are Koreans or their descendants who came to reside in Japan for various reasons during the 36 years (1910–1945) of Japan's so-called rule over Korea and held Japanese nationality during that period. They have continued to reside in Japan even after having lost their Japanese nationality due to the enforcement of the San Francisco Peace Treaty (April 28, 1952) after the World War II. The Korean residents are divided into those who have obtained the nationality of the Republic of Korea and those who have not, based upon their own will, under the current circumstances in which the Korean Peninsula is divided into the Republic of Korea and the Democratic People's Republic of Korea. These residents stay in Japan under the status of 'Special Permanent Resident'. They numbered 426,207 as of the end of 2007. (The total number of 'Special Permanent Residents' is 430,229, including 2,986 Chinese nationals and people of other nationalities) As for region of their

residence, about half of these Korean residents live in the Kinki region centering on Osaka, and approximately 23% of them live in the Kanto region such as Tokyo and Kanagawa Prefecture. The number of 'Special Permanent Residents' continues to decrease every year due to the settlement and naturalization of Korean residents in Japanese society. (United Nations Committee on the Elimination of Discrimination, 2009: 11–12)

Learner C8, for example, admitted to her own prejudice towards Korean residents in Japan, which she claimed was rooted in her parents' prejudice. When encouraged by the teacher to take social action outside the classroom to make a positive change in society, she researched the problem facing this social group and asked for information at the public office. She concluded, however, that they were not doing anything in particular to address the issues, despite constructing a new human rights building and suggested that they should take action for address problems facing not only Korean residents but also other minority groups. This conclusion is based partly upon a contradiction she claimed to have identified between what the public office claimed to be doing and what they seemed to be doing in practice. The identification of this contradiction appears to have stimulated recognition of the need for social change.

Learner C8: Week 20 Learner Diary

I researched about Korean residents. To be honest, I had a Korean residents prejudice, but not anymore. For the reason my parents have it strongly. I think they were told it from their parents. But somehow prejudice is ugly thing as a human. Then after I researched I could know about their problems partly. And those problems related to that each Japanese person. So I am thinking about what could I do for it. And the action for problem is the next homework. So, I will try to do something.

Learner C8: Week 20 Homework

I checked my citys' political manifesto about what are they doing for these problems. But there is no information of it. Therefore I asked about it to public office. And they replied that there is no counsel about Korean residents. Then I asked again that how ideal city do you want to make, and are you doing for it now? Then again they replied some common ideal city. And they are making new building for improvement the human rights problem. But actually they are doing nothing for it ... They should take action for improve that problems.

In this way, social action taken in the name of democratic citizenship may take the form of *communication* if learners find it easier to bring about change around them by communicating with people close to them, such as close family members, or with people in the community, such as public officers. Despite the positive action orientation displayed by learner C8 above, however, other learners may procrastinate and fail to carry out the task, not recognising the need for social action and claiming to have higher priorities, perhaps even refusing to carry out the project if they resent being pushed by the teacher, even if they recognise the value of the project. This was the position of learner C12 below who, while recognising the social problems facing the *burakumin* (部落民) community in Japan, refused to take social action to help them because she resented being forced by the teacher and rejected the teacher's view of citizenship. Notably, the *burakumin* community is not recognised as a racial minority in Japan because membership of the group is not defined by race. On their website, the Buraku Liberation League describes their definition and situation as follows, and the views of learner C12 are presented beneath.

What is *Buraku*?

Buraku is a Japanese word referring to village or hamlet. The word began to acquire a new connotation after the administration in Meiji era (1868–1912) started to use *'Tokushu Buraku'* (special hamlet) in reference to former outcaste communities. The intention was to negatively distinguish former outcaste communities from other areas. At present the word *'Buraku'* is usually referred to as communities where discriminated-against *Buraku* people reside. On the other hand, the term *'Tokushu Buraku'* has been figuratively used from time to time in distinguishing a different society from a so-called ordinary society as well as in describing *Buraku* areas, resulting in fostering discrimination against *Buraku* people.

Origin of the Discrimination

Buraku people or *Burakumin* (*min* refers to people) are the largest discriminated-against population in Japan. They are not a racial or a national minority, but a caste-like minority among the ethnic Japanese. They are generally recognized as descendants of outcaste populations in the feudal days. Outcastes were assigned such social functions as slaughtering animals and executing criminals, and the general public perceived these functions as 'polluting acts' under Buddhist and Shintoist beliefs. When the social status system was established in the 17th century (early Edo era) in the form of three classes (warrior, peasant, townsfolk), those outcastes, origin of the present *Buraku* people, were placed at the bottom of the society as *Eta* (extreme filth) and *Hinin* (non-human) classes. In 1871, the Meiji government promulgated the 'Emancipation Edict', declaring the abolition of the lowest social rank. Nevertheless, this has never gone further than a simple statement, without any effective measures.

Buraku Liberation Movement

Confronting the continued discrimination, the National Levelers Association was founded by *Buraku* people in 1922 to unite and fight against daily occurrences of discrimination. As Japan, however, moved toward militarism and took sides in World War II, the association was suppressed and stopped halfway. After the war, *Buraku* liberation movements were reunited in 1946 under the name of the National Committee for Buraku Liberation, which later evolved into the Buraku Liberation League (BLL), the present name. The Committee started to demand responsible local authorities to improve living environments of *Buraku* areas which were extremely poor as a result of the negligence of the government services. This struggle developed into a movement demanding a national policy on *Buraku* problems. As a result, the Cabinet *Dowa* Policy Council clearly stated that the solution of the *Buraku* problem was a State responsibility, in their recommendation of 1965. The Committee and subsequently the BLL successfully facilitated the national government to consecutively enact laws to improve the living environment of *Buraku* areas.

Reality of *Buraku* Discrimination Today

According to a 1993 government survey, there were about 1.2 million *Buraku* people at 4442 *Buraku* communities nationwide. These figures, however, only represent those areas classified as *Dowa* districts. (*Dowa* districts refer to *Buraku* areas in terms of government policy administration). Actual figures are estimated to as many as 6000 *Buraku* communities with over 3 million population. Although living standard of *Buraku* people became higher compared to the past, there are still gap between *Buraku* people and non-*Buraku* people. In addition, there are many incidents of discrimination, particularly in marriage and employment as well as discriminatory remarks and inquiries made by non-*Buraku* people, including public officials (Buraku Liberation League, undated).

Learner C12: Week 22 Homework

I chose the topic, the *burakumin* community. Because I had chance that I heard the feeling of my friend who lives in *buraku* community. When I was junior high school learner, she told us her experience as *burakumin*. It was very honest, and her insist was very impressed me. I know the *burakumin* community has the following problems. The burakumin are discriminated because of only one reason, that where they live in. For example, if we marriage with people who live in buraku, our parents or old people care about that, and sometimes old people don't admit this marriage because of prejudice toward *buraku*. And some prejudice will be happened when *burakumin* find employment. Sometimes it's hard for *burakumin* to be employed. Moreover, the security of the areas where *burakumin* live in is generally bad. In some road of *buraku* are very narrow, so the ambulance or fire engine can't pass that roads. It's very unfair and dangerous for people who live in this area. Through researching this problem, I decided my action. My democratic action is discussing this problem with my friends. Because we usually don't talk about such kind of topic. So I wanted to know their views toward this problem. Before the discussion I thought they have educated about this topic deeply. I tried to interview, but now I wander why I'm doing this action. And I don't want to do. Of course I understand why you suggest us to do this action. Maybe, you mean that we have to have a strong consciousness as one citizen. So I also thought I can have a citizenship thorough thinking other citizens who are suffered from prejudice and taking action for them. But I think I don't want to take action because of homework that was forced us. It's my honest feeling. And I also wonder why we only focused on people who are discriminated. I wonder I can't have citizenship through only thinking about such kind of people. I'm sorry, but I can't take action because of these reasons.

It is clear from the extract above that while learner C12 recognises the social problems facing the *burakumin* community in Japan, she is refusing to take social action to help them because she resented being forced by the teacher and rejected the teacher's view of citizenship. In this case, the teacher was requiring learners to take social action outside the class to help a selected minority group and learner C12 refused. This exemplifies a point made earlier in the book that teachers aiming to develop democratic awareness by prescribing, perhaps enforcing, certain values or evaluative tendencies may need to decide how to rank the following two types of learner, and learner

C12 clearly exemplifies the second. The two examples below clearly place the spotlight upon the issue of power dynamics:

- Learners who cooperatively select teacher-selected values and who are thus conforming to the will of the teacher as authority-figure.
- Learners who forcefully reject teacher-selected values or requirements for social action outside the classroom in the face of authoritarian teacher pressure exerted in the name of human rights and democracy.

Language, Ideology and Intercultural Dialogue in Practice

It was noted earlier in the book that as students proceed through the second stage of the ID model, they should systematically explore and describe the knowledge frameworks of others by deploying the skills of discovery and interaction, paying attention to linguistic and cultural influences in the process, while also actively looking for 'the hidden and the unexpressed' (Holliday, 2011: 27) and 'the "unsaid" (implicit propositions)' (Fairclough, 2010: 27) in which ideology tends to lie, and this also applies to the systematic exploration of discourse contained in written texts with which one can enter into an internal dialogue while reading. Barnett (1997) recognises that higher states of mind in academic life reside as much in *intra-student* dialogue as they do in consenting *inter-student* dialogue.

A definition of discourse which is meaningful here is 'a group of statements which provide a language for talking about – that is a way of representing – a particular kind of knowledge about a topic' (Hall, 1996: 201, citing Foucault). In this respect, the 'kind of knowledge' is governed by the ideology, which the discourse thus serves. A [useful] definition of ideology ... is 'a set of ideas put to work in the justification and maintenance of vested interests'. (Spears, 1999: 19) (Holliday, forthcoming)

But ultimately, through intercultural communication, and especially through social participation outside the classroom when one actively engages with discourses as they shape evolving social situations, individuals should be 'able to expand their repertoire of cultural engagement and carry practices from one society to another, to share underlying universal cultural processes with people from other societies, and to dialogue with the environment provided by national social structures' (Holliday, 2011: 36).

To this end, Holliday proposes an interpretivist methodology that involves the development of thick description, bracketing, making the familiar strange and reading critically. Developing thick description, which involves 'seeking the broader picture and looking for the hidden and unexpressed' by analysing 'all the facets of a social phenomenon that make up its full complexity ... is particularly relevant to sorting out truth and illusion in the discourses and ideologies of culture' (Holliday, 2011: 28–29). The systematic interrogation of ideology through texts in this way involves bracketing, or consciously identifying one's own prejudices and consciously putting them aside by adopting a non-judgmental stance, as noted earlier in the book. It also involves critical reading, through which the ideology and power relations characterising texts can be explored.

> Here, critical discourse analysis plays an important role in asking basic questions about the ideological intentions of the writer and the content. (Wallace, 2003 25–26, citing Fairclough, Kress and Halliday) (Holliday, 2011: 32)

As in any other field of social life, English language education has ideological dimensions that include the Western Othering of the non-West (Holliday, 2011) and native-speakerism (Holliday, 2005, 2006). However, the main focus of this book is neither critical discourse analysis nor the uncovering of ideology as ends in themselves, but the practice of intercultural dialogue by real people in real situations. Although, as Fairclough is careful to point out, critical discourse analysis 'is not just analysis of discourse (or more concretely texts), it is part of some form of systematic transdisciplinary analysis of relations between discourse and other elements of the social process' (Fairclough, 2010: 10). While it does involve the systematic analysis of texts, it also 'addresses social wrongs in their discursive aspects and possible ways of righting or mitigating them' (Fairclough, 2010: 11–12). The nature of the process is elaborated in further detail below:

> [I]deologies are first representations and discourses within relations of power, but dialectical processes of *enacting* such discourses as ways of (inter)acting, *inculcating* them as ways of being (or identities), and *materialising* them in the material world entail that actions and their social relations including genres, persons (or *subjects*) including styles, and aspects of the material world can also have ideological character. Moreover, ideology is first a relation between texts and power, but also a relation between orders of discourse and power, and between languages and power, because meanings of texts can achieve relative stability and durability in social practices and social structures. (Fairclough, 2010: 28)

The view taken in this book is that student autonomy should be enhanced through intercultural dialogue, and that the processes through which this takes place are dialectical in nature and potentially involve both personal and social change. Yet, in real life, people get trapped in contradictory situations and by ideological constraints that limit not only their potential to act, but also their choices and at a more basic level, their ways of perceiving the world.

There are many different kinds of ideology and different kinds of trappings and responses, but an example of an ideology that can trap English language teachers, including those classified as 'native' or 'non-native' teachers, is native-speakerism, a language-based form of prejudice that is prevalent in English language education. Native-speakerism has been defined as 'a pervasive ideology within ELT, characterized by the belief that "native-speaker" teachers represent a "Western culture" from which spring the ideals both of the English language and of English language teaching methodology' (Holliday, 2006: 385). It is close to the related concept of 'linguicism', which has been defined as 'ideologies, structures and practices which are used to legitimate, effectuate, regulate and reproduce an unequal division of power and resources between groups which are defined on the basis of language' (Skutnabb-Kangas, 1988: 13).

Houghton and Rivers (forthcoming) illuminate wide-ranging exclusionary attitudes and practices that can trap English language teachers classified as 'native speakers' that reflect 'native speakerism', 'linguicism' or 'othering' in English language education, particularly, but not exclusively, in the Japanese and Italian contexts, addressing notions of race and racism from theoretical and practical standpoints in relation to ideologies and attitudes, and their impact upon policies and practices at international, national and local/institutional levels. As real people get trapped in real and contradictory, ideologically laden situations, critical discourse analysis and the uncovering of ideology can play important roles in releasing oneself from unacceptable social situations through dynamic intercultural dialogue, autonomously and by choice, all of which may result in ongoing and incomplete, and perhaps imperfect, personal and social transformation.

Holliday (forthcoming) claims that ideology and discourse must be considered when researching native-speakerism, recommending the use of critical discourse analysis to expose what is concealed in everyday professional talk, to uncover and confront institutional complexities created and prejudiced by the 'native-speaker' status-label, and 'to drill down into the workings of a professional discourse in order to critique established positions' (Holliday & Aboshiha, 2009: 674).

As noted above, despite its broader, relational and politically oriented social dimensions, critical discourse analysis *does* involve the systematic analysis of texts (Fairclough, 2010). Hashimoto (forthcoming) clearly illustrates how this can be done in consideration of the construction of the 'Native Speaker' in Japan's educational policies for the teaching of English as a foreign language. Noting that in Japanese government publications, 'the term "native speaker" usually takes the form of the loanword "ネイティブ　スピーカー" (rather than the Japanese equivalent "母語話者", which literally means "mother tongue speaker"', Hashimoto points out that the 'crucial difference between the two terms is that the loanword is often used based on the assumption that it refers to foreigners who speak English, while the Japanese word does not specify the language or the speaker's background' (Hashimoto, forthcoming), taking the position that the view that a 'native speaker' of English is a foreigner has played a crucial role in the Japanese education system, and has contributed to restrictions on their functions within the system.

In the textual analysis that led to the expounding of this position, Hashimoto applied critical discourse analysis as a methodological tool by using both the original Japanese and the English versions of texts where available, comparing and contrasting them for wording and rhetoric when significant gaps existed while considering the conscious or subconscious production and reproduction of dominance through discourse (van Dijk, 1993) to explore and expose the roles that discourse plays in reproducing or resisting social inequalities (Richardson, 2007). Hashimoto contrasts critical discourse analysis with content analysis in the following way.

There are many studies of Japanese policy documents in the field of education (Beauchamp & Vardaman, 1994; Kawai, 2007; Okuno, 2007), and their approaches to policy texts predominantly involve content analysis. While content analysis assumes an interpretation of a text identical to the one intended by the policy maker, CDA allows us to see beyond the reading of policy documents that was intended by the policy maker, which is crucial to connect seemingly unrelated texts. In this way, CDA is likely to be an effective tool for revealing the mechanism for constructing the 'native speaker' within educational policy documents. (Hashimoto, forthcoming)

Moving away from textual analysis that is disconnected from the social situations in which the analyst is currently functioning, my own experience illustrates how critical analysis of the immediate social situation in which one is currently trapped can be used as a strategy to transform it, rendering it more acceptable in the process. Notably, the tension inherent in my own particular workplace in the early 1990s sparked the very case study based on action research described earlier in this book. In Houghton (forthcoming), I document and critically reflect upon my transition in employment status, over a decade of working at one university in southern Japan from a foreign lecturer as a *gaikokujin kyoushi* (外国人教師) to a language lecturer as a *gogaku kyoushi* (語学教師), and finally to a teacher of different languages and cultures as an *ibunka gengo kyouiku tantou kyouin* (異文化言語教育担当教員).

Starting with a legal background, I describe how, before the incorporation of national universities in Japan began in 2004, university employees were legally classed as civil servants. Such positions were reserved for Japanese citizens who were afforded permanent employment and although universities could employ foreigners as *gaikokujin kyouin* at their discretion, I was employed instead as a *gaikokujin kyoushi*, or foreign teacher, a position which pre-dated the *gaikokujin kyouin* category by almost a century and was originally defined by nationality (Worthington, 1999).

> The *gaikokujin kyoushi* were given full-time teaching duties, but were hardly involved in university administration, and were not treated as faculty members. While their employment on one-year (renewable) term limits rendered them ineligible for promotion, they were paid more than their Japanese counterparts because they were foreign. In 1992, the Japanese Ministry of Education issued a verbal directive to all national universities in Japan advising them not to retain *gaikokujin kyoushi* in the senior pay brackets to save money, which had a serious impact upon the older *gaikokujin kyoushi* in particular (Hall, 1998; JPRI, 1996), many of whom lost their jobs sometimes failing to qualify for their pensions. (Houghton, forthcoming)

In 2002, with the support of other *gaikokujin kyoushi* and the university labour union, collective effort was made to gather detailed and accurate information about employment conditions at the university concerned (Houghton, 2002). This started off with critical analysis of the terminology surrounding to employment status. Just as Hashimoto describes above, the original Japanese and the English versions of texts were used where available, and with the help of the union, they were compared and contrasted for wording and rhetoric when significant gaps existed while considering the conscious or subconscious production and reproduction of dominance through discourse. See Masden (forthcoming) for another example of the way this can be done in context. Such critical analysis revealed that at my university the word *gaikokujin* meant 'foreign' when it was used in the term *gaikokujin kyouin* and 'native speaker' of the language being taught when it was used in the term *gaikokujin kyoushi*. Technically, then, both 'Japanese' and 'non-Japanese' citizens who were native speakers of the language to be taught could become 'foreign' teachers. However, the university did *not* have a working definition of native speaker, leaving its definition in practice to those in charge of recruitment:

A *gaikokujin kyoushi* job advertisement written in English in the year 2000 (Arudou, 2009) did not make it clear to potential applicants that the word 'foreign' did not mean 'foreign' but 'native speaker', or that Japanese citizens who were also 'native speakers' of English could apply, and no standards were set for such applicants. No applications had ever been submitted by Japanese citizens who were also 'native speakers' of English, so none had ever been employed. Eligibility criteria for *gaikokujin kyoushi* positions included being a 'native speaker' of the language concerned, having some Japanese communication ability and being educated to Master's degree level (having been awarded the degree within the previous eight years, which effectively kept the *gaikokujin kyoushi* in the lower salary brackets by keeping them lower down on the pay scale). At the university concerned, they were employed to teach either the English or Korean languages on one-year contracts, renewable up to four times, and then they had to leave. (Houghton, forthcoming)

In the struggle to maintain continued employment, despite being classified as a 'native speaker' of either English or Korean, the *gaikokujin kyoushi* group used the Japanese Trade Union law (*roudou kumiai hou*) to initiate collective bargaining through a local labour union, chaired by myself, drawing upon not only domestic Japanese labour law but also on international human rights treaties as sources of internationally agreed standards. Generally persuaded by union argumentation, the university officially abolished the *gaikokujin kyoushi* position, replacing it with a new and improved, yet still peripheral and term-limited, employment category open either to 'native speakers' of English or Korean, ostensibly regardless of 'nationality'.

Conclusion

As explained briefly in the preface and in more detail in the introduction, the study described in this book was initially sparked by the troubling employment situation in which I found myself in the year 2000. Both this study and the gradual, albeit partial, resolution of the employment problems that ran in parallel to the study through labour union negotiations ultimately highlighted the need to place the dynamic concept of intercultural dialogue at the centre of foreign language education, which should take as its aim the development of criticality to help students respond communicatively, analytically and creatively to the increasingly culturally diverse – and often problematic – world that lies outside the classroom.

A great part of this challenge involves not only bridging the gap between theory and practice, but also building meaningful connections and pathways between the classroom and the world outside. In practice, this is not an easy task for foreign language teachers to achieve successfully, given the vast and multi-disciplinary nature of the intercultural communication field that necessarily extends its roots into interconnected and overlapping fields as distant and divergent as cognitive and social psychology, communication studies, foreign language education and sociology, all of which have shared yet differing terminologies, interests and priorities.

This book takes a rather circular yet ultimately holistic route through those fields by exploring, at the outset, the real and problematic world of a teacher–researcher engaging in research in the world, by initially placing a sharp focus on the mind of a single individual to explore the psychological and social psychological roots of value judgment in Part 1 of this book. Characterising the mind as an information handling system, the movement from the micro-level encompasses cognitive, moral and self-development within the individual, and the ethnocentric and ethnorelative dimensions that come into play when the individual is considered as a group member; however, the group(s) to which the individual belongs is/are defined. Understanding the underlying psychological and social psychological foundations of intercultural communication is necessary for foreign language teachers, but equally necessary is the need for both researchers and teachers working in different groups, social contexts and cultures around the world to work towards achieving greater terminological synchronization, since the range of terminology currently on offer tends to be group, context and/or culture bound to the point where the potency of the field of intercultural communication itself, taken as a broad and interconnected whole, is significantly weakened and undermined.

The lack of terminological clarity regarding the management of value judgment exposed in this book, initially identified in the first three years of the 21st century, largely remains unaltered at the end of its first decade, which indicates the almost glacial pace of conceptual development, despite Deardorff's (2009a) brave attempt to decentre the field. Concerning the management of value judgment in foreign language education, the nub of the problem seems to be largely, though not exclusively, two-fold.

First, residual problems partly revolve around persistent and ongoing disagreement between researchers from different backgrounds over whether the adoption of a non-judgmental stance vis-à-vis difference is viable and/or desirable. While some researchers still vehemently deny what has anecdotally been called 'the fiction of non-judgmental stance', there seems to be wide recognition between researchers across disciplines, contexts and cultures that the temporary suspension of judgment stance is a necessary part of not only decentring as 'students develop the ability to perceive their own and the other culture from the perspective of the other speaker' (Byram, 1989b: 5) but also critical thinking (Byram, 2008; de Bono, 1990; Dewey, 1997; Doyé, 2003; Holliday, 2011; Houghton & Yamada, forthcoming), the need for which in intercultural communication is hard to deny.

Second, residual problems also revolve around the role and relative importance given to the social context in intercultural communication. Polarising the argument briefly for the purposes of clarity, intercultural communication may be viewed primarily as being rooted in the socially functioning individual engaging in dyadic communication, a view that places limited attention upon the influences of and impact upon the social context. Or, intercultural communication can be seen primarily as the fundamentally human mechanism through which social transformation occurs either intentionally or unintentionally, a view that tends to prioritise the achievement of pre-determined social aims, in particular the active and democratic development of a newly emerging global society respectful of (supposedly) internationally agreed human rights. From this standpoint, foreign language education can be seen as an organised and carefully structured mechanism through which individuals are activated as critical social agents who are encouraged to act towards particular social and political ends.

A significant feature of this book is that it is written from the standpoint of a teacher–researcher who attempted not only to bridge the gap between theory and practice, but also to build meaningful connections and pathways between the classroom and the world outside paying attention to weaknesses inherent to the field of intercultural communication concerning the management of value judgment in the process. As noted in the introduction, the question of whether or not evaluation can be suspended for the purposes of perspective-taking is easily resolved when considered from the standpoint of materials design at the task level. Yes, it can, insofar as teachers can require learners to evaluate in some tasks and suspend it in others while doing other things. This is primarily a pedagogical decision, but such decisions should be theoretically sound. Providing teachers with the theoretical background they need to make such decisions in practice as they attempt to develop intercultural communicative competence in learners is an important aim of this book. To this end, the Intercultural Dialogue Model has been suggested as way of structuring teaching activities at the level of syllabus and task design following a series of particular learning objectives.

In this sequence, both the temporary suspension of judgmental and critical evaluation are reconciled within one overarching, systematic and very *practically-oriented* conceptual and pedagogical framework. This framework recognises the need for both, but at different stages of the teaching and learning process, starting with consciousness-raising which leads on to the critical analysis and evaluation of self and other in ways that can generate both personal and social transformation, but foregrounding identity-development in particular. While the Intercultural Dialogue Model is located first and foremost at the interface between self and other, and is rooted in real-time communication between real people, it was also shown how this focus can be shifted in order to address the interface between self and society for the purposes of social analysis and transformation through intercultural mediation, attention to propaganda, democratic citizenship and the exposure of ideology hidden behind language.

This focus on the social ultimately throws a loop back to the teacher-researcher's own life experience, making the flow of the book circular and holistic. Examples were provided of different ways in which intercultural dialogue can, and was, deployed in real life to address and overcome problems arising in real life that were at once personal, institutional and social in nature. Such complex problems can affect not only students but also teachers and researchers in the education sector not only in the particular social and cultural context of Japan but also further afield.

Epilogue

At an intercultural communication conference in China a few years ago, I surprised myself with my answer to a question. The topic of conversation revolved around living long term in Japan. Someone had heard of a Western man who, having lived in Japan for 15 years, suddenly packed his bags and left claiming that he would never understand 'these people'. This man had ostensibly lived in Japan longer than me and I was asked whether I had any form of identity crisis. As my entire study flashed through my mind in a split second, I found myself saying 'no', although to have almost completed a seven-year study rooted in an identity crisis, as outlined in the introduction, clearly contradicted that. But the correct answer at the time was still, and remains, 'no'. At that moment, I realised I had overcome the identity crisis that had initially triggered the study described in this book. 'How did that happen?' I asked myself.

Inability to overcome personal struggle drove me into research. While I was initially ill-equipped to deal with the problems I was facing, I managed to develop new understandings by exposing myself to the ideas of other teachers and researchers, developing a range of new conceptual tools along the way. While my problems were intensely personal, I did not retreat into them. Instead, I recognised not only their generic nature but also that I had a responsibility as a teacher to educate my students to deal constructively with intercultural issues. By teaching to the best of my ability, I used the opportunities provided by this thesis to learn how to do it myself.

In this, I am reminded of the words of Petrus' final words to Paolo in Coelho's (2008) story of his own pilgrimage along the road to Santiago in search of his sword. Having taught Paolo a series of lessons for life along the way, Petrus announces that after the next day, they would not meet again. As the time for the final lesson approached, Petrus imparted to Paolo the following secret:

On some future day, you will receive a message from me, asking you to lead someone along the road to Santiago, just as I have led you. Then you will be able to experience the great secret of the journey – a secret that I am going to reveal to you now, but only through words. It is a secret that has to be experienced to be understood . . .

The secret is the following, Petrus said. 'You can learn only through teaching. We have been together here on the Road to Santiago, but while you were learning the practices, I learned the meaning of them. In teaching you, I truly learned. By taking the role of guide, I was able to find my own true path'.

If you succeed in finding your sword, you will have to teach the road to someone else. And only when that happens – when you accept your role as Master – will you learn all the lessons in your heart. Each of us knows the answers, even before someone tells us what they are. Life teaches us lessons every minute, and the secret is to accept that only in our daily lives can we show ourselves to be as wise as Solomon and as powerful as Alexander the Great. But we become aware of this only when we are forced to teach others and to participate in adventures as extravagant as this one has been. (Coelho, 2008: 221–222)

The intertwining of teaching and learning in this way characterises my own experience of the process of developing the study described in this book within the context of my own life, in that I was a learner who was destined, indeed forced, to become a teacher in order to learn. By researching how language teachers can best help their students respond constructively to cultural difference, I learned to respond constructively to cultural difference myself. Further, I internalised many ideas and theories over time developing understandings that now seem like common sense to me.

In no corner of the inner or outer world do things stay completely the same. Things shift as entities and thoughts move harmoniously and dialectically to greater or lesser degree. We all play some small part in cultural evolution, even if only at the level of the unconscious, and have the potential to play a greater part, should we be disposed and able. What can be seen from one vantage point can always be seen from another. What seems like a whole can always be broken into smaller parts, and parts can be combined in new ways to make something different. What is labelled in one way can always be labelled differently, but the same label may mean two different things depending on 'the reader'. Wholes and parts may clash and contradict but can be evaluated from different vantage points, selected and rejected in whole or in part. Parts may integrate to form more integrated wholes, and spaces that open up between them can generate new options. To me, intercultural communication has become little more than a readiness to dive into this kaleidoscopic flux, swim around, make sense of it all and influence the shift. Some stability lies in recognising inner and outer world shift.

Turning the final spotlight of this thesis upon research methodology itself, what might one hope for method in a world where there are so many versions of the good? Such is the question posed by Law (2004: 154–156) whose claim that there is no general world and no general rules challenges researchers to face the possibility that the disappearance of the general necessarily accompanies the disappearance of both the universal and the local, for the local is a subset of the general.

After the subdivision of the universal, we need other metaphors for imagining our worlds and our responsibilities to those worlds. Localities. Specificities. Enactments. Multiplicities. Fractionalities. Goods. Resonances. Gatherings. Forms of craftings. Processes of weavings. Spirals. Vortices. Indefinitenesses. Condensates. Dances. Imaginaries. Passions. Interferences.

Metaphors for the stutter and the stop.

References

Abe, H. and Wiseman, R.L. (1983) A cross-cultural confirmation of the dimensions of intercultural effectiveness. *International Journal of Intercultural Relations* 7, 53–67.

Allport, G. (1954) *The Nature of Prejudice*. New York: Macmillan.

Anderson, J.R. (1985) *Cognitive Psychology and Its Implications*. New York: W.H. Freeman.

Anderson, L.W. and Krathwohl, D.R. (2001) *A Taxonomy for Learning, Teaching, and Assessing: A Revision of Bloom's Taxonomy of Educational Objectives*. New York: Longman.

Arudou, D. (2009) *Blacklist of Japanese Universities*. Online document: http://www.debito. org/kitakyushudata.html. Accessed 28.12.11.

Ashwill, M.A. and Du'o'ng, T. (2009) Developing globally competent citizens: The contrasting cases of the United States and Vietnam. In D. Deardorff (ed.) *The SAGE Handbook of Intercultural Competence* (pp. 141–157). Thousand Oaks, CA: Sage Publications.

Bachnik, J. (2007) Tatemae/Honne. In G. Ritzer (ed.) *Blackwell Encyclopedia of Sociology Online*. Accessed 6 January 2012 at http://www.sociologyencyclopedia.com/public/ tocnode?id=g9781405124331_yr2011_chunk_g978140512433126_ss1-14#citation

Barna, L.M. (1998) Stumbling blocks in intercultural communication. In M. Bennett (ed.) *Basic Concepts of Intercultural Communication: Selected Readings* (pp. 173–189). Yarmouth, ME: Intercultural Press.

Barnett, R. (1997) *Higher Education: A Critical Business*. Buckingham: Open University Press.

Beauchamp, E.R. and Vardaman, J.M. Jr. (1994) *Japanese Education since 1945: A Documentary Study*. New York: M.E. Sharpe.

Bennett, M. (1993) Towards ethnorelativism: A developmental model of intercultural sensitivity. In R.M. Paige (ed.) *Education for the Intercultural Experience* (pp. 21–72). Yarmouth, ME: Intercultural Press.

Blackmore, S. (1999) *The Meme Machine*. Oxford: Oxford University Press.

Blaxter, L., Hughes, C. and Tight, M. (2001) *How to Research*. Oxford: Oxford University Press.

Bloom, B., Englehart, M., Furst, E., Hill, W. and Krathwohl, D. (1956) *Taxonomy of Educational Objectives: The Classification of Educational Goals*. New York, Toronto: Longmans, Green.

Brewer, M. and Campbell, D. (1976) *Ethnocentrism and Inter-group Attitudes*. New York: Wiley.

Brislin, R.W. (1986) Prejudice and intergroup communication. In W. Gudykunst (ed.) *Intergroup Communication* (pp. 74–85). London: Edward Arnold.

Broughton, J. (1983) Women's rationality and men's virtues: A critique of gender dualism in Gilligan's theory of moral development. *Social Research* 50, 597–642.

Brown, P. and Levinson, S. (1987) *Politeness: Some Universals in Language.* Cambridge: Cambridge University Press.

Buraku Liberation League (undated) *What is Buraku Discrimination?* Online document: http://www.bll.gr.jp/eng.html. Accessed 28.12.11.

Byram, M. (1989a) *Cultural Studies in Foreign Language Education.* Clevedon: Multilingual Matters.

Byram, M. (1989b) Intercultural education and foreign language teaching. *World Studies Journal 7,* 4–7.

Byram, M. (1997) *Teaching and Assessing Intercultural Communicative Competence.* Clevedon: Multilingual Matters.

Byram, M. (2008) *From Foreign Language Education to Education for Intercultural Citizenship: Essays and Reflections.* Clevedon: Multilingual Matters.

Byram, M. (2009) Intercultural competence in foreign languages: The intercultural speaker and the pedagogy of foreign language education. In D. Deardoff (ed.) *The SAGE Handbook of Intercultural Competence* (pp. 321–332). Thousand Oaks, CA: Sage Publications.

Byram, M. and Zarate, G. (1997) Definitions, objectives and assessment of sociocultural competence. In M. Byram, G. Zarate and G. Neuner (eds) *Sociocultural Competence in Language Learning and Teaching. Studies Towards a Common European Framework of Reference for Language Learning and Teaching* (pp. 7–43). Strasbourg: Council of Europe.

Byram, M. and Guilherme, M. (2000) Human rights culture and language teaching. In A. Osler (ed.) *Citizenship and Democracy in Schools: Diversity, Identity, Equality* (pp. 63–78). Stoke-on-Trent: Trentham Books.

Byram, M. and Guilherme, M. (2010) Intercultural education and intercultural communication: Tracing the relationship. In Y. Tsai and S. Houghton (eds) *Becoming Intercultural: Inside and Outside the Classroom* (pp. 23–47). Newcastle: Cambridge Scholars Publishing.

Byram, M., Morgan, C. and colleagues (1994) *Teaching-and-Learning Language-and-Culture.* Clevedon: Multilingual Matters.

Byram, M., Gribkova, B. and Starkey, H. (2002) *Developing the Intercultural Dimension in Language Teaching: A Practical Introduction for Teachers.* Strasbourg: Council of Europe.

Byram, M., Barrett, M., Ipgrave, J., Jackson, R. and Mendez Garcia, C. (2009) *Autobiography of Intercultural Encounters.* Strasbourg: Council of Europe. Online document: http://www.coe.int/t/dg4/autobiography/default_EN.asp?. Accessed 28.12.11.

Call, M.E. (1985) Auditory short-term memory, listening comprehension and the input hypothesis. *TESOL Quarterly 19,* 765–781.

Canagarajah, A.S. (1999) *Resisting Linguistic Imperialism in English Teaching.* Oxford: Oxford University Press.

Carrell, P.L. (1983) 3 components of background knowledge in reading comprehension. *Language Learning 33,* 87–111.

Chen, G. and An, R. (2009) A Chinese model of intercultural leadership competence. In D. Deardorff (ed.) *The SAGE Handbook of Intercultural Competence* (pp. 196–208). Thousand Oaks, CA: Sage Publications.

Coelho, P. (2008) *The Pilgrimage.* New York: HarperCollins.

Cohen, L., Manion, L. and Morrison, K. (2000) *Research Methods in Education.* London, New York: Routledge.

Colombian Ministry of Education. Undated. Curriculum Guidelines: Education for Ethics and Human Values. http://www.mineducacion.gov.co/cvn/1665/articles-89869_archivo_ pdf7.pdf

Condon, J. and Yousef, F. (1975) *An Introduction to Intercultural Communication.* Indianapolis, IN: Bobbs-Merrill.

Convention for the Elimination of All Forms of Discrimination against Women (1979) Online document: http://www.un.org/womenwatch/daw/cedaw/. Accessed 28.12.11.

Convention on the Rights of the Child (1989) Online document: http://www.bayefsky.com/treaties/crc.php. Accessed 28.12.11.

Council of Europe (2001) *Common European Framework of Reference for Languages.* Strasbourg: Council of Europe. Online document: http://www.coe.int/T/DG4/Linguistic/Source/Framework_EN.pdf. Accessed 28.12.11.

Council of Europe (2008) *White Paper on Intercultural Dialogue: Living Together as Equals in Dignity.* Online document: http://www.coe.int/T/dg4/intercultural/Source/White%20Paper_final_revised_EN.pdf. Accessed 28.12.11.

Crain, W. (2000) *Theories of Development: Concepts and Applications.* Upper Saddle River, NJ: Prentice-Hall.

Creswell, J.W. (2003) *Research Design: Qualitative, Quantitative and Mixed Method Approaches.* Thousand Oaks, CA: Sage Publications.

Damen, L. (1987) *Culture Learning: The Fifth Dimension in the Language Classroom.* Reading, MA: Addison-Wesley Publishing Company.

Dawkins, R. (1989) *The Selfish Gene.* Oxford: Oxford University Press.

Deardorff, D. (2009a) Synthesising conceptualizations of intercultural competence. In D. Deardorff (ed.) *The SAGE Handbook of Intercultural Competence* (pp. 264–269). Thousand Oaks, CA: Sage Publications.

Deardorff, D. (2009b) Implementing intercultural competence assessment. In D. Deardorff (ed.) *The SAGE Handbook of Intercultural Competence* (pp. 477–491). Thousand Oaks, CA: Sage Publications.

Deardorff, D. (ed.) (2009c) *The SAGE Handbook of Intercultural Competence.* Thousand Oaks, CA: Sage Publications.

de Bono, E. (1969) *The Mechanism of Mind.* London: Cape.

de Bono, E. (1990) *Lateral Thinking.* Harmondsworth: Penguin Books. NOTE: Originally published: London: Ward Lock, 1970.

de Bono, E. (1991) *I am Right: You are Wrong.* Harmondsworth: Penguin Books.

Delors, J. (1996) *Learning: The Treasure Within.* Paris: UNESCO.

Devine, P.G. and Monteith, M.J. (1993) The role of discrepancy-associated affect in prejudice-reduction. In D.M. Mackie and D.M. Hamilton (eds) *Affect, Cognition and Stereotyping: Interactive Processes in Intergroup Perception* (pp. 317–344). Orlando, FL: Academic Press.

Dewey, J. (1997) *How We Think.* New York: Dover Publications.

Distin, K. (2005) *The Selfish Meme.* Cambridge: Cambridge University Press.

Donnelly, J. (2003) *Universal Human Rights.* Ithaca, NY: Cornell University Press.

Dörnyei, Z. (2005) *The Psychology of the Language Learner: Individual Differences in Second Language Acquisition.* Mahwah, NJ: Lawrence Erlbaum.

Dörnyei, Z. (2009) The L2 motivation self system. In Z. Dörnyei and E. Ushioda (eds) *Motivation, Language Identity and the L2 Self* (pp. 9–24). Bristol: Multilingual Matters.

Dörnyei, Z. and Ushioda, E. (2009) Motivation, language identity and the L2 self. In Z. Dörnyei and E. Ushioda (eds) *Motivation, Language Identity and the L2 Self* (pp. 350–356). Bristol: Multilingual Matters.

Dovidio, J.E., Brigham, J.C., Johnson, B.T. and Gaertner, S.L. (1996) Stereotyping, prejudice and discrimination: Another look. In C.N. Macrae, C. Stangor and M. Hewstone (eds) *Stereotypes and Stereotyping* (pp. 276–319). New York: Guilford Press.

Doyé, P. (2003) Foreign language education as a contribution to tertiary socialisation. Paper presented at the Durham Symposium on Intercultural Competence and Citizenship Education. Based upon Doyé, P. (1992). Fremdsprachenunterricht als Beitrag zu tertiare Sozialisation. In D. Buttjes, W. Butzkamm and F. Klippel (eds) *Neue Brennpunkte des Englishunterrichts [New Focal Points of English Education]*. Frankfurt: Peter Lang.

Edge, J. (1992) *Cooperative Development: Professional Self-Development through Cooperation with Colleagues (Teacher to Teacher)*. Harlow: Longman Publishing Group.

Endicott, L., Bock, T. and Narvaez, D. (2003) Moral reasoning, intercultural development and multicultural experiences: Relations and cognitive underpinnings. *International Journal of Intercultural Relations* 27, 403–419.

English Japanese Online Dictionary. Accessed 6 January 2012 at http://www.englishjapaneseonlinedictionary.com/

Fairclough, N. (1995) *Critical Discourse Analysis: The Critical Study of Language*. London, New York: Longman.

Fairclough, N. (2010) *Critical Discourse Analysis: The Critical Study of Language*. Harlow: Pearson Education Limited.

Fantini, A. (1995) Introduction – Language, culture and worldview: Exploring the nexus. *International Journal of Intercultural Relations* 19, 143–153.

Fauconnier, G. and Turner, M. (2002) *The Way we Think. Conceptual Blending and the Mind's Hidden Complexities*. New York: Basic Books.

Festinger, L. (1957) *A Theory of Cognitive Dissonance*. Evanston, IL: Row, Peterson.

Fiedler, F., Mitchell, T. and Triandis, H. (1971) The culture assimilator: An approach to cross-cultural training. *Journal of Applied Psychology* 55, 95–102.

Forgas, J. and Bond, M. (1985) Cultural influences on the perception of interaction episodes. *Personality and Social Psychology Bulletin* 11, 75–88.

Foundation for Critical Thinking (undated) *The Etymology and Dictionary Definition of 'Critical Thinking'*. Online document: http://www.criticalthinking.org/pages/index-of-articles/our-concept-and-definition-of-critical-thinking/411

Fowler, S. and Mumford, M. (1999) *Intercultural Sourcebook: Cross-Cultural Training Methods 2*. Yarmouth, ME: Intercultural Press, Inc.

Freire, P. (1990) *Pedagogy of the Oppressed*. London: Penguin Books.

Freire, P. and Macedo, D. (1987) *Literacy. Reading the Word and the World*. South Hadley, MA; Westport, CT: Bergin and Garvey Publishers.

Gardner, R.C. and Lambert, W.E. (1959) Motivational variables in second language acquisition. *Canadian Journal of Psychology* 13, 266–272.

Gilligan, C. (1982) *In a Different Voice*. Cambridge, MA: Harvard University Press.

Giroux, H. (2010) Teachers as transformative intellectuals. In A. Canestrari and B. Marlowe (eds) *Educational Foundations: An Anthology of Critical Readings* (pp. 197–204). Los Angeles: Sage Publications.

Goffman, E. (1959) *The Presentation of Self in Everyday Life*. Garden City, NY: Doubleday.

Goleman, D. (2004) *Emotional Intelligence and Working with Emotional Intelligence*. London: Bloomsbury.

Gruber, H. and Voneche, J. (1995) *The Essential Piaget: An Interpretive Reference and Guide*. Northvale, NJ: Jason Aronson Inc.

Gubrium, J.F. and Holstein, J.A. (1997) *The New Language of Qualitative Research*. New York: Oxford University Press.

Gudykunst, W. (1998) *Bridging Differences: Effective Intergroup Communication.* Thousand Oaks, CA: Sage Publications.

Gudykunst, W. and Hammer, M. (1988) Strangers and hosts: An extension of UR theory. In Y. Kim and W. Gudykunst (eds) *Cross-Cultural Adaptation* (pp. 106–139). Beverly Hills, CA: Sage Publications.

Gudykunst, W. and Kim, Y.Y. (2003) *Communicating with Strangers. An Approach to Intercultural Communication.* Boston, MA: McGraw-Hill.

Guilherme, M. (2002) *Critical Citizens for an Intercultural World: Foreign Language Education as Cultural Politics.* Clevedon: Multilingual Matters.

Guo, Y. (2010) The concept and development of intercultural competence. In Y. Tsai and S. Houghton (eds) *Becoming Intercultural: Inside and Outside the Classroom* (pp. 23–47). Newcastle: Cambridge Scholars Publishing.

Hall, E.T. (1976) *Beyond Culture.* Garden City, New York: Anchor Books.

Hall, E.T. (1990) *The Silent Language.* New York: Doubleday.

Hall, S. (1996) The West and the rest: Discourse and power. In S. Hall and D. Held (eds) *Modernity: An Introduction to Modern Societies* (pp. 184–228). Oxford: Blackwell.

Hall, I. (1998) *Cartels of the Mind: Japan's Intellectual Closed Shop.* New York: W.W. Norton & Company.

Hamilton, D. and Neville Uhles, A. (2000) Stereotypes. *Encyclopedia of Psychology* 7, 466–469.

Hardin, C. and Banaji, M.R. (1993) The influence of language on thought. *Social Cognition* 11, 277–308.

Hashimoto, K. (forthcoming) The construction of the 'Native Speaker' in Japan's Educational Policies for TEFL. In S. Houghton and D. Rivers (eds) *Native-Speakerism in Japan: Intergroup Dynamics in Foreign Language Education.* Bristol: Multilingual Matters.

Heine, S.J. (2001) Self as cultural product: An examination of East Asian and North American Selves. *Journal of Personality* 69, 881–906.

Hewstone, M. and Giles, H. (1986) Social groups and social stereotypes in intergroup communication: A review and model of intergroup communication breakdown. In W.B. Gudykunst (ed.) *Intergroup Communication* (pp. 10–26). London: Edward Arnold Publishers.

Higgins, E.T. (1987) Self-discrepancy: A theory relating to self and affect. *Psychological Review* 94, 319–340.

Higgins, E.T. (1996) The 'self-digest': Self-knowledge serving self-regulatory functions. *Journal of Personality and Social Psychology* 71 (6), 1062–1083.

Higgins, E.T., Klein, R. and Strauman, T. (1985) Self-concept discrepancy theory: A psychological model for distinguishing among different aspects of depression and anxiety. *Social Cognition* 3(1), 51–76.

Hoffman, E. (1989) *Lost in Translation.* London: Vintage.

Hofstede, G. (1980) *Culture's Consequences: International Differences in Work-Related Values.* Beverly Hills, CA: Sage Publications.

Hofstede, G. (2009) The moral circle in intercultural competence. In D. Deardorff (ed.) *The SAGE Handbook of Intercultural Competence* (pp. 85–99). Thousand Oaks, CA: Sage Publications.

Holliday, A. (2005) *The Struggle to Teach English as an International Language.* Oxford: Oxford University Press.

Holliday, A. (2006) Native-speakerism. *ELT Journal* 60, 385–387.

Holliday, A. (2011) *Intercultural Communication and Ideology*. Los Angeles: Sage Publications.

Holliday, A. (forthcoming) 'Native speaker' teachers and cultural belief. In S. Houghton and D. Rivers (eds) *Native-Speakerism in Japan: Intergroup Dynamics in Foreign Language Education*. Bristol: Multilingual Matters.

Holliday, A. and Aboshiha, P.A. (2009) The denial of ideology in perceptions of 'nonnative speaker' teachers. *TESOL Quarterly* 43, 669–689.

Hopkins, D. (2002) *A Teacher's Guide to Classroom Research*. Oxford: Oxford University Press.

Holmes, P. and O'Neill, G. (2010) Autoethnography and self-reflection: Tools for self-assessing intercultural competence. In Y. Tsai and S. Houghton (eds) *Becoming Intercultural: Inside and Outside the Language Classroom* (pp. 167–193). Newcastle-upon-Tyne: Cambridge Scholars Publishing.

Houghton, S. (2002) *Gaikokujindewanai gaikokujinkyoshi?* [Foreign lecturers who are not foreign] All current foreign lecturers are foreign. Where are the non-foreign foreign lecturers? *Forum: Journal of the University of Kitakyushu Union* 23, 54–31.

Houghton, S. (2007) Managing the evaluation of difference in foreign language education: A complex case study in a tertiary level context in Japan. PhD dissertation, Durham University.

Houghton, S. (2009a) Managing the evaluation of difference in foreign language education: A complex case study in a tertiary level context in Japan. PhD dissertation, Durham University. Online document: http://proquest.umi.com/pqdweb?did=1771 527591&Fmt=6&clientId=79356&RQT=309&VName=PQD. Accessed 28.12.11.

Houghton, S. (2009b) Intercultural mediation in the mono-lingual, mono-cultural foreign language classroom: A case study in Japan. *Cultus 2: Mediation and Competence 2*, 117–132.

Houghton, S. (2010) *Savoir se* transformer: Knowing how to become. In Y. Tsai and S. Houghton (eds) *Becoming Intercultural: Inside and Outside the Language Classroom* (pp. 194–228). Newcastle-upon-Tyne: Cambridge Scholars Publishing.

Houghton, S. (forthcoming) Intercultural communicative competence as an imperative. In S. Houghton and D. Rivers (eds) *Native-Speakerism in Japan: Intergroup Dynamics in Foreign Language Education*. Bristol: Multilingual Matters.

Houghton, S. and Rivers, D. (eds) (forthcoming). *Native-Speakerism in Japan: Intergroup Dynamics in Foreign Language Education*. Bristol: Multilingual Matters.

Houghton, S. and Yamada, E. (forthcoming) *Developing Criticality in Practice through Foreign Language Education*. Frankfurt-Am-Mein: Peter Lang Publishing Group.

Hubbard, R. and Power, B. (1999) *Living the Questions*. Portland, ME: Stenhouse Publishers.

Hunt, E. and Agnoli, F. (1991) The Whorfian hypothesis: A cognitive psychology perspective. *Psychological Review* 98, 377–389.

International Convention for the Elimination of All Forms of Racial Discrimination (1969) Online document: http://www2.ohchr.org/english/law/pdf/cerd.pdf. Accessed 30.12.11.

JPRI (1996) Foreign teachers in Japanese universities: An update. *JPRI Working Paper* 24. Online document: http://www.jpri.org/publications/workingpapers/wp24.html. Accessed 28.12.11.

Kachru, B.B. (1985) Standards, codification and sociolinguistic realism: The English language in the outer circle. In R. Quirk and H. Widdowson (eds) *English in the World: Teaching and Learning the Language and Literatures* (pp. 11–36). Cambridge: Cambridge University Press.

Kanagawa, C., Cross, S.E. and Markus, H.R. (2001) 'Who am I?' The cultural psychology of the conceptual self. *Personality and Social Psychology Bulletin* 27, 90–103.

Katz, D. (1960) The functional approach to the study of attitudes. *Public Opinion Quarterly* 24, 163–204.

Kawai, Y. (2007) Japanese nationalism and the global spread of English: An analysis of Japanese government and public discourses on English. *Language and Intercultural Communication* 7, 37–55.

Khan, H. (2003) Japan's foreigner crime fears. *The Asia Times online.* 14th November 2003. Online document: http://www.atimes.com/atimes/Japan/EK14Dh03.html. Accessed 28.12.11.

Kim, Y. (2009) The identity factor in intercultural competence. In D. Deardorff (ed.) *The SAGE Handbook of Intercultural Competence* (pp. 53–84). Thousand Oaks, CA: Sage Publications.

Kim, Y. and Gudykunst, W. (1988) *Theories in Intercultural Communication.* Newbury Park: Sage Publications.

Kingdom of Saudi Arabia Ministry of Education (2005) The executive summary of the Ministry of Education ten-year plan 1425-1435H (2004–2014). http://www.moe.gov.sa/pdf/english/moe_e.pdf

Kluckhohn, F. and Strodtbeck, F. (1960) *Variations in Value Orientations.* Evanston, IL: Row, Peterson.

Koester, J. and Olebe, M. (1988) The behavioural assessment scale for intercultural communication effectiveness. *International Journal of Intercultural Relations* 12, 233–246.

Kramsch, C. (1993) *Context and Culture in Language Teaching.* Oxford: Oxford University Press.

Lakoff, G. and Johnson, M. (1980) *Metaphors we Live by.* Chicago; London: University of Chicago Press.

Lantolf, J. (1999) Second culture acquisition: Cognitive considerations. In E. Hinkel (ed.) *Culture in Second Language Teaching and Learning* (pp. 28–47). New York: Cambridge University Press.

Law, J. (2004) *After Method: Mess in Social Science Research.* London: Routledge.

Leary, M.R. (2007) Motivational and emotional aspects of the self. *Annual Review of Psychology* 58, 317–344.

Lee, W.O. (2001) The emerging concepts of citizenship in the Asian context: Some reflections. *Keynote Presentation at the International Forum on New Citizenship Education Policies in Asian Context.* Hong Kong: Hong Kong Institute of Education.

Levine, R. and Campbell, D. (1972) *Ethnocentrism: Theories of Conflict, Ethnic Attitudes and Group Behaviour.* New York: Wiley.

Lippmann, W. (1922) *Public Opinion.* New York: Macmillan.

Lustig, M. and Koester, J. (1999) *Intercultural Competence: Interpersonal Communication across Cultures.* New York: Longman.

Maas, A. and Arcuri, L. (1996) Language and stereotyping. In C.N. Macrae, C. Stangor and M. Hewstone (eds) *Stereotypes and Stereotyping* (pp. 193–226). New York: Guilford Press.

Manian, R. and Naidu, S. (2009) India: A cross-cultural overview of intercultural competence. In D. Deardorff (ed.) *The SAGE Handbook of Intercultural Competence.* Thousand Oaks, CA: Sage Publications.

Markus, H. and Nurius, P. (1986) Possible selves. *American Psychologist* 41, 954–969.

Markus, H.R. and Ruvolo, A. (1989) Possible selves: Personalized representations and goals. In L.A. Pervin (ed.) *Goal Concepts in Personality and Social Psychology* (pp. 211–241). Hillsdale, NJ: Lawrence Erlbaum.

Markus, H. and Kitayama, S. (1991) Culture and the self: Implications for cognition, emotion and motivation. *Psychological Review* 98, 224–253.

Masden, K. (forthcoming) Kumamoto General Union vs. The Prefectural University of Kumamoto: Reviewing the decision rendered by the Kumamoto District Court. In S. Houghton and D. Rivers (eds) *Native-Speakerism in Japan: Intergroup Dynamics in Foreign Language Education*. Bristol: Multilingual Matters.

Matsuda, Y., Harsel, S., Furusawa, S., Kim, H. and Quarles, J. (2001) Democratic values and mutual perceptions of human rights in four Pacific Rim nations. *International Journal of Intercultural Relations* 25, 405–421.

Maynard, S. (1997) *Japanese Communication: Language and Thought in Context*. Honolulu: University of Hawaii Press.

Medina-López-Portillo, A. and Sinnigen, J.H. (2009) Interculturality versus intercultural competencies in Latin America. In D. Deardorff (ed.) *The SAGE Handbook of Intercultural Competence* (pp. 249–263). Thousand Oaks, CA: Sage Publications.

McDonough, J. and McDonough, S. (1997) *Research Methods for English Language Teachers*. London: Arnold.

Miller, G. and Steinberg, M. (1975) *Between People*. Chicago: Science Research.

Miyahara, A., Kim, M-S., Shin H-C. and Yoon, K. (1998) Conflict-resolution styles among collectivist cultures: A comparison between Japanese and Koreans. *International Journal of Intercultural Relations* 22, 505–525.

Modell, A.H. (2003) *Imagination and the Meaningful Brain*. Cambridge, MA: MIT Press.

Moosmüller, A. and Schönhuth, M. (2009) Intercultural competence in German discourse. In D. Deardorff (ed.) *The SAGE Handbook of Intercultural Competence* (pp. 209–232). Thousand Oaks, CA: Sage Publications.

Mouffe, C. (1992a) Democratic politics today. In C. Mouffe (ed.) *Dimensions of Radical Democracy: Pluralism, Citizenship, Community* (pp. 1–14). London: Verso.

Mouffe, C. (1992b) Democratic citizenship and the political community. In C. Mouffe (ed.) *Dimensions of Radical Democracy: Pluralism, Citizenship, Community* (pp. 225–239). London: Verso.

Naotsuka, R. (1981) *Mutual Understanding of Different Cultures*. Tokyo: Taishukan Publishing Company.

Nishida, H. (1985) Japanese intercultural communication competence and cross-cultural adjustment. *International Journal of Intercultural Relations* 9, 242–269.

Nishida, H. (1999) A cognitive approach to intercultural communication based on schema theory. *International Journal of Intercultural Relations* 23, 753–777.

Nwosu, P.O. (2009) Understanding Africans' conceptualizations of intercultural competence. In D. Deardorff (ed.) *The SAGE Handbook of Intercultural Competence* (pp. 158–178). Thousand Oaks, CA: Sage Publications.

Okuno, H. (2007) 日本の言語政策と英語教育 [*Japan's Language Policies and English Education*]. Tokyo: Sanyûsha.

O'Malley, J.M. and Chamot, A.U. (1989) Listening comprehension strategies in second language acquisition. *Applied Linguistics* 10, 418–437.

O'Malley, J.M. and Chamot, A.U. (1990) *Learning Strategies in Second Language Acquisition*. Cambridge: Cambridge University Press.

Olebe, M. and Koester, J. (1989) Exploring the cross-cultural equivalence of the behavioural assessment scale for intercultural communication. *International Journal of Intercultural Relations* 13, 333–347.

Oser, F.K. (2005) Negative morality and the goals of moral education. In L. Nucci (ed.) *Conflict, Contradiction and Contrarian Elements in Moral Development and Education.* Mahwah, NJ: Lawrence Erlbaum Associates.

Osler, A. (2000) *Citizenship and Democracy in Schools: Diversity, Identity, Equality.* Stoke-on-Trent: Trentham Books.

Osler, A. and Starkey, H. (1996) *Teacher Education and Human Rights.* London: David Fulton.

Parmenter, L. (2010) Becoming intercultural: A comparative analysis of national education policies. In Y. Tsai and S. Houghton (eds) *Becoming Intercultural: Inside and Outside the Classroom* (pp. 66–88). Newcastle-upon-Tyne: Cambridge Scholars Publishing.

Paul, R.W. and Elder, L. (2002) *Critical Thinking: Tools for Taking Charge of your Professional and Personal Life.* Upper Saddle River, NJ; Tokyo: Financial Times/Prentice-Hall.

Pennycook, A. (1994) *English as an International Language.* London: Longman.

Phipps, A. (2009) *An Agenda for Research in Intercultural Studies.* Durham Intercultural Studies (Cultnet) Meeting. Durham University, England, 26–29 March 2009.

Pinker, S. (1994) *The Language Instinct.* Harmondsworth: Penguin.

Pratkanis, A. and Aronson, E. (2001) *Age of Propaganda: The Everyday Use and Abuse of Persuasion.* New York: Henry Holt & Co.

Rathus, S.A. (1985) *Essentials of Psychology.* Fort Worth: Harcourt Brace College Publishers.

Rest, J., Narvaez, D., Bebeau, M. and Thoma, S. (1999) A neo-Kohlbergian approach: The DIT and schema theory. *Educational Psychology Review* 11, 291–324.

Richards, C. (1983) Listening comprehension: Approach, design and procedure. *TESOL Quarterly* 17, 219–239.

Richardson, J.E. (2007) *Analyzing Newspapers: An Approach from Critical Discourse Analysis.* New York: Palgrave Macmillan.

Rivers, D.J. (2011) Evaluating the self and the other: Imagined intercultural contact within 'native-speaker' dependent foreign language contexts. *International Journal of Intercultural Relations* 35 (6), 842–852.

Roberts, C., Byram, M., Barro, A., Jordan, S. and Street B. (2001) *Language Learners as Ethnographers.* Clevedon: Multilingual Matters.

Robinson, G.L.N. (1988) *Cross-Cultural Understanding.* New York: Prentice-Hall.

Rogers, C. (1951) *Client-Centred Therapy.* London: Constable.

Rogers, C. (1961) *On Becoming a Person.* London: Constable.

Rogers, C. (1980) *A Way of Being.* Boston: Houghton Mifflin.

Rokeach, M. (1973) *The Nature of Values.* New York: Free Press.

Rosch, E.H. (1978) Principles of categorization. In E. Rosch and B. Lloyd (eds) *Cognition and Categorization* (pp. 27–48). Hillsdale, NJ: Erlbaum Associates.

Rosenberger, N. (1992) *Japanese Sense of Self.* Cambridge: Cambridge University Press.

Ruben, B.K. and Kealey, D.J. (1979) Behavioural assessment of communication competency and the prediction of cross-cultural adaptation. *International Journal of Intercultural Relations* 3, 15–47.

Rubovitz, P. and Maehr, M. (1973) Pygmalion black and white. *Journal of Personality and Social Psychology* 25, 210–218.

Rumelhart, D. (1980) Schemata: The building blocks of cognition. In R.J. Spiro, B.C. Bruce and W.F. Brewer (eds) *Theoretical Issues in Reading Comprehension* (pp. 38–58). Hillsdale, NJ: Erlbaum.

Rumelhart, D. and McClelland, J. (1986) *Parallel Distributed Processing: Explorations in the Microstructure of Cognition*. Cambridge, MA: MIT Press.

Samovar, L. and Porter, R. (2004) *Communication between Cultures*. Belmont, CA: Wadsworth/Thomson Learning.

Schutz, A. (1970) *On Phenomenology and Social Relations*. Chicago: University of Chicago Press.

Schwartz, S.H. and Sagiv, L. (1995) Identifying culture-specifics in the content and structure of values. *Journal of Cross-Cultural Psychology* 26, 92–116.

Schwartz, S.H., Verkasalo, M., Antonovsky, A. and Sagiv, L. (1997) Value priorities and social desirability: Much substance, some style. *British Journal of Social Psychology* 36, 3–18.

Sercu, L. (2000) *Acquiring Intercultural Communicative Competence from Textbooks*. Leuven: Leuven University Press.

Simon, S., Howe, L. and Kirschenbaum, H. (1995) *Values Clarification*. New York: Warner Books.

Skutnabb-Kangas, T. (1988) Multilingualism and the education of minority children. In T. Skutnabb-Kangas and J. Cummins (eds) *Minority Education: From Shame to Struggle* (pp. 9–44). Clevedon: Multilingual Matters.

Soysal, Y. (1998) Toward a post-national model of membership. In G. Shafir (ed.) *The Citizenship Debates* (pp. 189–217). Minneapolis: University of Minnesota Press.

Spears, A.K. (1999) Race and ideology: An introduction. In A.K. Spears (ed.) *Race and Ideology; Language, Symbolism, and Popular Culture* (pp. 11–58). Detroit: Wayne State University Press.

Spitzberg, B. and Changnon, G. (2009) Conceptualising intercultural competence. In D. Deardorff (ed.) *The SAGE Handbook of Intercultural Competence* (pp. 2–52). Thousand Oaks, CA: Sage Publications.

Stenou, K. (2005) Cultural diversity and dialogue: An interface. In K. Stenou (ed.) *Dialogue: Cultural Diversity and Globalization: The Arab-Japanese Experience* (pp. 123–126). Paris, France: UNESCO.

Sumner, W.G. (1906) *Folkways: A Study of Mores, Manners, Customs and Morals*. Boston: Ginn.

Tajfel, H. (1982) *Social Identity and Intergroup Relations*. London: Cambridge University Press.

Tajfel, H., Billig, M.G., Bundy, R.P. and Flament, C. (1971) Social categorisation and intergroup behaviour. *European Journal of Social Psychology* 1, 149–178.

Taylor, D. and Nwosu, P. (2001) Afrocentric empiricism: A model for communication research in Africa. In V. Milhouse, M. Asante and P. Nwosu (eds) *Transcultural Realities: Interdisciplinary Perspectives on Cross-Cultural Relations* (pp. 299–311). Thousand Oaks, CA: Sage.

The Japan Times (2003) 32.4% of Japanese oppose increase in foreign tourists. *The Japan Times*, 2nd November 2003. Online document: http://www.japantimes.com/cgi-bin/getarticle.pl5?nn20031102a9.htm. Accessed 28.12.11.

Ting-Toomey, S. (2009) Intercultural conflict competence as a facet of intercultural competence development: Multiple conceptual approaches. In D. Deardorff (ed.) *The SAGE Handbook of Intercultural Competence*. Thousand Oaks, CA: Sage Publications.

Triandis, H. (1989) The self and social behaviour in differing cultural contexts. *Psychological Review* 96, 506–520.

Tronto, J.C. (1987) Beyond gender difference to a theory of care. *Signs: Journal of Women in Culture and Society* 12, 644–663.

Tsujigami, N. (2009) A 'gender backlash' in the midst of globalization: The dynamic of the 'anti-Cedawīyāt' in contemporary Saudi Arabia. *The Global Studies Journal 2*, 17–29.

Tsujigami, N. (2011) 現代サウディアラビアのジェンダーと権力―フーコーの権力論に基づく言説分析 [単行本] [*Gender and Power in Contemporary Saudi Arabia: A Discourse Analysis from the Perspective of Foucauldian Theory of Power*]. Tokyo: Fukumura Shuppan.

Turner, J.C. (1987) *Rediscovering the Social Group: A Self-Categorisation Theory.* Oxford; New York: Basil Blackwell.

UNESCO (1995) *Declaration and Integrated Framework of Action on Education for Peace, Human Rights and Democracy.* Paris: UNESCO.

UNESCO (2009) *UNESCO World Report: Investing in Cultural Diversity and Intercultural Dialogue.* Paris: UNESCO.

United Nations (undated) *Convention on the Elimination of Discrimination against Women: Declarations, reservations and objections to CEDAW.* Online document: http://www.un.org/womenwatch/daw/cedaw/reservations-country.htm. Accessed 28.12.11.

United Nations Committee on the Elimination of Discrimination (2009) *International Convention on the Elimination of Racial Discrimination. Reports submitted by states parties under article 9 of the Convention. Third to sixth periodic reports due in 2007. Japan. 19th August 2008.* Online document: http://www.bayefsky.com/docs.php/area/reports/treaty/cerd/opt/0/state/87/node/4/filename/japan_cerd_c_jpn_3_6_2008. Accessed 28.12.11.

Universal Declaration of Human Rights (1948) Online document: http://www.un.org/en/documents/udhr/. Accessed 28.12.11.

van Dijk, T.A. (1993) Principles of critical discourse analysis. *Discourse and Society 4*, 249–283.

Wallace, C. (2003) *Critical Reading in Language Education.* Basingstoke: Palgrave Macmillan.

Wallis, K.C. and Poulton, J.L. (2001) *Internalization: The Origins and Construction of Internal Reality.* Buckingham; Philadelphia: Oxford University Press.

Wetherell, M. (1982) Cross-cultural studies of minimal groups: Implications for the social identity theory of intergroup relations. In H. Tajfel (ed.) *Social Identity and Intergroup Relations* (pp. 207–240). Cambridge: Cambridge University Press.

Wierzbicka, A. (1997) The double life of a bi-lingual: A cross-cultural perspective. In M.H. Bond (ed.) *Working at the Interface of Cultures: Eighteen Lives in Social Science* (pp. 113–125). London: Routledge.

Wiseman, R.L., Hammer, M.R. and Nishida, H. (1989) Predictors of intercultural communicative competence. *International Journal of Intercultural Relations 13*, 349–370.

Worthington, C. (1999) Combatting discrimination at a Japanese university. *JPRI Working Paper 58.* Online document: http://www.jpri.org/publications/workingpapers/wp58.html. Accessed 28.12.11.

Wringe, C. (2007) *Moral Education: Beyond the Teaching of Right and Wrong.* Dordrecht, The Netherlands: Springer.

Yamada, E. (2010) Developing criticality through higher English language studies. In Y. Tsai and S. Houghton (eds) *Becoming Intercultural: Inside and Outside the Classroom* (pp. 146–166). Newcastle: Cambridge Scholars Publishing.

Zaharna, R.S. (2009) An associative approach to intercultural communication competence in the Arab world. In D. Deardorff (ed.) *The SAGE Handbook of Intercultural Competence* (pp. 179–195). Thousand Oaks, CA: Sage Publications.

Index

199